Division of Powers and Public Policy

RICHARD SIMEON
Research Coordinator

Published by the University of Toronto Press in cooperation with the Royal Commission on the Economic Union and Development Prospects for Canada and the Canadian Government Publishing Centre, Supply and Services Canada

University of Toront

Toronto   Buffalo

© Minister of Supply and Services Canada 1985

Printed in Canada
ISBN 0-8020-7308-5
ISSN 0829-2396
Cat. No. Z1-1983/1-41-61E

CANADIAN CATALOGUING IN PUBLICATION DATA

Main entry under title:
Division of powers and public policy

(*The Collected research studies / Royal Commission on the Economic Union and Development Prospects for Canada*,
ISSN 0829-2396; 61)
Includes bibliographical references.
ISBN 0-8020-7308-5

1. Federal government — Canada — Addresses, essays, lectures. 2. Federal-provincial relations — Canada — Addresses, essays, lectures.* 3. Political planning — Canada — Addresses, essays, lectures. 4. Canada — Economic policy — Addresses, essays, lectures. I. Simeon, Richard, 1943–   II. Royal Commission on the Economic Union and Development Prospects for Canada. III. Series: Research studies (Royal Commission on the Economic Union and Development Prospects for Canada); 61.

JL19.D58 1985 321.02'0971 C85-099126-9

PUBLISHING COORDINATION: Ampersand Communications Services Inc.
COVER DESIGN: Will Rueter
INTERIOR DESIGN: Brant Cowie/Artplus Limited

CONTENTS

FOREWORD

When the members of the Rowell-Sirois Commission began their collective task in 1937, very little was known about the evolution of the Canadian economy. What was known, moreover, had not been extensively analyzed by the slender cadre of social scientists of the day.

When we set out upon our task nearly 50 years later, we enjoyed a substantial advantage over our predecessors; we had a wealth of information. We inherited the work of scholars at universities across Canada and we had the benefit of the work of experts from private research institutes and publicly sponsored organizations such as the Ontario Economic Council and the Economic Council of Canada. Although there were still important gaps, our problem was not a shortage of information; it was to interrelate and integrate — to synthesize — the results of much of the information we already had.

The mandate of this Commission is unusually broad. It encompasses many of the fundamental policy issues expected to confront the people of Canada and their governments for the next several decades. The nature of the mandate also identified, in advance, the subject matter for much of the research and suggested the scope of enquiry and the need for vigorous efforts to interrelate and integrate the research disciplines. The resulting research program, therefore, is particularly noteworthy in three respects: along with original research studies, it includes survey papers which synthesize work already done in specialized fields; it avoids duplication of work which, in the judgment of the Canadian research community, has already been well done; and, considered as a whole, it is the most thorough examination of the Canadian economic, political and legal systems ever undertaken by an independent agency.

The Commission's Research Program was carried out under the joint direction of three prominent and highly respected Canadian scholars: Dr. Ivan Bernier (*Law and Constitutional Issues*), Dr. Alan Cairns (*Politics and Institutions of Government*) and Dr. David C. Smith (*Economics*).

Dr. Ivan Bernier is Dean of the Faculty of Law at Laval University. Dr. Alan Cairns is former Head of the Department of Political Science at the University of British Columbia and, prior to joining the Commission, was William Lyon Mackenzie King Visiting Professor of Canadian Studies at Harvard University. Dr. David C. Smith, former Head of the Department of Economics at Queen's University in Kingston, is now Principal of that University. When Dr. Smith assumed his new responsibilities at Queen's in September, 1984, he was succeeded by Dr. Kenneth Norrie of the University of Alberta and John Sargent of the federal Department of Finance, who together acted as co-directors of Research for the concluding phase of the Economics research program.

I am confident that the efforts of the Research Directors, research coordinators and authors whose work appears in this and other volumes, have provided the community of Canadian scholars and policy makers with a series of publications that will continue to be of value for many years to come. And I hope that the value of the research program to Canadian scholarship will be enhanced by the fact that Commission research is being made available to interested readers in both English and French.

I extend my personal thanks, and that of my fellow Commissioners, to the Research Directors and those immediately associated with them in the Commission's research program. I also want to thank the members of the many research advisory groups whose counsel contributed so substantially to this undertaking.

DONALD S. MACDONALD

At its most general level, the Royal Commission's research program has examined how the Canadian political economy can better adapt to change. As a basis of enquiry, this question reflects our belief that the future will always take us partly by surprise. Our political, legal and economic institutions should therefore be flexible enough to accommodate surprises and yet solid enough to ensure that they help us meet our future goals. This theme of an adaptive political economy led us to explore the interdependencies between political, legal and economic systems and drew our research efforts in an interdisciplinary direction.

The sheer magnitude of the research output (more than 280 separate studies in 72 volumes) as well as its disciplinary and ideological diversity have, however, made complete integration impossible and, we have concluded, undesirable. The research output as a whole brings varying perspectives and methodologies to the study of common problems and we therefore urge readers to look beyond their particular field of interest and to explore topics across disciplines.

The three research areas, *Law and Constitutional Issues*, under Ivan Bernier, *Politics and Institutions of Government* under Alan Cairns, and *Economics* under David C. Smith (co-directed with Kenneth Norrie and John Sargent for the concluding phase of the research program) — were further divided into 19 sections headed by research coordinators.

The area *Law and Constitutional Issues* has been organized into five major sections headed by the research coordinators identified below.

- Law, Society and the Economy — *Ivan Bernier and Andrée Lajoie*
- The International Legal Environment — *John J. Quinn*
- The Canadian Economic Union — *Mark Krasnick*
- Harmonization of Laws in Canada — *Ronald C.C. Cuming*
- Institutional and Constitutional Arrangements — *Clare F. Beckton and A. Wayne MacKay*

Since law in its numerous manifestations is the most fundamental means of implementing state policy, it was necessary to investigate how and when law could be mobilized most effectively to address the problems raised by the Commission's mandate. Adopting a broad perspective, researchers examined Canada's legal system from the standpoint of how law evolves as a result of social, economic and political changes and how, in turn, law brings about changes in our social, economic and political conduct.

Within *Politics and Institutions of Government*, research has been organized into seven major sections.

- Canada and the International Political Economy — *Denis Stairs and Gilbert Winham*
- State and Society in the Modern Era — *Keith Banting*
- Constitutionalism, Citizenship and Society — *Alan Cairns and Cynthia Williams*
- The Politics of Canadian Federalism — *Richard Simeon*
- Representative Institutions — *Peter Aucoin*
- The Politics of Economic Policy — *G. Bruce Doern*
- Industrial Policy — *André Blais*

This area examines a number of developments which have led Canadians to question their ability to govern themselves wisely and effectively. Many of these developments are not unique to Canada and a number of comparative studies canvass and assess how others have coped with similar problems. Within the context of the Canadian heritage of parliamentary government, federalism, a mixed economy, and a bilingual and multicultural society, the research also explores ways of rearranging the relationships of power and influence among institutions to restore and enhance the fundamental democratic principles of representativeness, responsiveness and accountability.

Economics research was organized into seven major sections.

- Macroeconomics — *John Sargent*
- Federalism and the Economic Union — *Kenneth Norrie*
- Industrial Structure — *Donald G. McFetridge*
- International Trade — *John Whalley*
- Income Distribution and Economic Security — *François Vaillancourt*
- Labour Markets and Labour Relations — *Craig Riddell*
- Economic Ideas and Social Issues — *David Laidler*

Economics research examines the allocation of Canada's human and other resources, how institutions and policies affect this allocation, and the distribution of the gains from their use. It also considers the nature of economic development, the forces that shape our regional and industrial structure, and our economic interdependence with other countries. The thrust of the research in economics is to increase our comprehension of what determines our economic potential and how instruments of economic policy may move us closer to our future goals.

One section from each of the three research areas — The Canadian Economic Union, The Politics of Canadian Federalism, and Federalism and the Economic Union — have been blended into one unified research effort. Consequently, the volumes on Federalism and the Economic Union as well as the volume on The North are the results of an interdisciplinary research effort.

We owe a special debt to the research coordinators. Not only did they organize, assemble and analyze the many research studies and combine their major findings in overviews, but they also made substantial contributions to the Final Report. We wish to thank them for their performance, often under heavy pressure.

Unfortunately, space does not permit us to thank all members of the Commission staff individually. However, we are particularly grateful to the Chairman, The Hon. Donald S. Macdonald, the Commission's Executive Director, Gerald Godsoe, and the Director of Policy, Alan Nymark, all of whom were closely involved with the Research Program and played key roles in the contribution of Research to the Final Report. We wish to express our appreciation to the Commission's Administrative Advisor, Harry Stewart, for his guidance and advice, and to the Director of Publishing, Ed Matheson, who managed the research publication process. A special thanks to Jamie Benidickson, Policy Coordinator and Special Assistant to the Chairman, who played a valuable liaison role between Research and the Chairman and Commissioners. We are also grateful to our office administrator, Donna Stebbing, and to our secretarial staff, Monique Carpentier, Barbara Cowtan, Tina DeLuca, Françoise Guilbault and Marilyn Sheldon.

Finally, a well deserved thank you to our closest assistants, Jacques J.M. Shore, *Law and Constitutional Issues*; Cynthia Williams and her successor Karen Jackson, *Politics and Institutions of Government*; and I. Lilla Connidis, *Economics*. We appreciate not only their individual contribution to each research area, but also their cooperative contribution to the research program and the Commission.

IVAN BERNIER
ALAN CAIRNS
DAVID C. SMITH

In a federation, a starting point for understanding the making of public policy is a constitutional division of powers. The studies in this volume bring together the perspectives of economics, law, and political science in an assessment of the structure and evolution of the sharing of responsibilities in a Canadian federal system. Each of the four papers brings a different approach to the common questions of how and why powers have evolved, and together the studies examine the implications of this evolution for future policy making.

Gérard Bélanger, Professor of Economics at the Université Laval, brings the public choice theory to bear on the division of powers. His models provide a strong, principled defence of the virtue of federalism and decentralization for the efficient performance of public responsibilities. They stress the advantages of intergovernmental competition and the ability of multiple levels of government to generate alternative "packages" of public services.

John Whyte, Professor of Law at Queen's University, focusses on the constitutional allocation of broad powers to regulate the economy. He finds embedded in the Constitution of 1867 two views of Confederation — one focussing on the need for strong central power for economic management and nation-building, the other on the need for protecting provincial communities and their capacity to manage their own economic and social development. The courts, he argues, have sought to balance these conflicting principles, and in so doing have refused to interpret federal powers such as trade and commerce as a mandate for plenary federal authority over economic policy. Whyte's central purpose is to find a set of constitutional "mediating principles" by which judges and all citizens can continue to maintain the balance, in the context of evolving domestic and international forces and their consequences for managing the economy.

Garth Stevenson, Professor of Political Science at the University of Alberta, provides a broad empirical survey beginning with the division of powers at Confederation and tracing changes resulting from major forces, including most important, the growth in size and role of government. He concludes that there is a large and growing disjunction between the formal division of powers in the Constitution and the actual roles governments play, and that there is, therefore, a strong case for a thoroughgoing reassessment.

Professor Frederick J. Fletcher and Donald C. Wallace of York University review and summarize what has become a large, dispersed literature on the consequences of federalism. Their focus is on the question, "What difference does federalism make empirically?" How can we assess whether or not it makes for more or less effective policy making . . . for more or less democratic policy making . . . for a greater or lesser ability to manage conflict? By looking at a large number of concrete case studies, Fletcher and Wallace show that the "complexities of federalism" have widely differing effects in various policy areas and that the consequences of the division of powers can be understood only in terms of mobilization of the social forces in society and the nature of intergovernmental relations.

Together, these papers constitute a compelling overview of the institutional capacity of federalism to respond to changing demands on government.

RICHARD SIMEON

1

The Division of Powers
in a Federal System:
A Review of the Economic Literature,
with Applications to Canada

GÉRARD BÉLANGER

Introduction

Economists have a distinct tendency to equate federalism with inter-governmental relations, as though all countries were federations by impli-cation, simply because their territories also contain municipal governments. Consequently, these analyses neglect the important constitutional aspects of the matter. Since the purpose of this paper is to describe the main themes of the economic literature on federalism, the constitutional aspects will not be totally ignored, but they will not receive all the attention they would warrant in another context.

While any classification of the literature on a given subject is always more or less arbitrary, economic studies of the division of powers in federal systems can probably be placed in one of two main categories: the con-ventional or orthodox approach, and the public choice approach. This paper is divided into one main section on each of the two approaches and a conclusion that summarizes the assessment of the material.

This review, which is by no means exhaustive, provides some applica-tions to the Canadian situation. Unfortunately, in spite of some references to local government, it tends to overemphasize relations between the cen-tral government and the provinces. This shortcoming is partly the result of the economists' lack of interest in the lower level of government.[1]

The Conventional or Orthodox Approach

The vast majority of economic studies of the division of powers in a federal system simply apply the precepts of welfare economics, or the normative foundation of economics. The approach of these economists is therefore conventional and highly orthodox.

This section briefly summarizes the orthodox approach and describes various applications of it to the federal system, along with their limitations.

The Normative Foundation of Economics

The central concept of welfare economics is efficiency, or the avoidance of waste: waste inevitably diminishes the welfare of the citizens, because it reduces the choices available to them. Waste can take a variety of forms, including the overuse of resources in production, poor distribution of goods and services among consumers, and production of goods and services that do not correspond to consumers' preferences.

Economists have sought to determine the conditions for avoiding waste. Without attempting an exhaustive analysis, it is useful to take a rapid look at two of those conditions. The first rule for avoiding waste is to ensure that the benefits of any activity are at least equal to its costs. Otherwise, the activity is a losing one for the economy. Consequently, when deciding whether to increase production, one must determine whether the benefit provided by the additional unit is at least equal to its cost. In fact, production is efficient at that quantity at which marginal cost equals marginal benefit. Beyond that point, the economy loses by an increase in production.

An appropriate price system, produced by a sufficiently competitive environment, allows this no-waste criterion to be met. In fact, it is in the interest of producers to increase production until the cost of one additional unit equals its selling price while, for consumers, the most recent unit available provides a benefit equal to its cost.

In the second place, if the price mechanism is to ensure there is no waste in a decentralized economy, decision makers — both producers and consumers — must internalize or take into account all the results of their decisions. Private benefits and costs must correspond to public benefits and costs for there to be no spillover effects. If such effects occur, the no-waste criterion requires correction of the pricing system so that decision makers do internalize these effects. That is why waste disposal should be subject to fees; it is a cost of any polluting activity.

Applications to a Federal System

Various economists have applied efficiency criteria to different aspects of the distribution of powers in a federal system. Although they are not unanimous, conventional economists do have a distinct bias in favour of the central jurisdiction, which is seen as the exogenous guardian of the national interest, as opposed to the parochial or selfish interests of the regional jurisdictions. In more technical language, the central government can use various instruments to ensure the internalization of spillover effects, while the regional governments are seen as making decisions that create such wasteful effects.

The bias in favour of the central jurisdiction is well illustrated by this quotation from W.E. Oates, the economist who has made the greatest use of the conventional approach in studying federalism:

> From an economic standpoint, the obvious attraction of the federal form of government is that it combines the strengths of unitary government with those of decentralization. Each level of government, rather than attempting to perform all the functions of the public sector, does what it can do best. The central government presumably accepts primary responsibility for stabilizing the economy, for achieving the most equitable distribution of income, and for providing certain public goods that influence significantly the welfare of all members of society. Complementing these operations, subcentral governments can supply those public goods and services that are of primary interest only to the residents of their respective jurisdictions. In this way, a federal form of government offers the best promise of a successful resolution of the problems that constitute the economic raison d'être of the public sector. It is in this sense that federalism may, in economic terms, be described as the optimal form of government. (Oates, 1972, pp. 14–15)

Thus, only matters of strictly regional or local interest should be within the purview of the lower levels of government; all matters of more general concern should be handled by the central government.

The centralizing bias ascribed above to the traditional approach might be countered by the supposed neutrality of its basic premise, which is that a choice must be made between the diversity required to satisfy multifarious private wants, and the centralized intervention required to take economies of scale and spillover effects into account. However, when it comes to the exercise of that choice, most economists reject for the public sector the resource allocation mechanism they advocate for the private sector — the mechanism of competition.[2] They would rather rely on a central jurisdiction said to pursue the national interest than study the competitive processes inherent in the idea of decentralization.

There are many applications of the traditional approach to the division of powers in a federal system, but they all deal with the central problem of economics: the organization of resources. While accepting R.A. Musgrave's breakdown of government activity into three functions — allocation, redistribution and stabilization — it seemed to me that the first of these warranted more detailed study in four parts. This gives a total of six applications in which both the advantages and limitations of the traditional approach to federalism can be examined:

- protection of the national common market;
- redistribution of income;
- economic stabilization;
- fiscal harmonization;
- equalization; and
- spillover effects or externalities.

PROTECTION OF THE NATIONAL COMMON MARKET

For more than two hundred years — especially since 1776 when two important works, by the Rev. Étienne Bonnot de Condillac and Adam Smith, were published — economists have been preaching the virtues of free trade as a source of prosperity. Free trade expands markets and decreases costs through a better division of labour and a more competitive climate. This is all the more important for a small region, which has more to gain from specialization and which, even in the short term, exerts no monopoly power in the international marketplace. Moreover, protectionism on the part of other governments does not warrant the use of protectionist measures by the domestic government because even unilateral free trade increases total income.

The constitutions of all federations prohibit the regional governments from erecting tariff barriers to imports from other countries or other regions of their own country. International and interregional trade is the exclusive domain of the central government, which can impose tariffs only on imported products. Therefore, federal constitutions aim at creating an internal common market, in other words, free trade in goods and services within the national boundaries.

However, tariff barriers are only one of many ways of hampering trade, and one whose relative significance is declining as a result of various negotiations, mainly under the GATT. Protectionism today is more likely to assume the form of non-tariff barriers — in particular quotas on various products, subsidies to domestic producers, preferential procurement policies, nationalization and, lastly, the regulation of various goods and services, especially with respect to labour. Thus a multiplicity of interventions by an omnipresent government would actually encourage the breakdown of a federation's internal common market. One example is the balkanization of the Canadian economy in recent years.[3]

The term balkanization, which seems to be synonymous with protectionism, needs to be defined precisely: it is the phenomenon by which government intervention dissociates the price of regional goods and services from the cost of producing them. Thus, balkanization is the regional dimension of inefficiency. Moreover, the balkanizing effect is just as strong when the price distortion applies to public sector goods and services. By altering relative regional prices, government intervention confers varying benefits and imposes varying costs on the people in the regions. These differences lead to balkanization.[4]

For example, the federal government's generous assistance to the nuclear energy sector has been of considerable advantage to Ontario, which has eleven of the thirteen nuclear generating stations currently in operation in Canada and all eleven of the stations that are under construction. The federal assistance has been a source of balkanization in the Canadian economy because it has distorted relative or regional prices in the country and has artifically weakened Quebec's natural advantage over Ontario in electricity.

The balkanization of the Canadian economy is a consequence not only of provincial protectionist policies, but also of the many central government programs that distort relative regional prices. It is not at all far-fetched to suggest that the central government has a stronger balkanizing effect than the other levels. Its discretionary power is greater than theirs because it is less subject to competition.[5]

Lessening Balkanization

If balkanization is the regional dimension of inefficiency, it would seem appropriate to reduce it. There are three possible approaches to this: limiting the powers of the lower levels of government; limiting the powers of all levels or government; or doing nothing directly.

Until recently, the literature on the balkanization of the Canadian economy was devoted almost exclusively to inveighing against the discriminatory policies of the provinces, and therefore it recommended strengthening the role of the central government in order to protect the integrity of the Canadian common market. The commerce clause in the American constitution was considered enviably broad in scope, compared with the similar provision of the British North America Act.

During the negotiations culminating in the Constitution Act, 1982, the federal government published a paper on the Canadian economic union and, in particular, advanced constitutional proposals for giving it greater protection (Chrétien, 1980). These provisions, which were rejected during the negotiations, would have considerably increased the powers of the central government. As Courchene notes:

> When these proposals were finally cast into draft sections of the new constitution, they amounted to a dramatic centralization of power in federal hands with little or no guarantee of any increase in the economic rights of individuals.
>
> (Courchene, 1984, p. 214)

The argument against limiting the powers of the central government is based on the fact that it represents every region in the country and internalizes all the effects of its decisions. Consequently, only the central government would be in a position to ascertain whether the net costs of balkanizing policies are warranted for reasons other than strict economic efficiency.

The second approach to reducing balkanization is to limit the powers of all levels of government. If the central government is viewed as the guardian of the national interest, as opposed to the limited interests of the regional governments, then asymmetrical constitutional constraints are warranted in order to protect the integrity of the common market. The challenge to this argument comes from the presence of imperfections in the political market that considerably limit the scope of the national interest. It would appear that the more concentrated or circumscribed the benefits of a government decision in relation to the distribution of the costs and the tax burden, the more likely that the decision will be made. It is not therefore surprising that political forces should lead to policies that do not meet the criteria of economic efficiency and that result in the balkanization of the national territory by the central government. For that reason, the constitutional provisions for protecting the integrity of the common market should limit the powers of all levels of government. This is the case with the Australian constitution, which prohibits both the state and federal (Commonwealth) governments from engaging in activities that involve regional discrimination. Section 93 says:

> The Commonwealth shall not, by any law or regulation of trade, commerce, or revenue, give preference to one State or any part thereof over another State or any part thereof.

The Australian constitution puts constraints on the central government, unlike the American constitution, which favours the federal government by limiting the discriminatory powers of the individual states.[6]

Nevertheless, while balkanization is the result of dissociating the regional prices of goods and services from their costs of production, the balkanizing effect is no less strong when the price distortion applies to public sector goods and services. Therefore, a constitutional amendment intended to protect the common market might have to be very broad in scope if it were to limit any state intervention with an internal discriminatory effect and encourage the setting of realistic rates for public services. Such an amendment would, in effect, be a type of charter of individual economic rights (Grubel, 1982).

The third approach to reducing balkanization is to do nothing directly, since constitutional provisions for protecting the common market may be considered inappropriate for various reasons. First, a number of authors prefer the British system, in which Parliament is supreme, with no formal constitution to override or limit it, to the American one, in which a group of nine individuals determines the important rules of society. Second, the real costs of provincial balkanization in Canada have been exaggerated, especially with regard to their spillover effects.[7] Since the provincial economies are very open, market forces prevent them from exporting any significant portion of the inefficiency costs arising from their governments' policies.

Nevertheless, it is important to be aware of the serious consequences the central government's protectionist policies can have by making the economy less open. On one hand, such policies have an effect on production allocation because rejecting free trade with other countries fosters the development of an industrial strategy or a "rationalization of production" at home; on the other hand, rejecting the use of immigration as a "pump primer" leads to recommendations for human resource planning policies. Moreover, a closed national economy can give the governments of the more populous provinces a certain monopoly power, enabling them to export part of the burden of their policies. In that sense, protectionism at the national level stimulates protectionism at the provincial level.

Lastly, if discriminatory policies reflect imperfections in the political market, it is preferable to correct them directly by improving the political processes or institutions: for example, by reforming the Senate, requiring more than a simple majority on certain questions and making more frequent use of referendums, with power of initiation by the public.

REDISTRIBUTION OF INCOME

The protection of the common market deals with the efficient allocation of resources without regard for what might be considered a desirable distribution of income. The public sector can play a significant role in altering the distribution of income so as to assist the less fortunate and provide income protection for the general population against socio-economic risks. In fact, many, perhaps most, government programs are created for their redistributive effects. By various means they take income away from some people and give it to others.

Unfortunately, it is very difficult to estimate the net effect of the various government interventions in this area with any accuracy. There are a number of reasons for this, including the decrease in private charity, the weakening of family ties, and alterations in the system of penalties and rewards for economic agents, such as explicitly or implicitly high tax rates and even incentives for fraud. However, one fairly widespread hypothesis suggests that redistribution policies have been of little help to the poorest one-fifth of the population — formerly the main concern of private charity — but have benefited the middle class, which forms the next two-fifths (Tullock, 1983).

As the quotation above from Oates illustrates so clearly, the conventional approach to federalism assigns the main redistributive function to the level of government furthest removed from the people. This prevents people from moving elsewhere in the country in order to minimize the cost of redistribution if they are net contributors, or to increase their benefits if they are on the receiving end.[8] In fact, if a municipal government wants to alter the distribution of income in its own territory (as the City of New York did during the 1960s, with its large network of free postsecondary institutions and municipal hospitals, an impressive stock of public housing and its social welfare program), it will have to raise its taxes in relation to the municipalities that do not wish to perform that function. The differences in tax rates will cause an exodus of individual and corporate taxpayers who were profitable to the municipality, while its generous assistance programs will promote an influx of potential beneficiaries, leading to increased expenditures. Consequently, the ability of the lower levels of government to redistribute income appears to be limited. The central government is better able to impose redistribution because taxpayers then find it relatively difficult to avoid their obligations by voting with their feet and gathering together with their peers to form a type of ghetto where lower tax rates are capitalized in higher land prices.

The redistribution of income to help the less fortunate can also be seen as a kind of collective good on which each individual's contribution has a negligible influence, but which is significantly affected by the aggregate contributions of all whose incomes are above a given level. Government action then becomes a mechanism for forcing individuals to contribute to the collective good that they really do want, even though their individual welfare prompts them to behave as "free riders," leaving it to others to assume the cost of the good they all seek. If it were generalized, this avoidance would block the redistribution, thus requiring constraining action on the part of government.[9]

The preceding argument — which is related to strictly technical, not economic, efficiency — does favour a strong role for the central government in income redistribution; however, for a number of reasons this role cannot be exclusive.[10] First, the conventional discussion of redistribution emphasizes the fact that it is imposed but neglects to mention that it is a type of good with some elements of supply and demand. Nevertheless, private charities still exist, although government redistribution policies have made them less important. Moreover, if sympathy for other people varies inversely with distance, and if mobility costs are relatively high, then there is a place for decentralized redistribution.[11] That is how small, very open countries can establish internal redistribution programs.

Standardized national redistribution policies very often involve significant inefficiency costs. For example, how can they take the sizable role of the non-monetary economy in a small community like a Newfoundland fishing village into account? Lastly, the increased convenience of having redistribution policies assigned to the central government simply reflects the greater discretionary power of this level, because the individual citizen cannot migrate elsewhere in the country in order to better satisfy his public sector preferences.[12] But how does that benefit the unfortunate?

ECONOMIC STABILIZATION

The last of the three major functions — allocation, distribution and stabilization — has still to be analyzed. According to Oates, this function, too, should be primarily the central government's responsibility. In the Keynesian models, the multiplier effects of variations in expenditures or taxes are smaller at the regional level than at the central level, because the lower-level economy is more open than the central one. Consequently, regional stabilization policies have spillover effects that prevent them from being optimal for the nation as a whole. Moreover, the regional government cannot turn to the monetary authority to finance its deficit, unlike the central government, which uses the central bank to absorb part of its debt.

This kind of analysis is open to various objections. First, the results of the central government's economic stabilization policies in Canada have not been very inspiring, even setting aside possible contradictory regional effects. One researcher who summarized seven analyses from various sources was able to conclude without hesitation, "Federal contracyclical fiscal policy performance during the postwar period was poor."[13] Nevertheless, he hastened to add, "The perverse fiscal policy actions of the postwar period may have been successful in assuring electoral gains."[14]

However, the main objection is the kind of model used by Oates and the other adherents of the conventional approach to analyze economic stabilization policies. The economy of a province like Quebec, and even that of a small country not unlike Canada, can be described as a very open one in which capital and commodities are significantly more mobile than labour. In such cases, economics teaches that government policies for combatting unemployment should pay little attention to aggregate demand management, concentrating rather on relative prices, especially labour costs.[15]

The existing Canadian Constitution leaves the provinces important instruments for altering regional wage levels. For the past 20 years, for example, in addition to raising taxes more rapidly than elsewhere, the various Quebec governments have increased the monopoly powers of unions, necessarily encouraging a relative increase in labour costs and, as a result, unemployment. Some of these measures are the unionization of, and province-wide negotiations with the right to strike in, the public and para-public sectors; until recently a very high minimum wage; employment restrictions and province-wide negotiations in the construction industry; and anti-strikebreaking legislation; not to mention the many decrees affecting tens of thousands of workers.

As a result, Quebec has presented a paradox since early 1980. In spite of a relatively plentiful labour force — revealed by its traditionally higher unemployment rate and the tendency of its natural population increase to be partially offset by net emigration — the average weekly earnings are higher in Quebec than in Ontario for the industrial composites, for nearly every component of the service sector and for the construction industry. Although the average earnings in the manufacturing sector are lower by 8.5 percent in Quebec, nearly 40 percent of employment in manufacturing is concentrated in the higher-paid subsectors. In addition to the large paper and printing industries, Quebec earnings are higher in industries usually considered "soft": leather products, nonsynthetic textiles, knitting mills, clothing and furniture.

This quick analysis of provincial policies that destroy jobs gives a good indication of the significant role a province can play in economic stabilization, particularly in a federal system in which labour legislation is mainly the responsibility of the regional jurisdictions.

So far, we have seen how the traditional approach is biased toward a strong central government for three of its functions: protection of the national common market, redistribution of income and economic stabilization. However, for each function I have tried to show that the arguments of the traditional approach raise potentially serious objections. This analysis of the traditional approach continues below with an examination of fiscal harmonization, equalization and, lastly, the subject that embraces all the others — spillover effects or externalities.

FISCAL HARMONIZATION

The question of fiscal harmonization is analytically related to the attempt to create a common market. The purpose of harmonization is to enable the various resources to be located and exploited wherever they will be most productive. Provincial government taxation can hamper the pursuit of efficiency by distorting the optimum geographic distribution of activities in the country. Therefore, taxation is not neutral.

Unfortunately, most work on fiscal harmonization in federal systems does not refer explicitly to the criterion of economic efficiency, but to that of uniformity.[16] The most direct way of achieving this objective is to have a single tax system for the whole country. Centralization produces harmonization because the tax rules are the same for everyone. Then, the central tax collector distributes revenues to the provincial governments, choosing among various criteria: amount collected in each province, population, standardized expenditures and so on. This is a good instance of what Gordon Tullock was already criticizing in the traditional approach to federalism fifteen years ago:

> Many students seem to think that a highly centralized government is the most effective government. It would be more accurate to say that centralized government is the most orderly government. . . . The most efficient goverment is not the most orderly looking government but the government that comes closest to carrying out the wishes of its makers.   (Tullock, 1969, p. 29)

Thus, by analogy many economists characterize the family as living in harmony when all its members think and behave identically, in all probability like the central authority, traditionally the father. Competition, discussion and tension between generations and sexes have no place in this "harmonious" family. Yet is this not a denial of the true family, just as uniformity is a denial of true federalism?

There are two other serious objections to fiscal harmonization through the use of a single, more or less pervasive tax system. First, such a system is hard to reconcile with the principle of the administrative responsibility of each level of government, which sees the revenue collected by each level as an indication of the quantity and quality of services the people want. Is this administrative responsibility not a prerequisite for minimizing waste or striving for efficiency?

Moreover, a centralized tax system is no assurance that the government will not distort prices within the country, since government intervention is not only restricted to taxation. To take the one example of budgetary operations, it is the net fiscal balance (the difference between the benefits derived from public expenditures and the costs of taxation) that should be the focus of harmonization.

The net fiscal balance can be harmonized throughout the country by making all income redistribution policies the preserve of the central government. Lower jurisdictions would then become mere purveyors of public services, making their taxes correspond as much as possible to the benefits received. They would not be involved in the redistribution function of the public sector. This situation is, for the most part, typical of the municipal level, which has lost many redistributive functions since the 1930s. The responsibility of municipalities for welfare policy has disappeared, or consists at most of administering provincial programs. The entire education sector, especially the financing of primary and secondary education, has gradually been taken over by the provinces.

Moreover, the various studies of the incidence of each jurisdiction's taxes are unanimous in agreeing that the central government has the most progressive tax system. In contrast, the municipal level makes greater use of pricing devices in financing public services, following the principle of taxation according to benefit received.

Nevertheless, the provinces retain considerable responsibility for the redistribution of income in Canada. For example, they must pay one-half the cost of their social assistance programs, with the federal government reimbursing the other half under the Canada Assistance Plan. This provincial responsibility for income redistribution can distort prices because, for a given level of income, the net fiscal balance is relatively unfavourable to residents of provinces with a tax base that is lower than average. This can lead to inefficient shifts of resources, needlessly penalizing the "have-not" provinces.

How can this situation be remedied? The simplest way is to limit the responsibility of the lower levels of government for income redistribution, since that is the source of the difficulty. Therefore, if they decide to take part in the redistribution function, they will have to be prepared to assume the consequences of their decision, as befits responsible governments. The use of equalization payments, the subject of the next section, is also proposed.

All in all, harmonization imposed by the central government is a source of monopoly power that increases the public sector's discretionary power over the individual by making it easier to collect taxes.[17] It runs counter to economic efficiency, which requires that the onerous nature of taxation not be disguised. On the other hand, harmonization can be the spontaneous result of governments' trying to minimize the inefficiency costs of their taxes. This situation should yield the optimal degree of harmonization, as illustrated by the example of federations in which the lower governments avoid significant differences in business taxes for fear the firms will move out of their territory.

Consequently, whether harmonization is good or bad depends on whether it is free and spontaneous, or imposed. In the first case, it is the result of competition and, in the second, it derives from a monopoly power, which is a source of constraints on the individual.

EQUALIZATION PAYMENTS

The rationale for government payments to individuals is the government's redistributive function. But what is the *raison d'être* for intergovernmental transfers such as the equalization payments Canada has had since 1957? These payments are unconditional grants from the central government, which effectively enable the have-not provinces to obtain per capita tax receipts equal to the average receipts of five provinces (excluding Alberta and the Maritimes) for all provincial and property taxes. This allows these provinces to provide an "average" level of public services, from the standpoint of both quantity and quality, without imposing a heavier tax burden on their residents.

Equalization payments can be appropriate in an imperfect world (according to the theory of "second best"). For example, if the provinces retain an autonomous role in income redistribution and their tax bases vary significantly, the net fiscal balance throughout the country for a given level of income will also vary, leading naturally to inefficient shifts in resources.[18] Consequently, equalization payments would appear to be a means of preventing this kind of mobility, which is a source of inefficiency or waste because the resources do not go where they would be most productive.[19] Was the purpose of entrenching the equalization principle in the Constitution Act, 1982, not to promote economic efficiency?

The problem of disparities among the provincial tax bases in Canada was brought into sharper focus by the increase in energy prices, in particular, oil. For example, the Alberta government had large receipts that enabled it to provide extensive public services with a minimal burden on its taxpayers. The very strong positive fiscal balance for residents of that province encouraged inefficient migration, that is, migration not entirely due to higher factor productivity in that province. Thus, migration became a way of dissipating the rent, or alternatively, a poor way of distributing it. Equalization payments can help indirectly to reduce this inefficiency.[20]

At least three objections can be raised with respect to equalization payments. First, while they make greater fiscal harmonization in the country possible, they do not guarantee it. That really depends on the policies of the provincial governments that receive the payments. Second, such payments — even in the form of unconditional grants — can lead to an overexpansion of the public sector by giving voters a false impression of the true marginal cost of provincial public services, assuming that voters take their average tax burden as the indicator of these marginal costs.[21] Lastly, why should the central government not let the provinces be fully responsible for their income redistribution decisions and tolerate variations across the country in the net fiscal balance for a given level of income?

SPILLOVER EFFECTS

So far, the entire analysis of the conventional approach to the distribution of powers in a federal system can be summarized as follows: the decentralized jurisdictions should handle the goods and services of exclusive or primary concern to their citizens, while the federal jurisdiction should intervene in everything that has broader implications. For example, spillover effects or externalities create inefficiencies in the decentralized allocation of resources and warrant intervention of some sort by a central jurisdiction.[22]

Unfortunately, a spillover effect can be found in any local or regional good. For example, the construction of a marina can be of interest to the central government, and eligible for financing by it, because it is located on an international or interprovincial waterway, or because the project can fit into some national program to fight unemployment, promote balanced regional development or provide infrastructure support to improve the quality of life for Canadians. There is no lack of ingenuity when it comes to finding arguments for grants, and much inspiration can be found in the analytical decision-making models developed by economists.[23]

What is, in my opinion, the very widespread conclusion of the conventional approach in favour of centralization has been reached by the same method listed by a legendary Roman emperor to judge between two singers. He listened only to the first one and awarded the prize to the second, on the assumption that the second could not possibly be worse! This has happened because the traditional approach implicitly assumes that the central jurisdiction will act as a benevolent despot to maximize the national interest. Only a lack of information about the strength of preferences for strictly local goods prevents the centralization of all powers in a single level of government. Just what mechanisms or processes will produce such a "benevolent" authority is not examined at all.[24]

Consequently, the conventional approach emphasizes the waste and inefficiencies resulting from the spillover effects of decentralized decisions but does not address the other side — the inefficiencies resulting from centralized decisions: the exporting of a very large part of the cost of regional services, standardization of services, increasing cartelization of government and a lack of experimentation and flexibility, to mention only a few.[25]

Nevertheless, there are ways in which the lower governments can partially export the burden of their policies through those of the central government. Although it is true in open economies like those of the provinces that market mechanisms are almost totally incapable of transferring the inefficiency costs of provincial and local policies, the transfer can still be partially achieved by the action of federal transfer and regional development policies. Courchene (1979) has described this situation:

> The incentives embodied in the transfer system are not conductive to ameliorating regional disparities. On the contrary, provinces are encouraged to enact legislation that is not in their long-run economic interest, nor in the interest of their citizens. In turn, these decisions can force Ottawa's hand in the type of legislation it enacts. (p. 32)

It may be useful to cite some cases of potential transfer of the burden of provincial policies, taking taxation as an example. First, since Crown corporations at all three levels of government are exempt from federal taxes, the proliferation of this type of organization at the provincial level is artificially promoted. Thus, one of the main reasons advanced by the government of Quebec for nationalizing the private electricity companies at the beginning of the 1960s was to repatriate the taxes paid to the federal government. Ottawa also bore the cost of Quebec's corporate tax reform. At the same time as provincial corporate income tax, which is not deductible from income taxable at the federal level, was significantly reduced, payroll taxes and taxes on paid-up capital of corporations, which are deductible from corporate income for federal tax purposes, were increased. This problem is even more significant in the United States, where state and local government taxes are deducted in calculating federal taxable income. This encourages the expansion of the lower levels of government. Put more generally, since any inefficient provincial policy reduces the federal tax base, the central government assumes part of the burden of such inefficiency.

In short, the federal government, through its protectionist policies and the stimuli provided by various other policies, can increase the lower government's ability to export the burden of their policies. Consequently, it should take this effect into account in designing its policies.

If the conventional approach to federalism favours centralization, does the opposite hold true for the other approach — the analysis of federalism from a public choice perspective? To answer this question, it is necessary to summarize the main contributions of this school of thought. That is the subject of the next section.

The Public Choice Approach to Federalism

Although the traditional approach to federalism is based on an exogenous governmental authority that can be described as a benevolent despot, public choice analysis, as the term is used here, covers all the studies that seek to make the public sector endogenous to the larger socio-economic system. The authors of these studies use traditional economic methodology — that is to say, economic agents acting in their own interests — to explain government activity. What the various points of view have in common is their economic approach to politics.

There are two parts to this section. The first is a very brief summary of the contribution made by Breton and Scott to the study of the distribution of powers in a federal system; the second examines the dynamics of competition between two levels of government.

The Viewpoint of Albert Breton and Anthony Scott

Breton and Scott address the question of the distribution of powers in a constitution directly, using the theory of the firm.[26] In order to obtain the various products it needs, the firm has to choose between producing them itself — purchasing the services of factors of production and using an internal control structure — and purchasing the products directly in the marketplace. This choice depends on organization costs and is somewhat flexible.

The two authors start with an imaginary constituent assembly in which representatives of highly diverse interests come together to negotiate. The purpose of this assembly is to determine the structure of the federal system, or the optimum level of decentralization, by seeking to minimize the organizational costs and inefficiencies that are pure losses. These organizational costs are of four types. The first two are borne directly by the voters: they are the costs of signalling their preferences by various means, such as voting and political pressure, and the costs of mobility between jurisdictions or "voting with their feet." The other two organizational costs are borne by governments: they are the costs of intergovernmental coordination of policies and internal administration costs.

This approach is interesting because it has the advantage of broadening the simplistic framework of the conventional analysis, and because, through the mechanism of the constituent assembly, it reintroduces the supremacy of the consumer. Unfortunately, the analysis is very abstract, partly owing to the lack of empirical information on the various aspects of organization costs.[27] Moreover, constitutional revisions are not produced only by constituent assemblies, as recent Canadian experience illustrates. Why would they be, when this instrument gives more power to the citizens? In fact, constitutions evolve indirectly, through such mechanisms as conditional grants, whereby the central government trades money for power.[28]

Competition in Federalism

In the private sector, competition is a powerful spur to efficiency. Viewed in the same way, a multiplicity of jurisdictions is a source, not so much of balkanization or disorder, as of choices for the citizen and a better approximation of public services to the varied preferences of the population.[29] The more decentralized the jurisdiction, the less discretionary power it has over the citizen. Therefore, decentralized federalism would appear to be a way of exercising control over the government, which is perceived as an exploiter or a new leviathan.[30]

If horizontal competition — competition among several governments at the same level — is seen as a source of choices and protection for the citizen, is vertical competition among various levels of government any different? Some writers believe this vertical competition has the same effect as competition in general and, consequently, that it provides the citizen with a better combination of public policies that take both national and regional considerations into account. As Riker says of the United States, "In function after function there is in fact no division of authority between constituent governments and the center, but rather a mingling."[31] In the same vein, West and Winer, instead of condemning duplication in government programs, say, "It is our view that an agreement between the federal government and the provinces over the division of power could be cause for concern by those who favour civil liberties."[32]

However, might the political process not favour the central authority, which would retain more of certain monopoly or discretionary powers? In the nineteenth century, two analysts had already noticed this tendency toward the hegemony of the central jurisdictions. Alexis de Tocqueville, in *Democracy in America*, said, "I am of the opinion that, in the democratic ages which are opening upon us . . . centralization will be the natural government." Lord Bryce, in *The American Commonwealth*, noted, "Federalism is simply a transitory step on the way to governmental unity." The history of federations tends to confirm these assessments. Federations do not owe their origin to decentralization of a unitary government, but rather to the incomplete fusion of previously separate units.[33]

A possible explanation of the increasing centralization and increasing standardization of services in federations may lie in the fact that the central jurisdiction can levy taxes more easily because it faces less competition and that it can trade money for power with the other levels of government when it does not have the power to intervene unilaterally.[34] The same explanation applies to the loss of autonomy by local governments.

In an imperfect world that encourages centralization, there is a place for a constitutional division of powers. Along with its role as potential guardian of individual liberties against government authority, the constitution can play a protective role against the forces of centralization.[35] This would necessitate placing constraints on the central jurisdiction instead of the reverse, as was done recently in the United States. In fact, the recent measures limiting the taxing power of municipalities — of which the best known is California's proposition 13 – affect the level of government with the least discretionary power, given the fact that local economies are wide open.

Nevertheless, it is legitimate to wonder whether constitutional constraints are adequate to the task. With the rapid growth of government intervention in the postwar period, and given the significant grey areas in the Constitution and the very broad general powers assigned to the federal government, Canada has witnessed — in the words of Ottawa's Federal-Provincial Relations Office — "a widespread, if not general, breakdown of traditional constitutional fences."[36] Unlike the Canadian Constitution, the American constitution assigns the residual powers to the states. But that provision has not prevented the American federation from becoming highly centralized.[37]

A system like Switzerland's, with a second federal chamber whose members represent the regions (the cantons), would seem to be a useful, but certainly not infallible, mechanism for restraining the centralizing tendency. Another way of doing that would be to prohibit the central government from intervening through conditional grants if a specified minimum number of provinces were opposed.[38]

The fact remains that the distribution of spending among levels of government is a poor indicator of the evolution of centralization in a federal state. Contrary to popular opinion, the significant decrease in the federal share, after transfers, of total public spending (from 60 percent between 1947 and 1952 to approximately 40 percent since 1967), certainly does not indicate a strong trend toward decentralization in Canada since 1945. What has occurred is a variety of transactions between the federal government and the provinces. The federal government established the broad framework of new programs in fields over which the provinces had primary constitutional authority in exchange for grants to the provinces. These included conditional and unconditional grants and even the transfer of tax points. The general powers assigned to the central government made it easier for that jurisdiction to obtain these exchanges or agreements. The period was also one during which the central government had the lion's share of taxes, which were not yet indexed, and with a yield growing faster than the economy. At the same time, the policies that appeared most popular were largely within the jurisdiction of the other levels of government. As a result, these exchanges allowed each level of government to improve its electoral image.

These exchanges placed severe constraints on the provinces' determination of their priorities. Since the provinces had to adjust their policies accordingly, the federal-provincial arrangements did not represent a step toward greater decentralization as far as the province was concerned. Nevertheless, that is how it appeared to the federal government, because it had to negotiate its interventions.

These two contradictory perceptions — one representing the central government's view and the other the provincial governments' — really bring out how difficult it is to obtain a reliable indicator of the degree of decentralization of the public sector and how pointless it is to calculate the comparative shares of each level of government for this purpose. Recent developments in the financing of established programs only confirm this.

Lastly, so as not to omit anything, there should be reference to the presumably different point of view of some other economists. This group would have their colleagues pay less attention to the normative aspects of the results of policies in a federal system and more to the improvements in organizational procedures that are likely to yield better outcomes.[39] For example, they recommend mechanisms such as formal meetings, at which all points of view are heard and every aspect of a question is examined in order to achieve better policy coordination. Unfortunately, this contributes very little to the study of procedures and in particular it ignores the fact that this very question is the central concern of the public choice approach, which studies the impact of various decision-making structures in the public sector.

Conclusion

As a conclusion to this summary of the two main approaches to the distribution of powers in a federal system, four general propositions can be stated:

- the distribution of powers is a "big question";
- the two approaches are very different, if not mutually exclusive;
- the conventional approach leads to fairly specific conclusions but its foundations are extremely weak; and
- the public choice approach provides a better definition of the questions requiring study, but its conclusions remain vague.

The distribution of powers is a "big question." The statement that the distribution of powers in federalism is a big question does not mean it is pointless to study it. On the contrary, the expression simply indicates (in addition to the scope of the question) a need to make use of ideas and beliefs about how various social mechanisms work. It is not surprising that different conceptions lead to different conclusions. Conclusions arise from premises.

Consequently, a true consensus on a big question is not to be expected among members of a given discipline. Were such a consensus to exist, it would be suspect because it could only be a reflection of the members' own interests. Moreover, it is perfectly normal for economists to alter their conclusions radically in the light of a new understanding of certain social mechanisms.[40]

The two approaches are very different, if not mutually exclusive. The economic literature on the distribution of powers in a federal system has been divided between two very different approaches. According to the conventional approach, government intervention is external to the political process. It is the result of decisions made by a sort of benevolent despot whose only concern is efficiency. On the other hand, the public choice approach includes studies that focus on government decision making, which is seen as the product of economic agents acting in their own interests.

These very different points of departure lead to differing conclusions on the division of powers. The first approach displays a clear centralizing bias, because only the central jurisdiction can maximize the national interest, as opposed to the parochial aims of the regional jurisdictions. The conclusions follow naturally from the premise.

The public choice approach, starting with individuals acting in their own interests, has the advantage of taking the study of federalism out of the realm of the abstract and into that of the concrete, examining it as a living institution in which the agents make their decisions according to the rules of the game. This approach generally displays a bias toward decentralization, as a means of enabling citizens to signal their various preferences more easily, and also of preventing the cartelization of the public sector.

The conventional approach has specific conclusions built on weak foundations. As the summary quoted from Oates at the beginning of this study indicates, the traditional approach yields specific conclusions that are very favourable to centralization. Why then, if economic efficiency requires this centralization, do so few policies of the central government meet efficiency criteria? Has this approach not generated a useless orthodoxy, as though players were trying to play poker by the rules of bridge? This approach sees centralization as the cure for the possible ills of decentralization, but does not examine the imperfections of the cure.[41] If it is to be of some relevance, the conventional approach will have to examine the mechanisms or processes by which the "benevolent" central authority implied in its rationale is created.

The public choice approach provides a good definition of the questions, but vague conclusions. The public choice approach adopts the terms used by traditional economic analysis (economic agents acting in their own interests) to explain government activity. The task of the economist is not to advise the benevolent despot (or prince), but to explain the impact of various decision-making structures. In that case, the relevant questions are: What is the effect of a federal system of government, in comparison with a unitary system or a system of unfederated units? Do constitutional provisions have a significant effect on policies? What mechanisms might improve the correspondence between public policy and the true preferences of the citizens in a heterogeneous society?

These very general questions illustrate the orientation of the public choice approach. Unfortunately, the answers are vague and will remain so for some time.[42] As yet little is known about such crucial matters as the importance of imperfections in the political market or of bureaucratic competition.

In spite of the huge gaps in our knowledge, however, the public choice approach contains a bias in favour of competition and, consequently, decentralization. In that, is it not consistent with what has been the principal tenet of economics for more than two hundred years?

Notes

This study is a translation of the original French-language text, which was completed in October 1984.

1. In my own defence, I refer the reader to my three papers: Bélanger (1976, 1980, 1984).

2. Breton (1983) recently expressed the same idea: "The general view among economists about intergovernmental competition is that it is not optimal. For that reason economists either favour a centralized form of government or, when they are forced by political necessity to accept the existence of federalism, they favour the maximum degree of policy harmonization" (p. 257).

3. See especially Safarian (1974, 1979).

4. The last two paragraphs are based on Migué (1983), p. 22.

5. This has been confirmed by a recent publication: "In fact, it is difficult to predict that central or unitary governments will be less prone to distort internal trade flows than lower levels of government. The evidence presented in this book suggests the opposite" (Trebilcock et al., 1983, p. 558).

6. The information in this paragraph is drawn mainly from a recent publication by Flatters and Lipsey (1983). These two economists favour borrowing the provisions of the Australian constitution to protect the Canadian common market.

7. A recent study of interstate barriers in the United States came to the same conclusion:

There are a large number and variety of interstate trade barriers. Two motivations for the observed barriers are theoretically examined. One reason state governments have for erecting trade barriers is there may be an opportunity to deflect costs to other states, or it may be possible to import certain benefits again at the expense of surrounding states. The alternative motivation examined is the potential for redistribution of income to one favored segment of the home state's population. The observed trade barriers are found to more closely correspond to the within-state redistribution motive. Thus, barriers to interstate trade are not found to be a product of the Federalist governmental structure, but are a result of the political economy of the individual state level governments.   (Craig and Sailors, 1983)

8. See Ladd and Doolittle (1982) as well as Usher (1980), who says: "Powers of government involving substantial redistribution of income from rich to poor should on that account be under the jurisdiction of federal rather than provincial government" (p. 668).

9. Private charity places the donor under a constraint by the mechanism of canvassing, which is not impersonal but nearly always involves someone the donor knows.

10. Breton and Scott (1978) have developed this point very well; see especially pp. 125-28.

11. This is analyzed in Pauly (1973).

12. Buchanan (1974, p. 38) gives a good summary of this: "There is more range of variation in the distribution of the gross gains-from-trade in the central government's provision of public goods and services than there is in the distribution of such gains from the provision of goods either through the market or through local government."

13. Gillespie (1979, p. 276). He adds: "The most charitable assessments found fiscal policy to be adequate no more than two-fifths of the time. The least favourable assessment (Gordon, 1983) found fiscal policy to be perverse (destabilizing) two-fifths of the time. Achieved budgetary policy did not even match the stated intentions and plans for budgetary policy."

14. Ibid., p. 276.

15. An excellent source on this point is Lindbeck (1976):

> Thus, an "improper" real wage rate, with a concurrent low profitability level, can be expected to be a more frequent reason for unemployment, low investment incentives, and a current account deficit in economies where the commodity market is open relative to the labor market than in economies where the degree of openness is about the same in both markets. This means that policies designed to influence the real wage rate will be more important for investment, employment, and the current account, the more open the commodity market is relative to the labor market. As an empirical generalization, I think it is safe to say that stabilization policy has suffered considerably in many countries from a neglect of relative prices — such as the real wage rate, the relative price between tradables and nontradables and in particular profitability — as compared to aggregate demand (pp. 4 and 5).

This approach to economic stabilization in a small country makes the popular distinction between cyclical and structural unemployment less relevant.

16. For the Canadian situation, refer to Thirsk (1980) and Forget (1983). Bird (1984) provides an excellent review of the literature on fiscal harmonization.

17. "Revenue sharing may represent some sharing of the fiscal monopoly of the federal government with state and local governments" (Wagner, 1983, p. 472).

18. This explanation first appeared in Buchanan (1950). In Canada, Boadway and Flatters have recently made frequent use of it. See, for example, Boadway and Flatters (1982).

19. Similar reasoning may warrant the use of zoning by municipalities. "If revenues are to be raised by a real-estate tax levied at the same rate on the market value of each dwelling, then land-use controls are required to ensure that each dwelling's market value is adequate to yield the appropriate tax payment" (Mills, 1979, p. 533).

20. See Dales (1983). The problem comes down to this: how can a rent be distributed efficiently, regardless of its source (be it petroleum or an exceptional location)? Should the federal government not tax all the rent, even that which is appropriated by provincial governments? If that is the case, to whom does this rent belong?
   Even when there is strong competition among local governments, they can still tax land rents to finance inefficient policies. "Competition among numerous jurisdictions is not sufficient to guarantee public sector efficiency. Though residents can 'vote with their feet', land is immobile. Hence, governments can usurp some land rents for their own ends. Increasing the number of jurisdictions limits but cannot completely eliminate the ability to exercise discretionary governmental power" (Epple and Zelenitz, 1981, p. 1197).

21. This explanation is advanced by Oates (1979) in an attempt to reconcile the traditional theory of unconditional grants (which anticipates a limited effect on the expenditures of the subsidized local government, equal to the effect of an increase in its taxpayers' income of the same amount as the grant) with the conclusions of a number of empirical

studies (which indicate the effect is significant). According to the theory, the effect should be between 0.05 and 0.10 per grant dollar, but the calculated effect is more than 0.40. This difference, known as the "flypaper effect," can also be partly explained by the lower inefficiency costs of taxes at the higher levels of government.

22. The central government does not have to produce the goods and services itself. It can use grants to induce the regional governments to reckon with the externalities generated by their activities:

Intergovernmental grants, here and in other federal countries as well, have become a widely used policy instrument. Federal governments have found them a very flexible fiscal tool that can be used to provide inducements for decentralized levels of government to respond appropriately where there are externalities or where the national interest is at stake, without the federal government's actually assuming full responsibility for the role. From an economic perspective, intergovernmental grants are typically seen as serving three different objectives. The first has to do with external effects, providing inducements such as matching grants for state and local governments to undertake or extend programs where there is a clear national interest at stake. Second, there is the role of providing relatively low-income jurisdictions with the ability to offer satisfactory levels of key public services while maintaining tax rates roughly equivalent to those elsewhere. Third, perhaps, is a revenue-sharing function, which essentially amounts to a substitution of part of the federal tax system for state and local taxes without assuming directly the expenditure role. By substituting part of the federal tax system for part of the state and local tax systems, one ends up with an overall tax structure that is, in some sense perhaps, more desirable in terms of its incidence, its pattern of payments, and also effects on the operation of the market system. For this third function, we are not trying to get state and local governments to provide specific services, so unconditional or "lump sum grants" as they are called, are appropriate. (Oates, 1983, p. 155)

23. For example Gordon (1983), in an analysis of taxation in a federal system, identifies seven externalities to taxation by a decentralized level of government:

The types of externalities that appeared in the equations resulting from a given community's decision were:

(1) Non-residents may pay some of the taxes.
(2) Non-residents may receive some of the benefits from public services.
(3) Congestion costs faced by non-residents may change.
(4) Tax revenues received in other communities may change due to the spillover of economic activity.
(5) Resource costs for public services in other communities may change.
(6) Output and factor price changes may favor residents over non-residents.
(7) Distributional effects among non-residents would be ignored (p. 580).

24. Brennan and Buchanan (1980) deliver a similar criticism of the traditional approach:

There would seem to be no reason why strictly localized public goods should not be provided by supralocal governmental units, which might, of course, decentralize administratively as the relevant externality limits dictate. . . . There is no analysis that demonstrates the superiority of a genuinely federal political structure over a unitary structure, with the latter administratively decentralized.

This result is not, in itself, surprising when we recognize that the "economic theory" of federalism is no different from standard normative economics in its implicit assumptions about politics. The normative advice proffered by the theory is presumably directed toward the benevolent despotism that will implement the efficiency criteria. No support can be generated for a politically divided governmental structure until the prospects for nonidealized despotism are acknowledged. Once government comes to be modeled either as a complex interaction process akin to that analyzed in standard public choice or, as in this book, in terms of Leviathan-like behavior, an argument for genuinely federal structure can be developed (pp. 174–75).

Breton (1983) states: "Very little of welfare economics can be salvaged once governing and nongoverning politicians are assumed to be motivated by their own interest" (p. 257).

25. The question that follows may be impertinent, but it is not unimportant. Why, instead of preaching genuine decentralization through the marketplace and responsible regional and local governments, do economists frequently prefer centralization — in other words the bureaucratization and standardization of decision making, with the resulting creation of interesting jobs? Do they find it only too easy to tailor their scientific thinking to their own interests? To answer these questions would simply involve applying their discipline to their own activities.

26. Breton and Scott (1978, 1980). The few lines devoted here to a summary of their two books do not go beyond their basic argument.

27. The situation may be somewhat better with respect to the division of powers between the constituent cities and the metropolitan government. Nevertheless, Breton and Scott's emphasis on organization costs is in fact only a return to the central concerns of economics, or as Knight (1935) put it: "Thus of the three main elements in economic life, wants, resources, and organization, economic theory deals directly with one aspect of the organization, and only incidentally with the other elements. Wants are in the province of psychology, sociology, and ethics; resources fall in various other sciences, and the technological aspects of organization to a vast number, and the internal organization of business to a special branch of economics" (p. 261).

28. "A grant-in-aid effectively changes the division of responsibility within the federal system. Grants involve a revision of the Constitution but without formal amendment" (Wagner, 1983, p. 466).

29. This is an application of the Tiebout (1956) model, which was developed in relation to municipal and metropolitan governments.

30. The political scientist Riker (1975) takes the opposite view: "States rights guarantee minority governing on national issues, if the minority differs from the majority in significant ways. That is, federalism permits minorities to impose very high external costs on the majority" (p. 158).

31. Riker (1975, p. 104). He refers to Grodzin's analogy between American federalism and a marble cake: "The American form of government is often, but erroneously, symbolized by a three-layer cake. A far more accurate image is the rainbow or marble cake, characterized by an inseparable mingling of different colored ingredients, the colors appearing in vertical and diagonal strands and unexpected whirls. As colors are mixed in the marble cake, so functions are mixed in the federal system."

32. West and Winer (1980, p. 14). The absence of an explicit distribution of functions in the Constitution does not mean that in practice there will not be one between the various levels of government. For example, there are no provincial fire fighters. By the same token, Pommerehne (1977) states: "Although the situation in the United States is formally one of complete competition, each of the three levels of government more or less monopolizes some tax sources. Thus, direct taxes go mainly to the federal government and indirect taxes to the state governments, while the communities rely primarily on wealth taxes" (p. 282).

33. The recent evolution of political institutions in Belgium would appear to be an exception.

34. In the words of Buchanan (1974): "The power of any government to extract income and wealth coercively from a person is related inversely to the locational alternatives that are available to that person" (pp. 22–23). See also Bélanger (1982).

35. As the American jurist Epstein (1984) notes, constitutional protection of civil liberties is not absolute:

> No constitutional provision, however, is self-executing. Its scope and application depend heavily on general attitudes that the Supreme Court uses to interpret it. With economic liberties, however, the court has deployed the so-called "rational basis" test to neutralize the constitutional protection of economic liberties. Under present law, if any conceivable set of facts could establish a rational nexus between the means chosen and any legitimate end of government, then the rational-basis test upholds the statute. In theory, the class of legitimate ends is both capacious and undefined, while the means used need have only a remote connection to the ends chosen. In practice, every statute meets the constitutional standard, no matter how powerful the arguments arrayed against it (p. 28).

36. Canada, Privy Council. (1979). It continues:

Although the frequency of the procedures and practices that we describe varied, they were sufficiently widespread to warrant the following observations:

(a) initial departmental responses to the question about the constitutional basis for the activity under review indicated that the majority of federal public servants concerned did not know what the relevant authority was;

(b) further enquiries at subsequent meetings, suggested that in many cases, if not the majority, the question of the distribution of powers had not been thoroughly considered when the activities were undertaken;

(c) more often than not, departments eventually indicated that the constitutional authority for activities was one or more of the following: the Peace, Order, and good Government (POGG) clause of section 91, even though in certain cases there was no enabling legislation justifying the reference to POGG; the federal spending power, derived in part from sections 91.1A. and 91.3.; or, least frequently, Parliament's power to declare works to be for the general advantage of Canada, section 92.10.(c);

(d) the *British North America Act*, and particularly the sections setting out the distribution of powers, did not appear to be a part either of the formal training of the public servants concerned, or, more significantly, of their governmental experience (pp. 9–10).

37. Political scientist Martin Diamond (1976) gives a good description of the importance of the constitution in restraining centralizing forces:

Perhaps it is necessary to remind ourselves why we should submit, from time to time, to the self-inflicted constraints of a constitution. With regard to the federal limitations, the following seems to me to justify the costs in constraint. We live in a centripetalizing and homogenizing age. All the social and economic forces of the age draw us in the direction of greater and greater centralization. And yet we are aware of the many advantages of preserving the strong decentralizing tendencies of our political system. Does not our saving decentralization, in all its informal varieties, depend upon the formal structural support that decentralization receives from the formal federal division of power in the Constitution? If we permit that formal federalism to be obliterated sub-silentio . . . will we not thereby have destroyed our own first barrier against executive centralization? And if the habitual willingness of Americans to accept certain self-imposed constitutional limitations is weakened, in the case of the federal limitations, will we not also have weakened that readiness of Americans to moderate any given policy preferences and urgencies in deference to other and perhaps even more valuable constraining features of the Constitution? (p. 193).

38. Applying the Niskanen (1978) formula to Canada, the minimum number could be the difference between ten and the number required for approval of a constitutional amendment, provided the total population of these provinces was at least half the population of the entire country.

39. According to Dafflon (1977):

In the theory of the political economy of federalism, we need to pay more attention to the organizational procedures that are likely to conduce to efficient outcomes and less attention to the prescription of the choices that "should" be made or to the shape of the outcomes themselves, although these must be relevant to an evaluation of the procedures proposed. Improved outcomes can be achieved only through improvements in the procedures that generate them, and improvements in such procedures in turn can be achieved only if their proper role in the whole structure of federalism is appreciated and understood (p. 54).

The inspiration for this idea is Wiseman (1964). It has also been taken up recently in Canada by Lemelin (1981).

40. Two economists whose work in public sector economics is widely quoted, J.M. Buchanan and C. McLure, are good examples of this. As we have seen, Buchanan (1950) argued in favour of equalization payments on the grounds of efficiency. Most likely, he would

see them today as an instrument of cartelization of the public sector. McLure, who concluded in his 1967 text that a considerable portion of the burden of local and state taxes was exported, has more recently suggested the opposite conclusion (see McLure, 1981).

41. At the same time, government intervention has been justified on the grounds of market deficiencies, without considering the deficiencies of non-market decision making.

42. In a recent text on a subject similar to this one, Carter (1983) concludes (translation):

> It would appear from the outset that the economist has very little to say about the setting up of some optimal political structure. The problems involved in the cost-benefit analysis of various political activities are insurmountable. While the economist may be able to identify the nature of the various types of costs and benefits associated with different political structures, he cannot measure their extent and thus determine an optimal solution. For example, considerations of economies of scale and externalities in consumption have often been used to justify centralizing powers in Ottawa, although the same considerations may offer even greater justification for making Ottawa disappear and setting up a North American federation. By the same token, the minimizing of preference signalling costs and satisfaction costs would seem to be an argument in favour of some decentralization of powers to the provinces, but there is no proof that such a decentralization is preferable to decentralization to the municipal level. Without measurements, the economist can only point out the advantages and costs of both centralization and decentralization, without being able to define some optimal solution (p. 604).

This conclusion is in contrast to that of the major economic study of federalism in Quebec by Lamontagne (1954), who wrote (translation): "The first law of federalism can be summarized in a formula that is in increasing use: *as much decentralization as possible, but as much centralization as necessary*" (p. 100).

Bibliography

Bélanger, G. 1976. *Le financement municipal au Quebec*. Québec: Éditeur officiel du Québec.

——. 1980. "La décentralisation municipale aura-t-elle lieu?" *Urban Forum/Colloque urbain* 4 (6): 4–8.

——. 1982. "Dans un système fédéral, le gouvernement central doit-il essayer d'imposer l'harmonisation fiscale?" *L'Actualité économique* 58 (4): 493–513.

——. 1984. *Fédéralisme et gouvernement local*. Quebec: Laval University, Department of Economics. Mimeographed.

Bird, R.M. 1984. "Tax Harmonization and Federal Finance: A Perspective on Recent Canadian Discussion." *Canadian Public Policy* 10 (3): 253–66.

Boadway, R., and F. Flatters. 1982. *Equalization in a Federal State: An Economic Analysis*. Ottawa: Minister of Supply and Services Canada.

Brennan, G., and J.M. Buchanan. 1980. *The Power to Tax: Analytical Foundations of a Fiscal Constitution*. Cambridge: Cambridge University Press.

Breton, A. 1983. "Federalism versus Centralism in Regional Growth." In *Public Finance and Economic Growth*, edited by D. Biehl et al. Detroit: Wayne State University Press.

Breton, A., and A. Scott. 1978. *The Economic Constitution of Federal States*. Toronto: University of Toronto Press.

——. 1980. *The Design of Federations*. Montreal: Institute for Research on Public Policy.

Buchanan, J.M. 1950. "Federal and Fiscal Equity." *American Economic Review* 40 (4): 583–99.

——. 1974. "Who Should Distribute What in a Federal State?" In *Redistribution through Public Choice*, edited by H.M. Hochman and G.E. Peterson. New York: Columbia University Press.

Canada. Privy Council. Federal-Provincial Relations Office. 1979. *Interim Report on Relations Between the Government of Canada and the Province of Quebec, 1967–1977*. Ottawa: FPRO.

Carter, R. 1983. "Séparation, annexion et fédéralisme." *L'Actualité économique* 59 (3): 596-619.

Chrétien, J. 1980. *Securing the Canadian Economic Union in the Constitution*. Ottawa: Minister of Supply and Services Canada.

Courchene, T.J. 1979. *Regional Adjustment. The Transfer System and Canadian Federalism*. Research Report 7903. London: University of Western Ontario, Department of Economics.

——. 1984. "The Political Economy of Canadian Constitution Making: The Canadian Economic Union Issue." *Public Choice* 44 (1): 201-49.

Craig, S.G., and J.W. Sailors. 1983. "Interstate Trade Barriers: Income Redistribution Among the States — Or Within the State?" Discussion Paper 83-5. Houston: University of Houston, Center for Public Policy.

Dafflon, B. 1977. *Federal Finance in Theory and Practice with Special Reference to Switzerland*. Berne: Verlag Paul Haupt.

Dales, J.H. 1983. "Distortions and Dissipations." *Canadian Public Policy* 9 (2): 257-63.

Diamond, M. 1976. "The Forgotten Doctrine of Enumerated Powers." *Publius, The Journal of Federalism* 6 (4): 187-93.

Epple, D., and A. Zelenitz. 1981. "The Implications of Competition Among Jurisdictions: Does Tiebout Need Politics?" *Journal of Political Economy* 89 (6): 1197-1217.

Epstein, R.E. 1984. "Asleep at a Constitutional Switch." *Wall Street Journal*, August 9 1984, p. 28.

Flatters F., and R.G. Lipsey. 1983. *Common Ground for the Canadian Common Market*. Montreal: Institute for Research on Public Policy.

Forget, C. 1983. "Quebec's Experience with the Personal Income Tax." In *A Separate Personal Income Tax for Ontario, an Economic Analysis*, edited by D. Hartle et al., pp. 157-78. Toronto: Ontario Economic Council.

Gillespie, W.I. 1979. "Postwar Canadian Fiscal Policy Revisited, 1945-1975." *Canadian Tax Journal* 27 (3): 265-76.

Gordon, R.H. 1983. "An Optimal Taxation Approach to Fiscal Federalism." *Quarterly Journal of Economics* 98 (4): 567-86.

Grubel, H.G. 1982. "A Canadian Bill of Economic Rights." *Canadian Public Policy* 8 (1): 57-68.

Knight, F.H. 1935. "The Limitations of Scientific Method in Economics." In *The Trend of Economics*, edited by R.G. Tugwell, pp. 229-67. New York: F.S. Crofts.

Ladd, H.F., and F.C. Doolittle. 1982. "Which Level of Government Should Assist the Poor?" *National Tax Journal* 35 (3): 332-36.

Lamontagne, M. 1954. *Le fédéralisme canadien*. Quebec: Presses de l'Université Laval.

Lemelin, C. 1981. "Dimensions of Fiscal Harmonization in Canada." Ottawa: Department of Finance. Mimeographed.

Lindbeck, A. 1976. "Stabilization Policy in Open Economy with Endogeneous Politicians." *American Economic Review* 66 (2): 1-19.

McLure, C. 1967. "The Interstate Exporting of State and Local Taxes: Estimates for 1962." *National Tax Journal* 20 (1): 49-77.

——. 1981. "The Elusive Incidence of the Corporate Income Tax: The State Case." *Public Finance Quarterly* 9 (4): 395-414.

Migué, J.L. 1983. "La centralisation, instrument de balkanisation du Canada." *L'Analyste* 2: 19-24.

Mills, E.S. 1979. "Economic Analysis of Urban Land Use Controls." In *Current Issues in Urban Economics*, edited by P. Mieszkowski and M. Straszheim, pp. 511-41. Baltimore: Johns Hopkins University Press.

Musgrave, R.A. 1959. *The Theory of Public Finance*. New York: McGraw-Hill.

Niskanen, W.A. 1978. "The Prospect for a Liberal Democracy." In *Fiscal Responsibility in Constitutional Democracy*, edited by J.M. Buchanan and R.E. Wagner, pp. 157-74. Boston: Martinus Nijhoff.

Oates, W.E. 1972. *Fiscal Federalism*. New York: Harcourt Brace Jovanovich.

——. 1979. "Lump-Sum Intergovernmental Grants Have Price Effects." In *Fiscal Federation and Grants-in-Aid*, edited by P. Mieszkowski and W.H. Oakland, pp. 20–23. Washington, D.C.: Urban Institute.

——. 1983. "Strengths and Weaknesses of New Federalism." In *Reaganomics: A Midterm Report*, edited by W.C. Stubblebine and T.D. Willet, pp. 153–57. San Francisco: Institute for Contemporary Studies.

Pauly, M.V. 1973. "Income Redistribution as a Local Public Good." *Journal of Public Economics* 2 (1): 35–58.

Pommerehne, W.W. 1977. "Quantitative Aspects of Federalism: A Study of Six Countries." In *The Political Economy of Fiscal Federalism*, edited by W.E. Oates, pp. 275–355. Lexington: D.C. Heath.

Riker, W.H. 1975. "Federalism." In *Governmental Institutions and Processes*, Handbook of Political Science, vol. 5, edited by F.I. Greenstein, pp. 93–172. Reading: Addison-Wesley.

Safarian, A.E. 1974. *Canadian Federalism and Economic Integration*. Ottawa: Information Canada.

——. 1979. "La crise constitutionnelle canadienne: un point de vue non conventionnel." In *Le Québec et ses partenaires économiques canadiens,* edited by L.N. Tellier et al., pp. 27–41. Montreal: Éditions Quinze.

Thirsk, W.R. 1980. "Tax Harmonization and Its Importance in the Canadian Federation." In *Fiscal Dimensions of Canadian Federalism*, edited by R. Bird, pp. 118–42. Toronto: Canadian Tax Foundation.

Tiebout, C. 1956. "A Pure Theory of Local Expenditures." *Journal of Political Economy* 64 (5): 416–424.

Tocqueville, A. de. 1951. *De la démocratie en Amerique*. Paris: Librarie de Médicis.

Trebilcock, M.J. et al. 1983. *Federalism and the Canadian Economic Union*. Toronto: University of Toronto Press for the Ontario Economic Council.

Tullock, G. 1969. "Federalism: Problems of Scale." *Public Choice* 6: 19–29.

——. 1983. *Economics of Income Redistribution*. Boston: Kluwer-Nijhoff.

Usher, D. 1980. "How Should the Redistributive Power of the State Be Divided Between Federal and Provincial Governments?" *Canadian Public Policy* 6 (1): 16–29.

Wagner, R.E. 1983. *Public Finance Revenues and Expenditures in a Democratic Society*. Boston: Little, Brown.

West, E.G., and S.L. Winer. 1980. "The Individual, Political Tension, and Canada's Quest for a New Constitution." *Canadian Public Policy* 6 (3): 3–15.

Wiseman, J. 1964. "The Political Economy of Federalism: A Survey and a Proposal." Report 20.6 for the Royal Commission on Taxation. Ottawa: The Commission. Mimeographed.

2

Constitutional Aspects
of Economic Development Policy

JOHN D. WHYTE

Introduction

Governmental regulation of the economy in Canada has been as much
constrained by the Constitution as by political conflict over the goals of
regulatory programs or by uncertainty over the best means of achieving
agreed-upon regulatory purposes. For example, in the cases of all three
of the early major federal regulatory initiatives — controlling the liquor
trade, responding to the trading distortions created by the First World
War, and stabilizing grain production and marketing — the primary
challenges and the dominant conflicts were constitutional in nature. In
all three cases the power of the federal level of government, while not
ultimately defeated, was conditioned,[1] restricted[2] or frustrated.[3] Canadian constitutional history shows that neither the choice of regulatory goal
nor the choice of regulatory method has been untrammelled; policy formation in both the development of regional and provincial economies and
in the improvement of the national economy has had to take account of
the idea of constitutional limit. However, in spite of the persistent constraint imposed by constitutional law on the formation of economic policy,
there is very little clear understanding of the force, content, or direction
of this law.

There are a number of reasons for the gap between knowledge *of* constitutional constraint and knowledge *about* constitutional constraint. First,
constitutional structure and language are highly indeterminate. Insofar
as the words of a particular section that allocates legislative power might
convey specific content and meaning, such clarity is typically confounded
by the juxtaposition in the Constitution of various sections, the various
intelligible meanings of which stand in conflict one to another. Even if
the language of the power-allocating sections contains coherent ideas, the
arrangement of those sections reveals competition between overlapping
themes and ideas. This is not the consequence of poor drafting or faulty

articulation of agreed-upon arrangements. Rather, the occurrence of conflicting political goals on the face of the Constitution reflects the unresolved tensions attendant upon the creation of a federal state.

In the Canadian context this tension is seen in the large number of powers conferred on Parliament and the federal government that indicate a political desire for a highly integrated nation with dominant central authority and, at the same time, the reservation to provinces of large, indeterminate powers that guarantee significant political authority. The scale of provincial government recognized by the *Constitution Act, 1867*, guarantees powerful political constituencies and interests. This, in turn, made the weakening of provincial and regional identification next to impossible. Consequently, development of the sense of national political community, which was the precondition to the effective operation of the centralizing powers, was forestalled. These centralizing powers — among them the power to appoint judges of provincial superior courts and to appoint provincial lieutenant governors, the power of reservation and disallowance, the capacity to enact laws for the peace, order and good government of Canada, and the power to declare works to be for the general advantage of Canada — all failed, even when used regularly, to weaken the hold of provincial political identification.[4]

The unresolved conflict between the urge to build a true nation and the desire to maintain strong local political communities is illustrated by other textual arrangements. Examples include the allocation to Parliament of legislative jurisdiction over trade and commerce, and to the provinces of legislative jurisdictions over property and civil rights, local works and undertakings and, generally, all matters of a local and private nature. Then there is the granting to Parliament of responsibility for criminal law and procedure, and the granting to the provinces of authority over the administration of justice. The scale of overlap in these legislative allocations is vast. Each allocation contains an idea of Canada, a vision of how the new nation should be organized politically (and, hence, economically and socially), but these visions are in sharp conflict with each other. The idea of confederation turns out not to be a single idea but, rather, a hope that somehow a nation will exist, will grow, and will become politically and economically one. Beyond that there were other ideas that must be made to fit together. It appears likely that those responsible for the creation of Canada had varying notions of what that fit would be and what the result would look like.[5]

The second cause of uncertainty over the precise nature of constitutionally based restrictions on the capacity to regulate is that there has been a tendency in Canadian constitutional adjudication to discern the present content of constitutional norms through the measurement of prior particular applications. What has often been lacking is the discovery of concepts, or underlying political goals, and the development of techniques for ascribing content that vindicates those concepts.[6] Furthermore, in dealing with what is clearly the normal situation of competing concepts, or the competing political aims of the Constitution, there has been inadequate judicial development of principles of mediation that would do justice to any deeper structural or organizing ideas of the Constitution that might exist.[7]

Canadian constitutional law has not often been marked by cases that are based on structural integrity.[8] There have, of course, been exceptions. The development of an implied bill of rights from the terms of the *Constitution Act, 1867*,[9] is an example of courts looking out for the deeper conditions of political life that the Constitution must have embraced. Likewise, the conflict in the *Winner* case — over the effect of Parliament's transportation jurisdiction on provincial bus regulation — between Mr. Justice Rand in the Supreme Court of Canada[10] and Lord Parker in the Judicial Committee of the Privy Council[11] reflects a search by two thoughtful judges for constitutional limits based on their sense of the concept that underlies the allocations of powers contained in s. 92(10) of the Constitution. For Mr. Justice Rand the range of immunity from provincial transportation regulation had to be defined in a manner that was consonant with the idea of the federal division of legislative responsibilities, or, in other words, in a way that left adequate, responsive, and effective regulatory room for both levels of government. Lord Porter, on the other hand, saw as fundamental the grant of constitutional immunity from provincial (and potentially parochial) regulation for those enterprises that engaged in the physical connection of the parts of Canada to each other and to the wider world; this immunity was extended to an entire enterprise rather than simply to the interconnecting activities of an enterprise because these enterprises, even when partially engaged in intraprovincial transportation or communication, were dedicated to constitutionally valued activity — helping to build a nation.[12]

This sort of discovery of underlying structure and themes has not been the usual stuff of Canadian constitutional adjudication.[13] Perhaps the tendency to see constitutional adjudication as a process of triangulation from previous outcomes, rather than as an opportunity to shape constitutive order according to the visions suggested by the constitutional text, is a product of the equation of constitutionalism with legalism.[14] Although this equation cannot be avoided, if constitutional order is to be authoritative and binding on all political actors,[15] it does not follow that because the Constitution creates legal limits, imposed through court adjudication, adjudication cannot be purposive and rooted in the political ideas that lie behind the constitutional text. Only when adjudication resorts to the constitutive concepts in allocating authority and in setting limits on legislative competence can there be a jurisprudence that both responds to the various political values that were meant to be reflected in public organization and provides intelligible guidance to political decision makers.

The language of Canada's Constitution, like that of most constitutions, tells only that certain human transactions, patterns and plans were reduced to a text from which only inexact re-creations and extensions are possible. It contains language that reflects an historical arrangement, a political agreement and certain hopes about the future look and structure of the country. In applying the Constitution, courts must catch both the history and the hope reflected in its terms. It is sadly true that to a great extent Canadian constitutional jurisprudence has failed to match the task. It has been marked by a futile search for definite and permanent meanings for constitutional phrases[16] and not by an attempt to come to grips with the purposes behind a head of power or the values represented by the juxtaposition of powers.

It may be that this state of constitutional jurisprudence is both inevitable and beyond redemption. In the first place, perhaps the reason for the history of limited constitutional jurisprudence stems from the feature of the Constitution already noted — its lack of unambiguous ideas; it is the presence of conflicting political visions that has driven courts to seek refuge in constitutional literalism. It is possible that the courts recognize that the underlying political tension can only be resolved through political accommodation, not through the futile search for coherent ordering principles hidden in the language and structure of the Constitution. Furthermore, it may be that a stage has been reached in Canada in which the factors of, first, unresolvable constitutional ambiguity and, second, the pattern of limited constitutional jurisprudence, preclude arriving at needed reforms in basic governmental structure through any means but constitutional amendment; if there is a need to release the federal level from some of the present constitutional constraints on its regulation of the nation's economic life (a question that will be explored later), then such a release must be produced by the federal government and the provinces engaging in formal constitutional amendment.

This paper, however, does not share in these pessimistic views, and therefore it is not directed to the question of which sort of basic structural changes should be made; nor is it directed to the search for an appropriate new constitutional text. Rather, the subject matter of the enquiry conducted in this paper is the reform in constitutional ordering that is possible through judicial interpretation of the Constitution as it presently stands. If the present constitutional jurisprudence in respect of trade regulation is inadequate in that it stands in the way of federal and provincial governments of Canada meeting challenges posed by a new economic order, and if no new constitutional text emerges out of federal-provincial discussions, it might prove to be prudent to have explored the possibility of judicial reconstruction of Canadian constitutional law. Of course, such an exploration may fail for a number of reasons. The textual limits created by the Constitution may not permit any real degree of reconstruction. Or, the raw meanings to constitutional provisions and the new principles of judicial mediation between conflicting provisions that are possible under the present text, may simply be unresponsive to the scale and nature of the economic regulatory powers that governments need in order to produce economic well-being. Or, finally, even if the present Constitution has sufficient room for a new constitutional jurisprudence of economic regulation, or even if the new powers needed were modest, the enterprise may falter because it is feared, by lawyers who argue cases and by judges who decide them, that the new, reshaped set of constitutional limits will only create regulatory uncertainty and chaos. Such fear may cause lawyers and courts to abstain from reconstucting constitutional jurisprudence.

Notwithstanding the reasons for pessimism and the uncertainties of the process, it would be a denial of serious constitutional analysis not to explore what is possible by way of rethinking the present division of powers in order to produce a jurisprudence that is both more subtle and more responsive to regulatory needs. If it is thought that the pattern of Canadian federalism that has been developed through a century and more of judicial construction of the *Constitution Act, 1867*, fits poorly the new economic reality and new economic forces, it is appropriate to search for deeper constitutive ideas that would support a sense of the constitutional division of powers under which state activity that is better able to meet current challenges might be sustained.

Constitutions are ethical documents, revealing and establishing basic ideas and values about the nations they order.[17] These ideas, as in the case of Canada, will not necessarily be all of a piece and they will not always be an appropriate reflection of the country's basic social values and social concerns.[18] However, a close examination of the most basic elements of the Constitution may show guideposts that can lead the country out of the present thicket of restraints on governmental regulation of the economy without requiring recourse to constitutional amendment. Furthermore, this examination may produce a constitutional law that is responsive to some ultimate and basic truth hidden in our constitutional history.

Federalism has not been the only major idea of Canadian constitutionalism. The idea of Canadian federalism is firmly located in the context of another idea, an idea of national survival. Clearly the general history of Canada is dominated by the theme of survival. So too the Constitution seems to be dominated by the idea of forging a single nation that succeeds and has the capacity to react to both short-term and long-term threats to its continued life and success. This idea, the concern for Canada simply to continue to be, should be seen as a cue to constitutional interpreters and to those who engage directly in political activity, to reconsider the ways in which federalism is to be reflected in public regulation of the economy, the ways in which the needs of the nation and respect for divided political authority may be harmonized. It may be that in applying the Constitution to our present circumstances we shall be able to see that the aspiration of the nation as inferred from the powers described and allocated in the *Constitution Act, 1867* is, in itself, a sufficient guide to allow us to meet our current needs.

Judicial Interpretation of the Constitution's Economic Powers

Canada's Constitution, the Act of 1867, is, notwithstanding Ivor Jennings' dismal view,[19] full of political theory. Not only does it embrace responsible government, democracy, and the separation of powers, it also clearly adopts a federalized governmental structure. It just as clearly contains the idea of the progressive merging of all significant authority in a powerful central, or national, government. These conflicting constitutional ideas reflect the unresolved competition in political ideas that was waged in Canada in 1867.

The inclusion in the *British North America Act* of 1867 of two disparate conceptions gave those whose responsibility it was to enforce the Constitution a choice of constitutional paradigms which, as it turns out, they exercised in favour of the idea of Canada as a "community of states." It would be wrong to consider this form of administration of the Constitution to be either non-textual or anti-purposive. Although the 1867 act contains a clear view about the special value of those enterprises that bind the country together, it also pays high regard to the autonomy of provinces to pursue their own interests and programs. It would be wrong to see in the federal arrangement spelled out in the *British North America Act* a belief that, for a country which lacks a single common set of political values, the only form of government that adequately protects against the tyranny and oppression of national majorities is federalism. The concerted attempts by the courts over the years to maintain the federal balance has been responsive to that sense of Canada that was based on the reluctance of the regions to be prey to the wishes of national majorities.

The chief targets of the judicial proponents of a strong federalism have been the two large general powers: peace, order and good government; and trade and commerce. The former has, by and large, been held not to sustain legislation in areas that are inherently of concern to the nation; and the latter has, by and large, not been allowed to sustain the general regulation of trading and other economic activity. These results are due to one dominant mediating idea: that recognition of some substantive content to the ideas of "inherent national concern" and "general trade" would necessarily entail the recognition of so much potential content that provincial jurisdiction based on such matters as property and civil rights, regulation of the local social environment, and the administration of justice, would not survive — except in radically diminished form.

The details of this interpretive method can be summarily explored in connection with the trade and commerce power. From the first decided cases on s. 91(2), the courts have limited the literal scope of "trade and commerce" in order to protect provincial autonomy. Thus in *Citizens Ins. v. Parsons*,[20] Sir Montague Smith held that federal regulation of the insurance industry, through the regulation of contracts of insurance, could not be sustained under s. 91(2). He said that:

> The words 'regulation of trade and commerce' in their unlimited sense are sufficiently wide, if uncontrolled by the context and other parts of the Act, to include regulation of trade ranging from political arrangements in regard to trade with foreign governments, requiring the sanction of parliament, down to minute rules for regulating particular trades.[21]

Accordingly, Sir Montague Smith came to his well known conclusion:

> Construing therefore the words 'regulation of trade and commerce' by the various aids to their interpretation above suggested, they would include political arrangements in regard to trade requiring the sanction of parliament, regulation of trade in matters of interprovincial concern, and it may be that they would include general regulation of trade affecting the whole dominion. Their Lordships abstain on the present occasion from any attempt to define the limits of the authority of the dominion parliament in this direction. It is enough for the decision of the present case to say that, in their view, its authority to legislate for the regulation of trade and commerce does not comprehend the power to regulate by legislation the contracts of a particular business or trade, such as the business of fire insurance in a single province, and therefore that its legislative authority does not in the present case conflict or compete with the power over property and civil rights assigned to the legislature of Ontario by No. 13 of sect. 92.[22]

It would seem that the "general regulation of trade" branch of Sir Montague Smith's definition of s. 91(2) must be given real regulatory content, otherwise, section 91(2) as a whole would become practically meaningless. The first branch, dealing with international and interprovincial trade, probably did not have to be specifically enumerated in s. 91 because it would not, in any event, have come within provincial jurisdiction. That is, s. 92(13)'s "Property and Civil Rights *in the Province*" and s. 92(16)'s "Generally All Matters of a merely local or private Nature *in the Province*" (emphasis added in both cases) could not, by their own terms, permit provincial regulation of international or interprovincial trade.

But ever since *Citizens Ins. v. Parsons*, it has been accepted that, whatever general regulation of trade might mean, s. 91(2) will not permit the detailed regulation of any particular intraprovincial trade. Thus, in *City of Montreal v. Montreal Street Ry.*,[23] Lord Atkinson made explicit the constitutional necessity of reading down s. 91(2) in the interests of preserving the scope of provincial autonomy. Lord Atkinson stated:

> Taken in the widest sense these words [the Regulation of Trade and Commerce] would authorize legislation by the Parliament of Canada in respect of several of the matters specifically enumerated in s. 92, and would seriously encroach upon the local autonomy of the province.[24]

He held that the trade and commerce power would not sustain a federal attempt to subject a provincial railway to the detailed regulatory regime established by statute of the Parliament of Canada, the *Railway Act*,[25] which included traffic and rate regulation and supervision by the federal Board of Railway Commissioners.

In *The King v. Eastern Terminal Elevators Co.*,[26] the Supreme Court of Canada struck down a federal attempt to regulate, in part, the business of grain elevator operators. As Mr. Justice Mignault observed, under the *Canada Grain Act*[27] all grain produced in Manitoba, Saskatchewan, Alberta and the Northwest Territories was to be "binned under the direction, supervision and control of the inspecting officer, who has full control of all grain in terminal elevators, and no grain is shipped out of, transferred or removed from any terminal elevator without his supervision."[28] The inspection was intended to ensure compliance with federal grading and quality standards. This limited regulatory objective in respect of a nationally significant product was seen as an intrusive attempt to regulate a particular occupation in the province.

Parliament's attempt to license insurance underwriters was held to be ultra vires, notwithstanding s. 91(2), in *A.-G. Can. v. A.-G. Alta.*,[29] Viscount Haldane held that:

> Their Lordships think that as the result of these decisions it must now be taken that the authority to legislate for the regulation of trade and commerce does not extend to the regulation by a licensing system of a particular trade in which Canadians would otherwise be free to engage.[30]

To this line of cases could be added others such as *A.-G. B.C. v. A.-G. Can. (Natural Products Marketing Reference)*[31] and *Can. Federation of Agriculture v. A.-G. Que. (Margarine Reference)*.[32] The theme of the series of cases as a whole is that s. 91(2) will not sanction the mandatory, intensive regulation of a particular trade or series of trades by Parliament.

One of the very few cases to give meaning to the second branch of Sir Montague Smith's definition of s. 91(2) — and so one of the few attempts to give meaning to s. 91(2) — is *John Deere Plow Co. v. Wharton*.[33] Viscount Haldane stated that:

> . . . the power to regulate trade and commerce at all events enables the Parliament of Canada to prescribe to what extent the powers of companies the objects of which extend to the whole Dominion should be exercisable, and what limitations should be placed on such powers. For if it be established that the Dominion Parliament can create such companies, then it becomes a question of general interest throughout the Dominion in what fashion they should be permitted to trade.[34]

The *Wharton* decision permits Parliament to define the powers of a company that operates in intraprovincial trade in several or even just one province. It must be admitted, however, that too much reliance cannot be placed on this case to support a federal jurisdiction over intraprovincial trades under the rubric of general regulation of trade. The *Wharton* decision involved companies that had, at the very least, formally stated objects that extended beyond any single province — indeed, extended to the whole of Canada.

In *A.-G. Ont. v. A.-G. Can. (Canada Standard Trade Mark Case)*,[35] the Privy Council upheld federal legislation that created the "Canada Standard" as a national trade mark and that permitted its application to any commodity that conformed to stipulated federal commodity standards. Even though the national standard could be used by a strictly intraprovincial trader, Lord Atkin upheld the legislation, pointing to s. 91(2) as "one obvious source of authority" for federal trade marks legislation in general.[36] While the standards involved under the Canada Standards program may have been fairly detailed, use of them was not legally or practically mandatory. The federal intervention in intraprovincial commerce and provincial autonomy was strictly limited by the legislation upheld in the *Canada-Standard* case, and no significant scope for federal power can be inferred from a decision which, in essence, holds only that Parliament may regulate one aspect of the economic activity of persons who decide to subject themselves to the regulation.

In *Labatt Breweries of Can. v. A.-G. Can.*,[37] Mr. Justice Estey wrote the majority opinion holding ultra vires the application of federal labelling regulations to a beer company under s. 6 of the *Food and Drugs Act*.[38] He held that the regulation was, in effect, an attempt to provide a "statutory recipe" for the basically local brewing industry. He reviewed much of the case law on s. 91(2) and concluded:

> In the end, the effort of the respondent here is simply to build into these Regulations a validity essentially founded upon the embryonic definition of the application of the trade and commerce heading in the *Citizens Insurance, supra, case*. That observation and the subsequent references thereto are all predicated upon the requirement that the purported trade and commerce legislation affected industry and commerce at large or in a sweeping, general sense. In the context of the *Food and Drug Act*, it follows that even if this statute were to cover a substantial portion of Canadian economic activity, one industry or trade at a time, by a varying array of regulations or trade codes applicable to each individual sector there would not, in the result, be at law a regulation of trade and commerce in the sweeping general sense contemplated in the *Citizens Insurance, supra*, case. That, in my view is the heart and core of the problem confronting the respondent in this appeal. Thus, the provisions regulating malt liquors relate either to a single industry or a sector thereof while other regulations appear to concern themselves in a similar way with other individual industries; the former being condemned by the *Citizens Insurance* case, and the latter does not rescue the malt liquor Regulations by reason of the *Board of Commerce* case, *supra*.[39]

Hence, the restrictive reading of s. 91(2) to disable Parliament from regulating the contracts of a single trade has been buttressed by decisions holding that Parliament is unable to legislate in relation to intraprovincial transactions and cannot enact laws which, in their administration, deal with trades or businesses individually.

As noted, the motive behind these carefully applied restrictions has been fear of a radical displacement of provincial jurisdiction in the realm of trade regulation. If the federal trade power were to be read apart from its juxtaposition with provincial powers, the resultant broad scope given to it would cause a corresponding narrowing of provincial jurisdiction over such things as local marketing, business practices, provincial economic development and the imposition of provincial charges on industrial or economic activity.[40] In short, the principle of constitutional interpretation (or the principle of mediation between conflicting constitutional ideas), which has been most actively and consistently at work in the area of trade regulation, has been the process of mutual modification — the limiting of the scope of two competing heads of power to leave some regulatory force to each. This mode or interpretation has, in a limited sense, been purposive in that it has been responsive to the federal principle.

The main object at work in this history of constitutional interpretation has been to maintain the balance in federalism from a functional perspective. However, the balance that has been sought has not been an *equal* judicial allocation of trade regulatory authority under the competing heads of regulatory power. In fact, s. 91(2) has done poorly in judicial allocation because jurisdiction over international and interprovincial trade could, strictly speaking, fall within the federal residual head, and because there has been virtually no judicial recognition of regulatory room under the rubric of "general regulation of trade." The interpretive balance has been of a different sort: the Judicial Committee of the Privy Council and the Supreme Court of Canada have allocated regulatory authority in terms that could not readily lead to a constant expansion of federal jurisdiction through the use of analysis based on the functional interrelatedness of detailed and extensive regulation to broad federal regulatory purposes.

Although the decision in any individual case that either struck down a regulatory scheme or, on the other hand, supported its constitutional validity, would not by itself be massively disruptive of present federalized patterns for regulating business and trade, it could be unbalancing for a court to base constitutional support for a scheme on a concept for which there is no ready limit and which, if carried as far as it can logically be extended, would erode the constitutional basis for trade regulation by the other level of government. It is clearly this caution about generating a principle of general regulation of trade which, in its conception, would contain no immediately apparent limit, that explains the reluctance of the Court in *Labatt Breweries* to permit the general regulatory idea of fixing certain standards for stipulated food goods. The danger that was perceived in permitting the fixing of national standards over the substance of goods is that such regulation would be indistinguishable, for constitutional purposes, from the imposition of standards in relation to trading processes.[41] If Parliament could regulate this, there would be little by way of economic activity that could not be brought within federal authority.

Likewise, in the Saskatchewan resources cases of CIGOL[42] and *Central Canada Potash*,[43] provincial legislative schemes designed, respectively, to meet legitimate provincial interests of collecting an economic rent from non-renewable resources in the province and of rationalizing production of an excessively available resource, were struck down because of their impact on interprovincial and international trade. In the particular instances of these cases, the strength of the provincial ground for validity was considerable, but the Supreme Court of Canada was doubtlessly fearful that, if the pursuit of valid provincial objects was allowed to burden interprovincial trade there would be no easily discoverable limit to the regulatory reach of provincial legislation designed to promote or protect provincial economies.

Consequently, the application of the constitutionally allocated powers over the economy has been balanced in the sense that no reading of the constitutional text has been permitted that would spark a series of unbalancing extensions. This form of balanced interpretation is not without merit; because it maintains the federal structure, it reflects the basic ideas of the Constitution. The question is whether there are other interpretive mechanisms appropriate to the application of the constitutional provisions relating to economic activity, mechanisms that would maintain the balance of legislative power within the federal union but would permit more coherent, less constrained and abridged federal regulatory authority.

The ambition behind this paper is to conceive of the federal power of economic regulation in ways that allow coherent national regulation of economic activity and the implementation of a national policy for economic development and, at the same time, do not transfer out of provincial competence all authority to pursue provincial economic goals. Is there a constitutional interpretive theory that recognizes both the appropriateness of detailed national economic regulation and the appropriateness in many instances of provincial authority over economic activity within the province?

The purpose behind such a proposal for reconstruction of the *Constitution Act, 1867*, is the creation of regulatory room in which regional and national economic development policies may be pursued and at the same time not result in debilitating and self-cancelling conflict.

Context of Federal Legislative Authority
General Economic Climate

The vast extent of Canada, the dispersed pattern of its population along its southern boundary and the proximity and vigour of the world's largest national market, have underscored both the need for and the problem of maintaining (or creating) a viable national economy.[44] Since pre-Confederation times governments in Canada have been called upon to play a leading role in economic development. Whether it be the building of a railway, the introduction of barriers to protect Canadian industries, the implementation of measures to buttress productivity during war years, the growth of state welfare, the cultural and political imperatives underlying the establishment of a national coast-to-coast broadcasting network, or the takeover of vital but floundering industries (such as the manufacturing of aircraft), government action has been considered essential. In this sense Canada and each of its component governments have always had an industrial strategy.

There are pressures for this to continue. In the first place, given the complexity and interdependency of the modern economy, the market's invisible hand does not guarantee (if it ever did) the very goal of efficiency that it was designed to produce. Moreover it is insensitive to, or conflicts with, other indispensable political, economic and social goals. These include regional economic equality, social insurance, education, pollution control, sustained employment opportunities, the maintenance of traditional ways of life and livelihood, health care and so on. In placing the realization of these diverse claims on the national economy, Canada is not unique in the world. For many of the world's nations the economy is the instrument for promoting well-being, liberty and fairness, while at the same time these nations want the strongest, most competitive, economies possible.

The governments of Canada face some unique problems in developing feasible programs for economic development. For one thing, the Canadian economy, in what it produces, what it consumes, how it markets its products, and how it finances its operation, has followed the larger, more competitive and, arguably, more efficient economy of the United States. Canada has not sought to carve out for itself a distinct economy except insofar as it has been heavily reliant on natural resources — from furs to uranium. Second, the quasi-colonial status of the Canadian economy has meant that there has not been marked innovation in terms of general structure or in terms of technology, product and distribution. Third, insofar as Canada's economic well-being has depended on a strong international demand for its natural resources, two phenomena have produced disarray. First, the other nations of the world are producing more of the sorts of natural resources in which Canada has specialized; and, second, the demand for Canadian natural resources has fallen. This second feature has probably been caused by a higher and higher share of the world's trading dollars being dedicated to energy resources (mostly oil) as a result of the rapid escalation of energy prices following the cartelization of oil sales in the early 1970s.

A fourth problem for the Canadian economy is that the highly developed welfare state has made production quite simply expensive. If Canada were a self-contained economy, the only outcome of welfare activism would be a tolerable redistribution of wealth in Canada. However, it is not, and Canada's competitive position, with respect to consumer goods, is weak. Notwithstanding these costs, transportation and servicing considerations might make Canadian manufacturing competitive within the Canadian market, without a great deal of assistance by way of governmental protection of the local market (and even this assessment is likely too sanguine); but in the vital matter of selling Canadian goods in the world market, success has not been commonplace without the aid of governmental inducements. These have included interest-free loans to international purchasers, massive subsidization of the domestic product and trade arrangements under which Canada is committed to purchasing foreign goods.

Other strains of the Canadian economy are of a second generation sort. As Canada's economic fortunes have, first, been dislocated and, then, fallen, there have followed consequences such as intense federal-provincial conflict, interprovincial economic competition, high unemployment, inflation and high interest rates. These problems have now become part of the agenda in the reform and revitalization of the Canadian economy.

The reform of the Canadian economy is not likely to be easy and is not likely to be achieved except through a series of small changes. The task; therefore, is to discover what these small changes need to be. For the purposes of this paper, such small changes are those made possible through changes in the constitutional normative order.

Intergovernmental Economic Competition

The small changes addressed through constitutional law are those that are responsive to federal-provincial conflict and interprovincial competition. There is a sense that the Canadian economy is battered by regulatory uncertainty, the result of lack of clarity over which level of government has authority to engage in which sorts of economic regulation. In fact, there have been and continue to be doubts over such threshold questions as which level of government owns a natural resource and which level of government has primary regulatory jurisdiction over a resource, or over a particular technology, or over a transportation system, or over a sector of servicing.

There is an even stronger sense that economic performance in Canada is debilitated by provincial governments' pursuit of economic development programs that serve well the interests of the regulating province but produce, in the Canadian economy generally, wasteful duplication, disharmony in regulatory objectives (and methods), blatant protectionism and, generally, intolerably high levels of economic inefficiency. Industrial policy as practised by the provinces is seen to be a zero-sum game: the economic goals of each province seem to assist that province's economy at the expense of another province or region within Canada. Usually these goals are perfectly laudable in themselves. They include diversification, in order to ameliorate the boom and bust cycles of economies based on world trade in natural resources, and integration by way of developing industrial capacities that support or complement the extraction, or harvesting, of natural resources. In any event, the dominant features of Canada's present industrial strategy are perceived to be decentralization and intense intergovernmental conflict.

These negatives should not be exaggerated. Provinces do much less to create barriers in interregional trade of goods, services, capital and labour than they could; furthermore, interregional conflict is not nearly as costly as it would be if the various regions of Canada were not pursuing distinct and, to a large extent, complementary industrial strategies. Nevertheless the interests of provinces, coupled with their constitutional capacities as well as their political will to act in order to maximize their economic advantage, mean that national economic goals are not easily pursued, and national solutions to Canada's economic malaise are not easily formulated or implemented.

Constitutional Amendment

Constitutional reform might reduce federal-provincial conflict and might lead to a lessening of the harm caused by interregional competition. Certainly if there were a transfer to Parliament of new jurisdictions relating to economic regulation, the fields of federal-provincial combat would be altered. If, for example, there were an amendment to s. 91(2) of the *Constitution Act, 1867*, to give Parliament jurisdiction over competition policy,[45] the sort of constitutional debate that took place in argument (but not in the actual decision) in *A.-G. Can. v. Law Society of B.C.* and *Jabour v. Law Society of B.C.*[46] would not recur; provinces would be foreclosed from arguing on the basis that the application of federal competition policies was tantamount to regulation of entirely intraprovincial business activity. This, of course, does not mean that the processes of challenging, classifying and locating the essential constitutional character of federal and provincial laws would not continue. In a division of legislative powers the process of locating the true constitutional aspect of legislation is unavoidable unless, of course, one level of government possesses such general and overarching powers that the federal arrangement is less a matter of legal imperatives than it is the reflection of a tradition of voluntary accommodation.

Such an amendment transferring new economic powers might have a beneficial impact on the problems of federal-provincial wrangling, interprovincial competition and provincial protectionism, but it would have the negative consequence of unbalancing the present structure of Canadian federalism. Although formally redesigning the Canadian federation would not necessarily be undesirable, it would, in the context of economic regulation and development, be unfortunate. An overriding indeterminate federal authority over these matters would either cause provincial economic development measures to be extra-jurisdictional and, hence, invalid; or, if large areas of concurrent jurisdiction over economic regulation were judicially recognized, it would make provincial statutes and economic plans subject to federal policies. The influence of provinces over the economic structure and over economic activity would be conditioned by the requirement that their plans fit with, or track, federal policies.[47] In other words, provincial policies, regardless of their appropriateness in terms of shaping a provincial economy, could be modified or overridden by federal policies with which they were in conflict.

Accordingly, responding to the problem of a weak or inadequate federal general trade jurisdiction by creating a new constitutional text that conferred broad regulatory powers on Parliament,[48] would in all probability create the same problem of imbalanced federalism that has, for over a century, so assiduously driven the adjudicators of the Canadian constitutional system to give constrained readings to the federal trade power.

This is not to say that there could not be some formal constitutional amendment that would lessen this problem. For instance, there could be the creation, in the Constitution, of an intergovernmental structure that could control destructively competitive provincial economic strategies and sanction exercises of provincial regulatory authority which, although not meeting federal norms, did not pose a threat to the efficiency of the national economy.[49] Such a structure would have responsibility for discerning which discriminating or protective governmental practices were not tolerable in light of stipulated economic goals and which were allowable because their benefit to regional economic development outweighed injury to national economic goals.

The Alternative of Judicial Reconstruction

The purpose of this paper is not to explore in detail new constitutional texts relating to economic regulation or new constitutional structures. Rather, the analytical ambition of this study is to suggest a new style of constitutional interpretation, or constitutional mediation, in respect of the present allocation of legislative power. The purposes behind such new interpretations are to expand the scope for national general trade policy so that interprovincial economic competition, when it leads to unacceptable inefficiencies, can be checked, and so that federal-provincial conflict, when it creates confusing regulatory competition, can be resolved. At the same time, new interpretations of the constitutional powers over economic regulation should not lead to the devastation of provincial ambitions to develop economic and social strategies.

Federal general powers have been interpreted so that the scope of legislation they can support is controlled and limited. This has been done by paying strict attention to the idea of Canada as a true federation: two levels of government each acting within its own sphere and neither possessing such power that would permit unilateral control over the economic, cultural, political or social life of the community. The idea of Canada that has been rejected is the idea of a strong central government with power to unify, harmonize and integrate any, or all, of the aspects of community life. Now Canada is at the stage of its economic and political history where arguably it must act as an integrated whole in respect of economic regulation and industrial policy. Does our present constitutional arrangement permit this while preserving federalism? Is it possible to derive from the Constitution a more effective federal power without producing a constitutional concept that will prove to have overwhelming centralizing force?

Constitutional Theory for a Revised Trade Power

New Principles of Constitutional Adjudication

The prime obstacle to national economic regulatory authority is the recognition that there are no manifest dividing lines between the regulation of general trade and the regulation of all aspects of the nation's economic activity. If Parliament may enact legislation which, as in *MacDonald v. Vapor Canada Ltd.*,[50] requires persons engaged in any form of business activity to conduct their business affairs according to "honest industrial and commercial usage in Canada,"[51] then, so the concern goes, it may enact legislation requiring business to do or desist from doing anything regardless of how small the enterprise, how local its economic impact, how limited its market. The constitutional powers of provinces over "property and civil rights" (the power over contracting) and "matters of merely local and private nature" (the power to develop provincial social and economic environments), would be obliterated. What is needed is a conception of federal power that enables national standards, goals and policies to be pursued while leaving room for provinces to stipulate certain conditions and features for the provincial marketplace.

Let us first state a conception of the Canadian federal state that would support a federal, general economic power and still leave provinces constitutional room to determine their own economic patterns. That conception is expressed in the *Constitution Act, 1867*, and is based on that document's clear concern with nation building — with activities that produce a nation state that despite its illogicality in terms of geography, will function as a single state and as an economically viable whole. This view explains the limited form of economic union represented by s. 121 of the *Constitution Act, 1867* and the special place of interconnecting (or nation-creating) transportation and communication systems created by s-ss.(*a*), (*b*) and (*c*) of s. 92(10). Economic survival and economic viability are implicit aims in the structure of the division of powers. If Canada's economic survival in the last decades of the 20th century demands increased coherence in the governmental shaping of economic activity, then the implicit message of ss. 91 and 92, it is argued, is that the economic regulatory powers to meet this need must be seen to be present. The power, in s. 91(2), of regulation of trade and commerce may mean something limited throughout much of the 1900s; but it can mean something different and more intrusive when there are increased demands for governmental management of economic development.

In this way it might be appropriate to make an analogy between the potential of the federal trade and commerce power and the potential of the peace, order and good government clause. Both heads of power could, by a literal reading of their terms, sustain immense realms of legislative authority. Both heads, out of the need to preserve some scope for provincial autonomy, have been read in limited ways. At times the meaning given to these large general powers has been extremely limited. The peace, order and good government clause has been equated to a federal emergency power,[52] and the trade and commerce power has been held to be auxiliary to other heads of federal power.[53] Yet for both heads there have been other roles recognized; the general trade regulation capacity of s. 91(2) has never been denied at a theoretical level, and the peace, order and good government clause has occasionally sustained legislation in matters of a national dimension.[54]

The analogy is even more direct. The national dimension idea of peace order and good government is the right idea by which we can understand federal jurisdiction over trade and commerce. When the governmental management of trading activity is in response to a generally experienced need, and when it can be demonstrated that the mechanisms of state involvement in the economy are general mechanisms dependent on national implementation and national coordination, then the general trade idea of trade and commerce will be properly available as constitutional support.

The generality and genuineness of need for national trade regulation are, however, only the background conditions for judicial recognition of substantive content to Parliament's general trade jurisdiction under the trade and commerce power. More precise conditions for this recognition need to be spelled out. These conditions should include, first, the requirement that actual federal regulation be general in conception — that it be directed toward economic goals that transcend the needs of specific economic or industrial sectors. This is not to say that the administration of policies that have been developed to satisfy the general goals cannot entail specific sectoral applications. It is, of course, a truism that even generally expressed standards or proscriptions must be applied in particular instances. The tolerance for sectoral application of general federal trade policies goes further. It would permit regulations and even primary legislation to be expressed in terms of specific industries, occupations or activities, so long as the legislation was clearly relatable to general economic goals or was clearly an application of a general economic strategy.

A second condition for the exercise of federal authority would be the recognition of some form of provincial paramountcy. General federal regulation is tolerable only as long as it does not disrupt established provincial patterns of economic organization. The establishment of a doctrine of provincial immunity from federal trade regulation is based on the great value of provincial trade regimes in the sense that, for many aspects of trading activity and economic regulation, the provinces are best situated to determine what is appropriate for the circumstances and what is likely to be effective. When, through provincial legislation, a pattern of economic activity has been established — for example, the creation of a monopoly within the province, or the allocation, by public authority, of segments of markets to certain traders — federal policies ought not to disrupt those patterns except in the most compelling circumstances.

The third condition follows from the second; provincial paramountcy must itself be set aside in circumstances in which Parliament has expressly determined that its policies must, for compelling reasons of economic health, prevail and be in force in the nation without any exceptions.

Effect of New Principles

Before we explore how these mediating principles can be drawn from the present constitutional text, closer examination must be given to the operation of this set of ideas. For discussion purposes, we can consider the national regulation of competition in economic activity. The *Combines Investigation Act*[55] is an attempt to regulate trade and commerce in Canada with the goal of reducing anti-competitive activities. Its object is to improve the overall efficiency of the entire Canadian economy by reducing anti-competitive practices in all sectors of the economy. Restrictive trade practices in a local service industry may not in themselves be of national interest, but the total adverse impact on the Canadian economy, caused by anti-competitive practices in local trades and businesses throughout Canada, may add up to a problem of national concern.

The *Combines Investigation Act* does not attempt to regulate any particular trade or business. It attempts to regulate one aspect of all trades and businesses — their anti-competitive practices. If the application of the *Combines Investigation Act* to intraprovincial trade and commerce is allowed under the federal trade powers, that would not necessarily open the way for serious federal intrusions upon provincial autonomy. That Parliament may be able to prevent insurance companies in Saskatchewan from forming mergers and combines does not mean it can regulate any other aspect of the insurance business in Saskatchewan. Hence, recognizing the applicability under s. 91(2) of the *Combines Investigation Act* to local trades and businesses would not open the way for Parliament to regulate intensively provincial trades and businesses by passing laws of general application.

The questions that arise are whether there are cases, other than anticombines legislation, in which it would be feasible for the federal government to pass laws that would apply throughout Canada to all trades and businesses, and whether these other cases would have a more drastic impact on local trading activity. Some examples, such as requiring all trades and businesses to comply with federal trademark laws, do not seem to involve great intrusions upon provincial jurisdiction. A further example of a law applying generally to one aspect of all trades and businesses would be a general prohibition on misleading advertising. Indeed, s. 37 of the *Combines Investigation Act* contains such provisions. On the reasoning just advanced, s. 37 might be sustained under s. 91(2). Indeed, in the Federal Court of Appeal decision in *MacDonald v. Vapor Canada Ltd.*,[56] Jackett C.J. was prepared to uphold, on the basis of s. 91(2), s. 7 of the *Trade Marks Act*,[57] which condemned generally a number of false and misleading trade practices. Laskin C.J. indicated in his Supreme Court judgment that the "general trade" power might provide a basis for the public regulation of the s. 7 kind, but that since the remedies actually created were civil only, the subsection could not be sustained.[58]

This question of what other sorts of economic regulation could be supported under the rubric of laws applying generally to one aspect of all trades and businesses is, of course, vital to the issue of whether this sort of resurrection of the trade power is sufficient for the task of national economic survival that is before the country. A tentative answer is that federal standards of economic fairness and efficiency, as well as federal controls over province-serving economic policies, could be framed to fit within the general and limited standards theme which, it is argued, properly forms part of the federal trade power. Much of the federal regulation needed to control interprovincial competition and provincial protectionist policies could take the form of competition legislation. This legislation could grant power to a federal agency to monitor and control governmental decisions that impose false (non-market) costs on trading activity or that create inducements to trade in inefficient ways. In this way, provincial policies that distort the market, even though motivated by a reasonable desire to protect and encourage the provincial economy, would be controllable by a federal authority. The preservation of competitive trading conditions, which is the policy behind federal competition legislation, would satisfy the test of generality and would also be sufficiently comprehensive to meet those dislocating problems, currently experienced in the Canadian economy, that are attributable to economic provincialism.

Hence, s. 91(2) can be given genuine force by recognizing it as a constitutional basis for the *Combines Investigation Act* and other general trade regulations without unduly endangering provincial autonomy over local trading. After all, the regulation of market activity in only one respect is contemplated, albeit that it would apply to intraprovincial as well as interprovincial and international trade and commerce.

It does not do to be too sanguine about the effect of an expanded federal trade power. Even a limited role for federal trade jurisdiction could do much to interrupt the exercise of provincial rights under ss. 92(13) and 92(16) of the *Constitution Act, 1867*. For example, in relation to the application of the provisions of the *Combines Investigation Act*, there would be a grave interference with provincial policies if those provisions were permitted to apply to the activities of persons and organizations that are authorized by constitutionally valid provincial legislation. The answer would seem to be that the federal constitutional authority to take measures to improve the economic efficiency of the market should not be constitutionally permitted to disrupt provincial schemes based on valid provincial purposes such as regulating professional conduct, ensuring fair distribution of incomes to producers in an interprovincial market, limiting an oversupply of persons in one economic area and so on. Of course, the line between these ostensibly legitimate provincial goals and provincial protectionism would not be easy to draw. Such a distinction could not always be made on the basis of the scale of distortion of market activity produced, even if agreement on the quantification of economic costs were possible. For this reason, it is essential that there be a further refinement in the operation of provincial paramountcy. This refinement is that provincial economic regimes inconsistent with federal standards and created by express provincial legislation would be allowed to operate subject to Parliament's capacity to insist formally that its policies prevail against provincial regimes.

Claims Against Provincial Paramountcy

Two claims will be made against the proposal for provincial paramountcy. The first is that "federal paramountcy" requires that federal anticompetitive policy, or any other general economic policy at the federal level, override relevant and conflicting provincial policies. However, s. 91(2) has always been strictly construed so as to preserve the scope of provincial autonomy; indeed, it has, so far, been given very little independent force. It seems far preferable that mediating principles be adopted that strike a balance between giving s. 91(2) its full literal force — which the courts have never done and, barring some complete reorientation in constitutional ideology, are not likely to do — and making it totally ineffectual — which the courts seem to have been completely willing to do. In the field of anti-combines regulation this balance can be achieved by limiting the ambit of anti-combines laws to the provincially unregulated market. This argument amounts to a claim for provincial paramountcy, at least in relation to encroachments on the trade and commerce area, because the federal trade and commerce power, when considered in juxtaposition with provincial powers that bear on economic regulation, is of such a nature (i.e., general and indeterminate) that if the two mediating principles governing its operation were, first, to give it a wide substantive content and, second, to allow it to enjoy the operation of federal paramountcy, the resultant impact on provincial heads of power — and on the provincial interests they represent — would be devastating. In other words, in designing the system of constitutional trumps it makes far greater sense to allocate pre-eminent authority according to the nature of the competing powers than to make the allocation according to the general tenet of federal paramountcy.

The second point is that if, under some conceptions of the judicial function, the idea of having a system of shifting constitutional paramountcies entails judicial invention of too great a magnitude, the proposal to subject federal, general trade policies to provincially legislated economic regimes could be stated another way. It could be expressed in terms of a more familiar doctrine: the federal trade and commerce power permits regulation of the market; the anti-combines legislation is about improving the market environment; insofar as a province has regulated an area, it could be said to be no longer part of the "market"; an area of activity regulated by a province cannot be considered part of the overall "trade and commerce" of Canada subject to general regulation under s. 91(2).

Development of a Federal Overriding Power

It is necessary to consider a further mediating principle. The suggestion for the pre-eminence of provincial regulatory arrangements will, in normal circumstances, not significantly detract from, or neutralize, the increase in Parliament's regulatory powers produced through recognizing the validity of general trade policies and trade standards. However, there are circumstances in which federal policies over trade and economic development ought not to be made subject to overriding provincial regulatory regimes. This would be because the federal regulatory plan absolutely requires universal application for its effectiveness, or because the quantity and intrusiveness of provincial economic schemes that are to be exempted from application of the federal scheme would be too damaging to the federal objectives. This problem can be addressed through judicial mediating devices under which conditions for overriding federal authority can be identified, or through a legislative mechanism under which Parliament would identify that a compelling national interest is being served by its scheme. If it was thought necessary that this form of legislative identification of the federal trump against provincial paramountcy be invariably effective against any court challenge that might be launched against overriding inconsistent federal legislation, then the Constitution would need to be amended to stipulate that federal legislation carrying a statement that it was passed in response to a compelling national interest would not be reviewable by courts. More reasonably, it could be established merely through judicial decision-making that a clear legislative declaration of compelling national interest would be taken by reviewing courts as presumptively establishing that any economic activity regulated under inconsistent provincial law would be subject to federal law, and that provincial law would not apply.

These interpretive ideas require considerable innovation. Although that fact ought not to be intimidating once it is accepted that the function of constitutional interpretation is to give the normative utterances of the last century relevant prescriptive force in today's context,[59] it is essential to show how these ideas are derived from established ideas about constitutional adjudication. Two interpretive strategies have been suggested. The first is that this set of mediating principles best meets traditional judicial anxiety about unlimited and unchecked expansion of the federal power. The brief survey of trade and commerce jurisprudence shows this judicial anxiety to have become constitutive. Consequently, devices that meet this problem head-on can be seen to be operating within the realm of constitutional antecedents.

The second strategy is a definitional one under which federal competition policy is excluded from operating against provincial economic or trade arrangements. Under this strategy it could be claimed that the prerequisite market environment for the operation of competition law is not present whenever provincial laws have prevented its development. This strategy can be generalized. It could be argued that when provinces have created a controlled economic environment, either by way of establishing a chosen instrument or by way of establishing especially favourable marketing conditions for local enterprises, there is no longer a normal trade relationship being conducted. Parliament's trade power is designed to operate in the market and control trading and commercial activity. When trading has been infused with false impediments (from the perspective of economic theory), or false rewards through provincial regulation, the situation can no longer be classified as a trading situation. Rather, it has become a situation of which the dominant constitutional aspect is pursuit of provincial objectives. Clearly, however, this strategy achieves too much. It exempts from overriding federal regulation any provincial policy, regardless of its protectionist motives or economically costly effects.

Furthermore, any federal trade regulation, even that accompanied with a parliamentary declaration of compelling national interest, could not, under the idea that provincial economic promotion is a conclusive constitutional head of power, be classified as trade legislation when applied to regimes operating under provincial legislation. Accordingly, it is necessary to develop the further interpretive principle that the classification of provincial legislation as being in respect of the provincial head of power and not in respect of the federal trade and commerce power, can only be a prima facie classification. This classification can be displaced if the effect of the provincial economic and social strategy is to produce significant trading consequences. In other words, the initial leading aspect of provincial legislatively created economic development schemes is not trading (not even intraprovincial trading) but rather the shaping of the provincial social and economic environment. However, as in normal aspect analysis in Canadian constitutional law,[60] the effect of legislative and governmental activity can produce a characterization that does not reflect the initial intention behind the legislative scheme.[61] In the context of economic development this would happen when provincial regulation operated, so as to confound in serious ways any federal regulatory scheme declared to be of grave importance. This finding, in respect of provincial legislation, of a trade aspect, a finding that removed the jurisdictional underpinning of the provincial scheme, would be possible even though, in the initial creation by the province of the offending economic structure, there had been neither intention to create, nor awareness of, conflict with federal general trade policies. In fact, under the proposed set of mediating principles, the federal trade strategy need not have been implemented, or even conceived of, at the point that the provincial pattern was established. The normal exemption for provincial economic structures from federal, general trade policy, or, in other words, the operation of a limited provincial paramountcy, would simply no longer occur once Parliament were to declare that there was an overriding or compelling need for uniform general application of its policy.

The precise analytic account by which such a result may be reached under aspect analysis proceeds by way of observing that when Parliament states that its general trade policy must apply in all relevant circumstances, without exemption for provincial patterns, the primary aspect of inconsistent provincial regulation is federal trade power. This is because Parliament has established a new constitutional condition. Whereas, normally, existing provincially created monopolies, for example, do not carry the aspect of general trade, once Parliament has identified — through the use of a declaration of compelling interest — that that provincial scheme is significantly undermining the federal economic goals with respect to, say, efficiency or competition, the aspect of the provincial scheme becomes trade. Any legislatively supported arrangement that breaks down the goals that are identified as vital trade goals itself carries a trade aspect.

However, in cases in which Parliament has expressed a trade policy (for example, in respect of national standards or the encouragement of infant, or sunrise, industries) but has not established (by declaring a compelling interest) that the policy must be uniformly applied in order to be worthwhile or effective, provincially mandated economic structures would not carry the trade aspect. As suggested earlier, such structures normally carry a constitutional aspect within s. 92 of the *Constitution Act, 1867*, the most likely specific head of power being s. 92(16): "Generally all matters of a merely local or private nature in the Province." That the continued operation of such a provincial scheme would present an instance in which federal, general trade policy did not hold sway would not in itself transform the constitutional aspect of the scheme if there had been no declaration that the federal policy need prevail uniformly. Provincial economic structures do not carry a general trade aspect when there has not been sufficient identification of a general trade interest in the scheme's operation. In this way the exact content of the various provincial and federal heads of power are determined, as always, by specific social contexts,[62] and the context in relation to trade interests is established through self-conscious parliamentary declarations about the overriding need, or lack of it, for a particular program of economic regulation.

A further aspect of the federal overriding power needs brief canvassing: to what extent should parliamentary declarations of compelling national interest be controlling in the judicial process of determining primary constitutional aspect? In other words, should exercise of the federal overriding power provide a complete answer to constitutional challenges to the declaration? There are two instances in Canadian constitutional law in which parliamentary declarations suspend the normal autonomy of the courts in determining the proper characterization of challenged laws. These are, first, in respect of declarations under s. 92 (10) (c) of the *Constitution Act, 1867*, that works are for the general advantage of Canada,[63] and, second, of declarations of an emergency used by Parliament to support legislation under the emergency conception of the peace, order and good government clause of s. 91.[64] The former declarations are not reviewable, and the latter, theoretically, are.[65] However, judicial deference to declarations of emergency has been high, and it would seem likely that such a degree of deference would persist in respect of declarations of compelling national economic interest that were included in legislation that created general trade regulation. This would, of course, be especially so if there were an express recognition in the constitutional text of such a declaratory power,[66] but the proposal under consideration is premised entirely on judicial elaboration of mediating principles that would include judicial creation of the test that a declaration of compelling national interest for uniformly applied economic regulation should normally end the operation of provincial paramountcy.

In the context of judicially created interpretive rules, it is conceivable that courts could be satisfied of the presence of a compelling national interest even without express statutory language to that effect; and, when there was clear evidence that it was Parliament's intention to have its scheme apply against provincially mandated economic and social structures, judges would need to be satisfied that there was insufficient evidence supporting the claim that it was necessary to disrupt established provincial patterns. However, in respect of this latter interpretive rule, it should be remembered that the emergency conception of the federal residual power is also a judicial construct and that Canadian courts have not taken an active role in ensuring that parliamentary use of the concept has been fully warranted.[67] In fact, in instances in which a court became satisfied that Parliament truly thought that universal application of its policy was essential, it would be a brave court that undertook fully to re-examine that conclusion and to substitute its own opinion. This is not to say that colourable or underhanded uses of a compelling national interest standard would not be subject to court interference.[68] In the application of basic constitutional norms, courts are not likely to abandon their ultimate authority to determine the real quality of challenged governmental conduct or allow themselves to be governed by mere legislative or executive stipulation that an essential constitutional condition has been satisfied.[69]

Operation of Provincial Paramountcy

Apart from the exercise of Parliament's power to override provincial legislation that sets up schemes to regulate, restrict or encourage economic activity, such legislated schemes will not be touched by inconsistent federal legislation establishing standards for economic activity. The question that arises with respect to this degree of provincial paramountcy, or provincial immunity, is whether it should be available only in respect of schemes that are in place at the time the federal, general trade legislation comes into force. Should provincial economic structures that are created *after* a valid federal trade policy has been put in place, and that are inconsistent with it, not enjoy a provincial constitutional classification and not prevail over the federal policy?

There are reasons why the appropriate mediating principle between conflicting federal and provincial schemes should be that provincial economic or trading arrangements created subsequent to the federal policy invariably be struck down. In the first place, even when Parliament has not implicitly or explicitly represented an aspect of its economic program to be vital and to demand universal application, provincial arrangements which, when enacted, are known to be in conflict with federal economic goals, could reasonably attract the characterization of trade regulation. Furthermore, it might be undesirable if Parliament, having failed to declare that its policies must prevail for reasons of compelling national interest, signalled that non-conforming provincial practices would be tolerated and then — on discovering that there is a growing number of provincial schemes that deviate from national trade policies — was forced to change the legislation to mandate universal application of its policy. This would be unfortunate if the result of the potential added legislative burden produced by such a principle were to be that Parliament would be induced to use the compelling-national-interest terminology indiscriminately in all of its economic regulatory legislation. This might be a particularly powerful temptation in light of the difficulty experienced by recent governments in controlling the legislative timetable. In addition, it would be unfair if traditional provincial schemes were to fall prey to parliamentary declarations once the latter were induced by the appearance of new nonconforming provincial regulations. A province's choosing to pass legislation conflicting with federal policy would become the indirect cause of the overturning of other provinces' economic management shemes that had been established prior to the federal law.

Notwithstanding the strength of these arguments, it would be better if the mediating principle developed to deal with legislative conflict were to be that any provincially mandated economic arrangement be immune from the operation of federal rules governing trading activity. There are four reasons for this. First, it would be a pity to induce provinces to maintain economic regimes that are outmoded and inappropriate on the ground that federal legislation enacted since the establishment of the now obsolete regime precluded the development of substitute schemes. Furthermore, in many cases it would be impossible to tell whether the provincial scheme was simply undergoing amendment and minor revision, in which case the constitutional immunity for it would continue, or was, in effect, being repealed and replaced, in which case the immunity from federal standards would be lost.

Second, it would likewise be a mistake to develop mediating principles that caused both federal and provincial governments to rush to legislate. Under a mediating principle based on the temporal priority of conflicting pieces of legislation, the incentive to create quickly both large federal regulatory regimes and many special provincial marketing arrangements could lead to the disaster of widespread, poorly conceived and unnecessary regulation of trade activity.

Third, the requirement that provincial market schemes be created prior to federal regulatory legislation in order to be immune is unnecessary in light of Parliament's capacity to respond to unacceptable levels of exemption from its standards. Parliament's power to override provincial schemes through the use of its declaratory power obviates the need to provide a guaranteed field of operation.

Finally, and most important, the great contribution of provinces in the Canadian federal system is that they are the units of government that have the greatest incentive to engage in regulatory innovation and experimentation. The pressures on provincial governments to respond to local and regional economic problems are considerable. The stream of regulatory initiative that provinces have provided ought to continue. When new provincial regulation becomes too costly for the nation, Parliament, under this doctrinal scheme, may respond. In the meantime the multifaceted effort to fashion strong and efficient regional economies is permitted to continue. Hence, in terms of rationality and in terms of realizing the fundamental virtue of permitting competition in the accommodation of political interests, it is preferable to permit provincial paramountcy to operate in respect of all expressly legislated economic regimes, unless Parliament has chosen to insist on the primacy of its economic goals over all other governmental schemes.

Constitutional Antecedents

The last matter to be considered concerns antecedents for the development of sets of mediating principles of this sort in constitutional interpretation. In the first place, the doctrine of federal paramountcy is itself a judicial construct not specifically mandated in the text of the *Constitution Act, 1867*. However, it is a principle needed to deal with an interpretive phenomenon not generally recognized at the original point of enactment — the problem created when legislative arrangements can be characterized as being just as much in relation to a federal matter as to a provincial matter.

Apart from being a rule in a situation in which *some* rule is necessary, federal paramountcy tracks the rule that is textually established in those cases in which concurrent jurisdiction is expressly created.[70] Furthermore it catches the tone of primacy of federal authority, which is established by the concluding words of s. 91.[71] However, it is important to note that the concluding words of s. 91 do not expressly present a rule of federal paramountcy in situations of concurrent jurisdiction. The concluding words of that section are literally directed to the enterprise of defining exclusive jurisdictions and not to the problem of resolving conflict in concurrent jurisdictions. Hence, the traditional rule of federal paramountcy is the product of, first, the need to develop some principle for mediating between competing claims and, second, the desire to reflect basic structures of the *Constitution Act*. Likewise, the mediating principles suggested in this paper are legitimated, first, by functional necessity to generate a more elaborate constitutional jurisprudence than has hitherto been in place and, second, by their appropriateness in terms of what the constitutional text and Constitutional history suggest about honouring realms of provincial autonomy. There is a third point of legitimation: these interpretive principles provide the surest way to respect the basic structure of federal balance which is created by ss. 91 and 92 in respect of legislative powers (and which is matched in respect of judicial powers by ss. 92(14) and 96 of the *Constitution Act*).

Other instances of judicial creativity may be cited. Arguably, the gradual elaboration of the content of the separation of powers doctrine culminating in *McEvoy*[72] is an example of the court developing constitutional norms based on sparsely outlined structures.[73] A further instance is the judicial development of a tolerance for legislative schemes that encroach on the jurisdictions of the other level of government when those encroachments are necessary to the integrity of a particular scheme. Another way of viewing this judicial strategy is that the court will permit constitutional encroachments in legislation when the challenged scheme represents the least drastic means of achieving an otherwise valid objective. An example of this interpretative process can be seen in the Supreme Court of Canada's decision in *A.-G. Ont. v. Barfried Enterprises*.[74] In that case, the Ontario legislature's attempt to provide remedies for exploitive credit transactions was challenged because one of the forms of market exploitation for which the legislative remedy was available was exorbitant interest rates. The earlier case of *A.-G. Sask. v. A.-G. Can.*[75] had clearly established that relief against interest payments was not within the provincial domain merely because the credit transactions were in relation to commodities and activities that fell within the provincial jurisdiction and were vital to provincial interests. However, relief against high interest rates by way of substituting more reasonable rates was allowed in *Barfried*, notwithstanding the placing of interest under federal jurisdiction by s. 91(19) of the *Constitution Act, 1867*, since the primary element of the legislative scheme (the regulation of contracts for the lending of money) was within provincial competence. The treatment of interest rates and interest payments in the provincial statute was a tolerable encroachment because it was an encroachment needed to maintain the integrity of the borrower protection scheme.[76]

Another example of the willingness of the Supreme Court of Canada to refine constitutional principles in order to produce a more adaptive jurisprudence is found in the decision in *Fulton v. Energy Resources Conservation Board and Calgary Power Ltd*.[77] Chief Justice Laskin, writing for the Court, upheld the constitutional authority of Alberta's Energy Conservation Board to issue a permit to construct an electrical transmission line to the Alberta–British Columbia border to be connected with a transmission line in British Columbia. It is clear that regulatory authority over interconnecting works, such as the proposed power line, belongs to the federal level. It is also clear that, normally, this jurisdiction is considered to be exclusively federal.[78] Notwithstanding, in this case Chief Justice Laskin ignored the implications of the case law, which had recognized exclusive federal authority, and decided that since in the circumstances of the actual case there was no existing federal regulatory authority, the provincial permit granting regime should operate. The novel cast to constitutional doctrine that this result illustrates was underscored by the confusing observation that there was "no operative federal legislation to underscore exclusiveness or to support federal paramountcy."[79] The chief justice went on to state: "Although exclusiveness may arise even in the absence of federal legislation, I do not regard the situation presented here as providing a basis for its assertion."[80] By these passages Chief Justice Laskin avoided finding that the jurisdiction in question in this case was concurrent and, at the same time, avoided the consequences of finding exclusive federal power.[81] This decisional strategy is not to be scorned, however, as it reveals a number of doctrinal virtues. In the first place it allows provincial regulation over a matter with which Parliament has not shown an interest in dealing. In the second place, the regulatory objective of the province (controlling the location of high voltage transmission lines) is patently desirable and is highly suitable for provincial regulation. Finally, since the decision is not based on concurrent regulatory authority, a provincial regulatory regime that was more restrictive (or defeating of the interconnecting enterprise) would not necessarily have to be tolerated even in the face of continued regulatory abstinence by Parliament. These features of the decision were available only through judicial adaptation of the mediating principles traditionally at play in Canadian constitutional law.

The *Barfried* and *Fulton* cases are, therefore, evidence that Canadian courts have sometimes been willing to generate norms for the interpretation of constitutional powers that produce a reasonable allocation of authority measured both by the need for coherent and effective regulation and the need to maintain the basic federal structure.

Likewise, it is reasonable to assume that if the context of economic regulation has changed to place new importance on national regulation designed to promote efficient players in the marketplace, then reconstruction of the methods of constitutional interpretation and application are within the best traditions of our constitutional law. A set of principles for resolving constitutional conflict in a way which permits general coherent regulation, which is not tied to interprovincial marketing patterns and which respects provincial plans to generate rational provincial economic development and activity, is within our grasp under present constitutional arrangements.

New Constitutional Theory in the Making

The 1983 decision of the Supreme Court of Canada in *A.-G. Can. v. Can. National Transportation*[82] was concerned primarily with the troubling constitutional question of which level of government has jurisdiction over criminal prosecutions. The precise issue raised by this case was which level had prosecutorial authority in respect of offences under the *Combines Investigation Act*. The operating assumption in Canadian law had been that the prosecution of federal offences enacted under Parliament's criminal law power was the responsibility of provincial attorneys general.

That assumption was challenged by the federal government in its argument in the 1979 case of *R. v. Hauser*.[83] However, in that case the Supreme Court of Canada neither upset nor confirmed this assumption. The challenge to provincial prosecutorial authority over criminal offences in that case was side-stepped by the Court's finding that the offences in question, offences under the *Narcotic Control Act*,[84] were an exercise of Parliament's authority arising under the peace, order and good government clause of s. 91 and were not, in fact, criminal offences. The same challenge to the assumption of provincial authority was again made in the *Canadian National Transportation* case, and it was generally thought that avoidance of the issue would not be so easy, since there had been a number of cases which had established that legislative authority to create the offences found in the *Combines Investigation Act* arose under Parliament's criminal law power.[85] The majority decision in the case, written by Chief Justice Laskin, did, in fact, confirm those previous cases; the offences of the *Combines Investigation Act* were held to be exercises of criminal law. The majority went on to hold in this case and in the companion case of *R. v. Wetmore*[86] that prosecutorial authority over criminal offences was not within the jurisdiction of provinces under s. 92(14): "The Administration of Justice in the Province. . ." but fell within federal authority under s. 91(27): "The Criminal Law, except the Constitution of Courts of Criminal Jurisdiction, but including the Procedure in Criminal Matters."[87]

Had the decision stood at that point, it would have been of no interest to the process of elaborating an understanding of the constitutional arrangement over economic regulation. However, Mr. Justice Dickson wrote a concurring opinion in which he held that the *Combines Investigation Act* is valid federal legislation under both the criminal law power and the federal trade and commerce power under s. 91(2). It followed from this finding, and the holding in the *Hauser* case, that prosecutorial authority over *Combines Investigation Act* offences fell to the federal government. However, what is important in Mr. Justice Dickson's decision is his elaboration of the federal trade and commerce power and his demonstration of how it supports general trade regulation such as that found in the *Combines Investigation Act*. It is that portion of this opinion which needs closer examination. Such examination shows that virtually all of the elements of the mediating principles sketched in the earlier sections of this paper were touched upon, albeit lightly, by Mr. Justice Dickson.

The opinion on this issue contains ten distinct passages that show the process by which the present understanding of the competing trade powers were arrived at and, further, demonstrate how this understanding can be modified to produce a sounder jurisprudence in the area of trade regulation. The ten passages are set out below with a short commentary following each.

1. In deciding how much ought to be subtracted from the full literal meaning of s. 91(2) in order to preserve proper constitutional balance between the federal government and the provinces the Courts have developed a number of indicia of the respective federal and provincial competences.[88]

Commentary   This passage reveals that sheer literalism is not appropriate, at least with respect to the interpretation of the trade powers of the *Constitution Act, 1867*, and that preservation of the federal structure created by the Constitution requires mutual modification of the literal meaning of the heads of power.

2. The difficult underlying task facing a court determining the constitutional status of federal economic regulation is, without passing on the substantive merits of the legislation, to assess whether and how far it encroaches on the degree of local autonomy contemplated by the Constitution. It is not surprising that the tenor of what constitutes such an encroachment has varied over time.[89]

Commentary   Clearly the devices that the Judicial Committee of the Privy Council and the Supreme Court of Canada have used for ascribing constitutional meaning are not unalterable. It is worth noting that Mr. Justice Dickson does not simply state that those legislative schemes that have constituted an encroachment have varied over time, but rather that the *tenor* of what has constituted an encroachment has varied. By this, he means that the way of thinking about balancing the competing heads of power has been subject to alteration and revision. This, of course, is certainly true with respect to the regulation of interprovincial trade in commodities.[90] The tests for tolerable encroachment in this area have become considerably less stringent over the years. It has not been true in respect of what is permissible under "general regulation of trade." This claim by Mr. Justice Dickson of the potential for varying conceptions of constitutional norms sets the scene for adaptation in our constitutional jurisprudence with respect to general trade.

3. If every economic issue that could be characterized as a "question of general interest throughout the Dominion" were to fall under federal competence by virtue of s. 91(2), then the extent of the power would be on a literal reading of the words "regulation of trade and commerce" alone. There is hardly an economic issue which if only by virtue of its recurrence in locations around the country could not be characterized as a matter of general interest throughout the Dominion.[91]

Commentary   This passage reveals the nature of the historically dominant judicial anxiety with respect to ascribing content to the trade and commerce power apart from the regulation of interprovincial and international trade. Since there is no readily apparent limitation to the idea of "general regulation of trade," giving it any meaning at all runs the risk of obliterating provincial powers over trade and economic activity.

4. (iii) Regulating the Contracts of a Particular Business or Trade.[92]

Commentary   This is a title of a portion of Mr. Justice Dickson's opinion and reveals the nature of the chief analytical device used to check the application of the general trade power. In this portion of the opinion he shows how federal regulation, which can be seen to be the regulation of a single trade or industry, notwithstanding that the regulation is expressed in more general terms, has failed to pass constitutional muster.

5. Every general enactment will necessarily have some local impact, and if it is true that an overly literal conception of "general interest" will endanger the very idea of a local, there are equal dangers in swinging the telescope the other way around. The forest is no less a forest for being made up of individual trees.[93]

Commentary   Mr. Justice Dickson reveals the potential fallacy of the limitation that has been imposed upon the "general regulation of trade" power of s. 91(2). All legislative schemes that are not self-executing (and in economic regulation it would be typical that regulatory schemes would require administration of some sort) will depend on a series of individual applications that will invariably have local impact. That the implementation of a general scheme will consist of a series of individual and local applications directed to a particular enterprise or economic activity cannot by itself be reason to disqualify the legislative scheme as invading a provincial head of power.

6. Were that the test, then no economic legislation could ever qualify under the general trade and commerce power. Such a conception is merely the obverse of the equally unacceptable proposition that economic legislation qualifies under the general trade and commerce rubric merely because it applies equally and uniformly throughout the country.[94]

Commentary   What is established here is the need for the development of a new analytical device for achieving a balanced federal arrangement for the exercise of economic regulatory powers.

7. A different situation obtains, however, when what is at issue is general legislation aimed at the economy as a single integrated national unit rather than as a collection of separate local enterprises. Such legislation is qualitatively different from anything that could practically or constitutionally be enacted by the individual provinces either separately or in combination. . . . The line of demarcation is clear between measures validly directed at a general regulation of the national economy and those merely aimed at centralized control over a large number of local economic entities.[95]

Commentary   What is clear is that there is a qualitative test for any legislation that purports to be valid under Parliament's trade and commerce power. The test, as suggested by Mr. Justice Dickson in the last sentence of the above extract, is that the idea behind the regulation must be one of general appropriateness regardless of region or particular economic activity.

8. To this list [of indicia of general trade] I would add what to my mind would be even stronger indications of valid general regulation of trade and commerce, namely (i) that the provinces jointly or severally would be constitutionally incapable of passing such an enactment, and (ii) that failure to include one or more provinces or localities would jeopardize successful operation in other parts of the country.[96]

Commentary   Mr. Justice Dickson cited the indicia suggested by Chief Justice Laskin in *MacDonald v. Vapor Canada Ltd.*[97] that exercises of the national regulatory power required surveillance by a regulatory agency. He also added the test that the provinces not jointly or severally be able to pass the desired regulatory legislation. These indicia seem sensible and unremarkable. However, the next indicium is troublesome for the thesis of this paper. It suggests that any operation of provincial paramountcy, even an operation as constrained as that described in this paper, would be inconsistent with the precondition for general trade power, which is that any nonconformity within provinces would jeopardize the regulatory scheme. The passage may not, however, be as fatal to the set of mediating principles devised in this paper as first appears. In the first place, the range of exemption from the scheme alluded to in the passage is the removal from the application of the federal scheme of a whole province or whole provinces. Under the scheme suggested in this paper, provincial paramountcy would exempt from the operation of the federal scheme only precise economic arrangements created by provincial legislation. Therefore, it is not as if the total of a province's economy would escape from the regulatory ambitions of Parliament. Only particular, legislatively recognized, trading activities — for example, the delivery of professional legal services or the sale of natural gas — would not be subject to the federal scheme. In the second place, the test advanced by Mr. Justice Dickson does lend support to the proposition that the central question to be asked in relation to the scope of application (and the range of possible exemptions) to any federal economic regulatory scheme is the cost of noninclusion (or exemption) to the integrity of the scheme. This is precisely what is at the heart of the mediating principles suggested in this paper. If an exemption for an existing provincial economic arrangment would not jeopardize the operation of the federal scheme, then it should be allowed. If it would jeopardize such a scheme, then Parliament is free to indicate that universal application is a significant element of its scheme, and no exemptions would be allowed.

9. The above does not purport to be an exhaustive list nor is the presence of any or all of these indicia necessarily decisive.[98]

Commentary   This passage underscores the fluid nature of the constitutional principles being developed to bring rational constitutional organization to this area. For Mr. Justice Dickson the indicia of the previous paragraph were by no means final; more sophisticated elaboration of mediating principles is not foreclosed and is, in fact, invited. More to the point, it is clearly in Mr. Justice Dickson's contemplation that this further elaboration is one that will take place through the operation of constitutional adjudication. It would be institutionally unusual for a justice of the Supreme Court to suggest constitutional amendment. It is clear that, in the context of constitutional powers over the economy, Mr. Justice Dickson does not consider developments that would support a wider range of federal regulatory jurisdiction to be at all dependent upon constitutional amendment.

10. The basis of these inclusions and exclusions [of trading activity from the application of the *Combines Investigation Act*] cannot be said to be the moral or ethical quality of the acts in question. The purpose of these specifications seems to be to include the kinds of acts and agreements that are considered to have economically harmful consequences while ignoring the same kinds of acts and agreements when their consequences are beneficial or at least domestically harmless.[99]

Commentary   Although, in this passage, Mr. Justice Dickson is talking about the basic regulatory idea behind the *Combines Investigation Act*, the passage does reveal that, in his opinion, federal economic regulation will not necessarily be general and uniform. It follows from this description that there is no constitutional requirement that exercises of federal authority be uniformly applied. As indicated earlier in this paper, there are both good and bad trade discriminations, good and bad provincial economic development policies, and good and bad restraints on free trade; the Constitution cannot be read as conveying the message that all impediments to a truly free market imposed by provincial regulation are contrary to constitutional value. Clearly, Mr. Justice Dickson's description of the *Combines Investigation Act* cannot be raised to the level of constitutional theory, but it is fair to draw from this passage judicial recognition that uniformity in trade regulation is not an unquestioned value. Just as the *Combines Investigation Act* can be seen as sensitive to economic context, there is no reason why the application of the constitutional division of powers may not be similarly sensitive. The point in respect of this passage is that the economic sophistication that underlies it will also inform judges when they undertake the important task of reconstituting the powers to regulate economic activity. There can be no ready assumption that any set of mediating principles which allows for exemption, deviation or diversity is contrary to the ideas of constitutional ordering found in the Act of 1867.

Although the decision of Mr. Justice Dickson in *Canadian National Transportation* is the decision of only a minority of the Supreme Court,[100] it represents a way of thinking about the relationship between provincial authority over economic development and the federal trade and commerce power that promises great opportunity for enhanced federal regulatory authority. Futhermore, it does so while leaving open the door for further principles of constitutional interpretation that do not threaten the basic constitutional structure underlying Canadian political life, a structure which has been so assiduously preserved for well over 100 years and which, by its facilitation of innovation and competition, has been a strong contributor to national economic health.

Notes

This study was completed in February 1985.

1. In the case of the liquor trade the federal power to create zones of prohibition recognized in *Russell v. The Queen* (1881–82), 7 App. Cas. 829 (J.C.P.C.), was conditioned in the later case of *Attorney General of Ontario v. Attorney General of Canada* (the *Local Prohibition* case), [1896] A.C. 348 (J.C.P.C.), by the statement that federal regulation reached local matters (i.e., the liquor trade) only when the matter "attain[ed] such dimensions as to affect the body politic of the Dominion . . . " (at p. 361).

2. Federal regulation of the wartime and postwar economy, the validity of which was recognized in *Fort Frances Pulp and Paper Co. v. Manitoba Free Press* (1923), A.C. 695 (J.C.P.C.), was restricted to taking measures to meet grave emergencies "such as that arising out of war . . . " (at p. 705). See also *Re Board of Commerce Act, 1919* [1922], 1 A.C. 191 (J.C.P.C.) for an instance of severe restrictions placed on federal wartime regulation.

3. In *The King v. Eastern Terminal Elevator Co.*, [1925] S.C.R. 434, federal legislation regulating the grain trade was struck down as violating provincial legislative powers notwithstanding that most of Canada's grain production was sold outside the provinces in which it was grown. Duff J., through quoting counsel for the Government of Canada, reported that " . . . the trade in grain is largely an external trade (between seventy and eighty percent, apparently, of the grain produced in the country is exported)" (at p. 446).

4. For a telling account of the power of local culture and local political identification during the first decades of Canadian Confederation, see J.A. Corry, *My Life and Work: A Happy Partnership* (Kingston: Queen's University Press, 1981). Corry describes his place of growing up as an "independent republic" whose "citizens had to rely on themselves almost completely and were little subject to outside intervention. . . . We. . . were free of the present day corroding resentment about decisions that affect us intimately and deeply being made by distant authorities whom we do not know, have no direct effective control over, and no power to warn off" (at p. 23).

5. Evidence of the irreconcilability of specific visions of the new nation of Canada is provided in the historical essay on the role of the British colonial secretary in the drafting of the *British North America Act, 1867*. See P. B. Waite, "Edward Cardwell and Confederation" (1962), 43 *Canadian Historical Review* 1, reprinted in *Confederation*, edited by Ramsey Cook (Toronto: University of Toronto Press, 1967), p. 23.

6. Concepts as a term to describe constitutional values, is suggested by Ronald Dworkin. He emphasizes the distinction between concepts and specific conceptions pointing out that "'vague' constitutional clauses" should be read "as representing appeals to the concepts they employ. . . ." See R. Dworkin, *Taking Rights Seriously* (Cambridge: Harvard University Press, 1977), pp. 133–37.

7. An extremely ambitious account of what it means to look for the "deeper," historical significance of constitutional texts is found in R. Cover, "Foreword: *Nomos* and Narrative" (1983–84), 97 Harv. L.Rev. 4.

8. For a description of structuralist constitutional jurisprudence under the United States Constitution, see Charles Black, *Structure and Relationship in Constitutional Law* (Baton Rouge: Louisiana University Press, 1969), pp. 3–32.

9. See, e.g., the judgments of Duff C.J. in *Re Alberta Legislation*, [1938] S.C.R. 100 at pp. 132–37, and Rand J. in *Saumur v. City of Quebec*, [1953] 2 S.C.R. 299 at pp. 329–33.

10. [1951] S.C.R. 887 at pp. 916–25.

11. [1954] A.C. 541 (J.C.P.C.).

12. Admittedly these notions were not explicitly developed by Lord Porter in his decision in *Winner, ibid*. However, the constitutional prescription against treating interconnecting enterprises as indivisible is a clear theme of his opinion, as it was in Lord Macnaghten's opinion in *Toronto Corp. v. Bell Telephone Co. of Can.*, [1905] A.C. 52 (J.C.P.C) on which Lord Porter relied.

13. Recognizing that the identification of specific instances of weak constitutional interpretation is perhaps both insidious and unfair, I would nevertheless mention the conclusory opinion of Martland J. in *Carnation Co. Ltd. v. Quebec Agricultural Marketing Board*, [1968] S.C.R. 238, and the long but unilluminating opinion on the scope of provincial jurisdiction over the administration of justice in the province, of Laskin C.J. in *A.-G. Can. v. Can. National Transportation Ltd.* (1983), 3 D.L.R. (4th) 16 (S.C.C.).

14. For a description of the intellectual limits associated with the ideology of legalism, see Judith Shklar, *Legalism* (Cambridge: Harvard University Press, 1964), pp. 1–28.

15. The consequence of finding a constitution to be a legal document was first articulated by Chief Justice John Marshall of the United States Supreme Court in *Marbury v. Madison*, 5 U.S. (1 Cranch) 137 (1803).

16. A recent example of literalist, non-purpose interpretation is *Province of Manitoba v. Air Canada*, [1980] 2 S.C.R. 303, in which the meaning of "Direct Taxation within the Provinces . . ." under s. 92(2) of the *Constitution Act, 1867*, is applied in a manner detached from consideration of the intended role of the provincial taxing power, as well as from the leading authority in this area, *Bank of Toronto v. Lambe* (1887), 12 App. Cas. 575 (J.C.P.C.). For a criticism of the *Air Canada* decision see James MacPherson, "Developments in Constitutional Law: The 1979–80 Term" (1981), 2 Supreme Court L.R. 4 at pp. 98–99.

17. See Philip Bobbitt, *Constitutional Fate: Theory of the Constitution* (New York: Oxford University Press, 1982), pp. 93–124, for a description of the interpretational significance of considering constitutions to be ethical documents, by which Bobbitt means that constitutions are expressive of a nation's fundamental character (at pp. 94–95).

18. Examples of the Constitution being changed in order to meet new social and political realities are the *Constitution Act, 1940*, adding para. 2A: "Unemployment Insurance" to s. 91, and the *British North America Act, 1951* (repealed by the *Constitution Act, 1982)*, replaced with *Constitution Act, 1964*, conferring jurisdiction over "Old Age Pensions" on Parliament.

19. See Ivor Jennings, "Constitutional Interpretation — the Experience of Canada" (1937-38), 51 Harv. L. Rev. 1: "The British North America Act, 1867, is a strictly businesslike document, it contains no metaphysics, no political philosophy and no party politics" (at p. 1).

20. (1881-82), 7 App. Cas. 96 (J.C.P.C.).

21. Ibid., at p. 112.

22. Ibid., at p. 113.

23. [1912] A.C. 333 (J.C.P.C.).

24. Ibid., at p. 344.

25. 3 Edward 7, c. 58.

26. Supra, note 3.

27. 2 George 5, c. 27.

28. Supra, note 3, at pp. 453-54.

29. [1916] 1 A.C. 588 (J.C.P.C.).

30. Ibid., at p. 596.

31. [1937] A.C. 377 (J.C.P.C.).

32. [1951] A.C. 179 (J.C.P.C.).

33. [1951] A.C. 330 (J.C.P.C.).

34. Ibid., at p. 340.

35. [1937] A.C. 405 (J.C.P.C.).

36. Ibid., at p. 417.

37. (1979), 110 D.L.R. (3d) 564 (S.C.C.).

38. R.S.C. 1970, c. F-27.

39. Supra, note 37, at p. 626.

40. Case authority in the trade and commerce area has established that very little jurisdictional overlap is recognized. In other words, little scope has been given, in this area of constitutional adjudication, to the concept of concurrent legislative powers. Displacement of any provincial jurisdiction over matters within the federal sphere of trade and commerce was demonstrated in the Supreme Court of Canada decisions in Can. Industrial Gas & Oil Ltd. v. Govt. of Sask., [1978] 2 S.C.R. 545, and Central Can. Potash Co. Ltd. v. Govt. of Sask., [1979] 1 S.C.R. 42.

41. The Supreme Court of Canada had already decided that the trade and commerce power could not sustain the legislative establishment of standards of trading activity. See MacDonald v. Vapor Can. Ltd., [1977] 2 S.C.R. 134.

42. Supra, note 40.

43. Ibid.

44. The discussion of the current Canadian economic context in this section is drawn largely from Debra Simpson, "Water Tight Compartments Spring Leaks: Towards a Re-Thinking of the Court's Role in Economic Regulatory Activity" (Kingston: Faculty of Law, Queen's University, unpublished LL.B. major research paper, 1984). See also Michael Jenkin, The Challenge of Diversity: Industrial Policy in the Canadian Federation (Ottawa: Science Council of Canada, 1983), and A.E. Safarian, Canadian Federalism and Economic Integration (Ottawa: Information Canada, 1974).

45. Such a proposal was made by the Government of Canada during the federal-provincial constitutional negotiations which took place during the summer of 1980. The federal position on constitutional reform with respect to the amendment to confer jurisdiction over competition on Parliament, is discussed in Roy Romanow, John Whyte and Howard Leeson, Canada . . . Notwithstanding: The Making of the Constitution 1976-1982 (Toronto: Carswell/Methuen, 1984), p. 70.

46. [1982] 2 S.C.R. 307.

47. One view of the conditions under which provincial legislation is allowed to co-exist with federal legislation in concurrent areas is described by Rand J. in Johnson v.

A.-G. Alta., [1954] S.C.R. 127. Rand J.'s description, although expressed purposively in terms of the need for provincial legislation not to weaken or confuse the enforcement of federal law, falls within the dominant sense of the operation of federal paramountcy. That sense is that, apart from direct operational conflict, provincial law in a concurrent field will be allowed to operate. Under this view of the operation of paramountcy it could be that provincial legislation would not need to fit with, or complement, federal policies; provincial legislation would need only not confound federal economic strategy.

However, another sense of how concurrency operates, how laws from the two legislative levels should be reconciled, is possible. This view is that provincial law is either not appropriate at all once the federal government has legislated with repect to a matter, or, at least, must be supportive of the same general goals.

The former narrow notion of federal paramountcy has been developed almost entirely in respect of exercises of Parliament's criminal law power. Insofar as this head of power has been seen more as an instrumental head of power and less as a substantive head of power, it makes sense that Parliament's exercise of it not readily be allowed to displace substantive provincial regulatory policies. However, legislation enacted under other heads of federal power, such as the peace, order and good government clause, or proposed new federal economic powers, could be seen as requiring greater protection against the effects of provincial regulation than the narrow idea of paramountcy allows. This account of shifting conceptions of how federal paramountcy works might explain that part of the judgment of Rinfret C.J. in *Johannesson v. Mun. of West St. Paul*, [1952] 1 S.C.R. 292, in which he decided that the general statement of ministerial responsibility in the *Aeronautics Act*, R.S.C. 1927, c. 3, as am., occupied the entire field of aeronautics and eliminated any provincial legislation (at p. 303). It should, however, be noted that the legislation in that case expressed a clearer intent to occupy the whole field than might normally be found in legislation passed under an expanded head of power over economic regulation. Nevertheless, it is not beyond reasonable speculation to recognize the possibility that the mediating principles that would be developed in respect of concurrent federal and provincial powers over economic regulation would differ from traditional notions of how concurrency works, and that new principles might develop which would require provincial law to fit with, or track, federal policies.

48. The proposed constitutional text in respect of powers over the economy proposed by the federal government during 1982 is discussed in Romanow, Whyte, and Leeson, *Canada . . . Notwithstanding, supra*, note 45, pp. 68–73. See also, Thomas J. Courchene, "Analytic Perspectives on the Canadian Economic Union" in *Federalism and the Canadian Economic Union*, edited by M.J. Trebilcock et al. (Toronto: Ontario Economic Council, 1983), at pp. 51–55.

49. A proposal for the constitutional creation of an intergovernmental agency for monitoring economic regulation is discussed in Richard Simeon, "Some Observations on the 'Powers over the Economy'" (Kingston: Queen's University, Institute of Intergovernmental Relations, unpublished paper, 1980).

50. *Supra*, note 41.

51. *Trade Marks Act*, R.S.C. 1970, c. T-10, s. 7 (*e*).

52. See *Toronto Electric Commissioners v. Snider*, [1925] A.C. 396 (J.C.P.C.), at pp. 412–14.

53. See *Re Board of Commerce Act, 1919, supra*, note 2, at p. 198.

54. See, e.g., *Johannesson v. Mun. of West St. Paul*, [1952] 1 S.C.R. 292, and *Munro v. National Capital Commission*, [1966] S.C.R. 663.

55. R.S.C. 1970, c. C-23, as am.

56. (1972), 33 D.L.R. (3d) 434 (F.C.A.).

57. *Supra*, note 51.

58. *Supra*, note 41, at p. 158. It should be noted that because misleading advertising is analogous to fraud, it could, in any event, be supported under Parliament's criminal law power under s. 91 (27) of the *Constitution Act, 1867*.

59. This purpose of constitutional review was implicitly expressed by Viscount Sankey in *Henrietta Muir Edwards v. A.-G. Can.*, [1930] A.C. 124 (J.C.P.C.). In this case the

constitutional provision relating to membership of the Senate was read to permit the appointment of women notwithstanding that women would not have been considered to be qualified for appointment in 1867. This result was reached by seeing the textual provisions relating to the legislative branch as reflecting, above all, the conditions of responsible government and responsibility which, by the late 1920s, women enjoyed.

60. For a full discussion of aspect analysis in constitutional law, see William R. Lederman, "The Balanced Interpretation of the Federal Distribution of Legislative Powers in Canada" in *The Future of Canadian Federalism*, edited by P.A. Creapeau and C.B. MacPherson (Toronto: University of Toronto Press, 1965), at pp. 93–100.

61. See, e.g., the result in *CIGOL*, *supra*, note 40. The background to the challenged legislation in CIGOL is discussed in John Whyte, "A Constitutional Perspective on Federal-Provincial Sharing of Revenues from Natural Resources" in *Fiscal Federalism and the Taxation of Natural Resources*, edited by Charles McLure and Peter Mieszkowski (Lexington, Mass.: D.C. Heath, 1983), at pp. 207–11.

62. For an example of a detailed contextual analysis for the purpose of determining the limits of a federal power (in this instance, the federal aeronautics power), see the judgments of Beetz, J. and Laskin, C.J. in *Construction Montcalm Inc. v. Minimum Wage Commission*, [1979] 1 S.C.R. 754.

63. E.g., *Canadian Wheat Board Act*, R.S.C. 1970, c. C–12, s. 45, declares that "flour mills, feed mills, feed warehouses, and seed cleaning mills, whether heretofore constructed or hereafter to be constructed" are works for the general advantage of Canada. This prospective declaration under s. 92(10)(c) was found to be constitutionally valid in *Jorgensen v. A.-G. Can.*, [1971] S.C.R. 725.

64. See, e.g., the various Orders in Council made under the *War Measures Act*, 5 Geo. 5, c. 2, which were considered in *Fort Frances Pulp and Paper Co. v. Man. Free Press*, *supra*, note 2.

65. For a discussion of the reviewability of declarations of emergency, see Herbert Marx, "The 'Apprehended Insurrection' of October 1970 and the Judicial Function" (1972), 7 U.B.C. L. Rev. 55.

It is likely that courts have an even greater responsibility to review both the reality of a declared emergency and the reasonableness of the legislative response to it when challenged legislation abridges rights or freedoms under the *Canadian Charter of Rights and Freedom*. This would seem to be required by the language of s. 1 of the Charter, ss. 1–34, *Constitution Act, 1982*.

66. An antecedent for a constitutional compelling national interest test is found in proposals for a new constitutional provision relating to the management of resources that were developed during federal-provincial constitutional negotiations held from time to time between November, 1978 and February, 1979. For a description of the proposal see Romanow, Whyte and Leeson, *Canada . . . Notwithstanding, supra*, note 45, pp. 24–29.

67. The most notable recent example of judicial deference in the face of a declared "serious national concern" are the judgments of a majority of the Supreme Court of Canada in *Reference re Anti-Inflation Act*, [1976] 2 S.C.R. 373.

68. Colourable legislation is a recognized form of constitutional invalidity. It describes legislation which has the form of legislation that is constitutionally permitted to the enacting authority but that, in substance, is in relation to a subject assigned to the other level of government. For example, the Supreme Court of Canada held that what appeared to be taxation legislation passed by British Columbia was, in light of all the provisions, an intolerable burden on the production of minerals that were not processed in British Columbia. Hence the true substance of the legislation was the regulation of international and interprovincial commerce. See *Texada Mines Ltd. v. A.-G. B.C.*, [1960] S.C.R. 713.

69. The courts' fundamental unwillingness to accept preclusions of their review jurisdiction is shown by their treatment of legislative privative (or preclusive) clauses. For a discussion of judicial response to privative clauses, see *Administrative Law: Cases, Text and Materials*, 2d ed., edited by J.M. Evans et al. (Toronto: Edmond-Montgomery Ltd., 1984), pp. 528–31, 535–36.

70. S. 95, *Constitution Act, 1867*, which creates concurrent legislative jurisdiction in relation to immigration and agriculture, concludes by stating:

> . . . any Law of the Legislature of a Province relative to Agriculture or to Immigration shall have effect in and for the Province as long and as far only as it is not repugnant to any Act of the Parliament of Canada.

71. The concluding clause of s. 91, *Constitution Act, 1867*, states:

> And any Matter coming within any of the Classes of Subjects enumerated in this Section shall not be deemed to come within the Class of Matters of a local or private nature comprised in the Enumeration of the Classes of Subjects by this Act assigned exclusively to the Legislatures of the Provinces.

72. *McEvoy v. A.-G. N.B. and A.-G. Can.* (1983), 148 D.L.R. (3d) 25 (S.C.C.).

73. The doctrine of separation of powers had, however, been developed some 27 years prior to the *McEvoy* decision by W. R. Lederman. See William Lederman, "The Independence of the Judiciary" (1956), 34 Can. Bar Rev. 769 and 1139.

74. [1963] S.C.R. 570.

75. [1949] A.C. 110 (J.C.P.C.).

76. *Supra*, note 74, at pp. 557–78.

77. (1981), 118 D.L.R. (3d) 577 (S.C.C.).

78. See *A.-G. Ont. v. Winner, supra*, note 11, in which an interconnecting undertaking was held to be outside provincial authority. There are a number of additional cases which support federal exercises of regulatory authority in respect of interconnecting works; see, e.g., *Luscar Collieries Ltd. v. McDonald*, [1927] A.C. 925 (J.C.P.C.), *Campbell-Bennett Ltd. v. Comstock Midwestern Ltd.*, [1954] S.C.R. 207, and *Re Sask. Power Corp. and Transcanada Pipelines Ltd.*, [1979] 1 S.C.R. 297.

79. *Supra*, note 77 at p. 585.

80. Ibid.

81. This same ambiguity concerning exclusivity is also present in the decision of Rinfret C.J. in *Johannesson v. Municipality of West St. Paul, supra*, note 47.

82. *Supra*, note 13.

83. [1979] 1 S.C.R. 984.

84. R.S.C. 1970, C. N–1.

85. *Proprietary Articles Trade Association v. A.-G. Can*, [1931] A.C. 310 (J.C.P.C.); *Reference re Dominion Trade and Industry Commission Act*, [1936] S.C.R. 379; *A.-G. B.C. v. A.-G. Can.*; *Reference re s. 498A of Criminal Code*, [1963] S.C.R. 368; *R. v. Campbell* (1968), 58 D.L.R. (2d) 673n; affg. (1964), 46 D.L.R. (2d) 83 (Ont. C.A.); *Goodyear Tire and Rubber Co. v. The Queen*, [1956] S.C.R. 303; and *A.-G. Can. v. Law Society of B.C.*; [*Jabour v. Law Society of B.C.*,] *supra*, note 46.

86. *R.v. Wetmore and A.-G. Ont.* (1983), 2 D.L.R. (4th) 577 (S.C.C.).

87. This aspect of the *Can. National Transportation* case and the decision in the *Wetmore* case have been criticized in John Whyte, "The Administration of Criminal Justice and the Provinces" (1984), 38 C.R. (3d) 184. See also comment, *supra*, note 13.

88. *Supra*, note 13, at p. 57.

89. Ibid.

90. Compare *The King v. Eastern Terminal Elevator Co.*, *supra*, note 3, with *Murphy v. C.P.R. and A.-G. Can.*, [1958] S.C.R. 626.

91. *Supra*, note 13, at p. 58.

92. Ibid., at p. 59.

93. Ibid., at p. 61.

94. Ibid.

95. Ibid., at p. 62.

96. Ibid.

97. *Supra*, note 41, at p. 165.

98. *Supra*, note 13, at p. 62.

99. Ibid., at p. 67.
100. Beetz and Lamer JJ. wrote a short separate opinion concurring with Dickson J. They stated that they found themselves in "substantial" agreement with the reasons for judgment of Dickson J. See ibid., at pp. 73–74.

3

The Division of Powers

GARTH STEVENSON

Introduction

Among modern writers on federalism, the division of powers between the central and regional governments is usually regarded as a fundamental attribute of a federal constitution. "The distribution of powers," according to A.V. Dicey, "is an essential feature of federalism."[1] K.C. Wheare views the existence of a constitutionally entrenched division of powers as the primary feature that distinguishes federal from unitary states, and defines the federal principle as "the method of dividing powers so that the general and regional governments are each, within a sphere, co-ordinate and independent."[2] For W.H. Riker, "The essential institutions of federalism are, of course, a government of the federation and a set of governments of the member units, in which both kinds of governments rule over the same territory and people and each kind has the authority to make some decisions independently of the other."[3] Depending on how many kinds of decisions the central government can make alone, Riker classifies particular federalisms as centralized or peripheralized.

Canadian federalism in recent years, and indeed throughout most of its history, has been characterized by conflict and controversy regarding the division of powers. Federal and provincial governments have sought to expand their de facto, and at times de jure, sphere of legislative power at one another's expense, and have frequently accused governments at the other level of trespassing on the powers guaranteed them by the Constitution. Private interests have often challenged the actions of governments by arguing that such actions violated the constitutional division of powers, while at other times private interests have encouraged the expansion of governmental activity without much regard for whether the jurisdiction of the other level of government was being invaded. Repeatedly, the judiciary has been called upon to define the scope of legislative powers confided to one or the other level of government, with results that have rarely failed to cause disappointment or resentment among some of those interested in the outcome. Formal changes in the division of powers have been rare, difficult and controversial, although in recent years at least there has been no lack of suggestions concerning changes that might be made. Clearly for Canadians the division of powers is an important subject.

Three variables tend to determine the extent of a citizen's preoccupation with the division of powers within a federal state. The first variable is the seriousness and significance of real or perceived conflicts of interest among territorially based subnational groupings. Such conflicts may be based on ethnocultural differences or on the economic division of labour between regions. Where both types exist, as in Canada, they are likely to be particularly insoluble. The more acute such conflicts are, the more controversy is likely to surround the division of powers, since the division of powers between levels of government will have an impact on the balance of power between competing collectivities associated with the various governments.

A second variable, related to the first, is the extent to which opposing interests are perceived to be represented within the two levels of government. Only to the extent that significant interests lack influence within a level of government are they likely to display a marked preference for the other level of government; and only if these interests have such a preference are they likely to become preoccupied with the division of powers. In Canada, a variety of economic or functional interests, and some of an ethnocultural nature, perceive either the federal or a provincial government as likely to be unsympathetic to their demands, and thus they seek to redistribute powers from that government to the other level.

The third variable, which may be less obvious than the two major ones, is the scope and extent of activities that are carried on by the state. The greater the extent of state intervention, the more questions are likely to arise as to whether a particular function should be performed by one or the other level of government. An interventionist state can confer more benefits, and also cause more deprivations, than a non-interventionist state. Therefore, the stakes will be much greater in any controversy over which level of government should have the power to act.

Over the last several decades, the scope and extent of state activities have increased sharply in all the industrialized liberal democracies, and so one would expect that the division of powers would be a far more significant issue in modern federalism than in federalism of the 18th or 19th centuries. It is noteworthy and, from a modern perspective, surprising, that at the conferences leading up to Confederation the division of powers was the object of less debate and controversy than were matters that now seem much less important, such as statutory subsidies and the distribution of seats in the Senate. The contrast with constitutional discussions between 1968 and 1981 is rather striking.

Over the years, the proliferating functions of the state have caused the formal specification of the division of legislative powers to become increasingly complex and verbose, reflecting the times in which a federal constitution was first enacted. The constitution of the United States, framed in 1787, specified only 18 legislative powers of Congress, and 6 of these pertain to national defence. The Canadian federal Constitution, enacted 80 years later, specified 31 powers of Parliament, including the concurrent powers over agriculture and immigration. The Australian constitution, enacted in 1901, specified 42 powers for that country's parliament. The constitution of India, enacted in 1950, specified no less than 144 powers for the national parliament.

In response to the growth of state activity and intervention, federations whose constitutions were drafted at a time of lower expectations in this regard have occasionally resorted to formal amendment, inserting new powers in the list of those assigned to the central, or more rarely to the subcentral, level of government. Canada amended its Constitution to increase the powers of Parliament in 1940, 1951 and 1964, and to increase the powers of the provincial legislatures over natural resources in 1982. More frequently, however, new subjects requiring state intervention have been dealt with through a combination of informal intergovernmental collaboration, judicial interpretation, or unilateral extensions of authority by whichever level of government is the one to take the initiative. The result has typically been a de facto division of powers that bears an increasingly small resemblance to the division provided in the formal Constitution, and that singularly lacks the virtues of logic, precision and predictability. Dissatisfaction with this state of affairs is certainly a reason, although perhaps not the only one, why Canada, Australia and Switzerland have all recently engaged in extensive efforts to review and update their federal constitutions.

Even in 1867 the problem of dividing legislative powers in a federal constitution was not an easy one, as an examination of sections 91 through 95 of the Constitution Act, 1867 suggests. Although these sections show signs of the political and conceptual difficulties encountered by their authors, sections 91 through 95 nonetheless command respect as a serious and reasonably successful effort to deal with the problems of their time. Today, however, their adequacy has been undermined by new technologies, economic developments, urbanization and changing expectations concerning the role of the state. Of the numerous proposals to replace or update the existing division of powers, few if any have shown much evidence of careful thought or sound theoretical underpinnings. It is probably time for a systematic reexamination of the whole subject.

The present paper aims to provoke such a reexamination by introducing some of the main aspects of the problem, embellished by whatever insights and suggestions the author can provide as a result of several years' preoccupation with Canadian and comparative federalism. The first section of the paper suggests some conceptual frameworks for classifying the various "powers" that must be divided among levels of government. Fundamental to the argument of this section, and indeed of the paper as a whole, is the belief that only by sorting "powers" into distinct categories can the subject be properly understood. The second section is devoted to the techniques for distributing legislative powers in a federal constitution. The third section examines various criteria for assigning powers to one or the other level of government, with particular reference to Canadian conditions. The fourth section examines the de facto evolution of the division of powers from the 1930s to the 1980s. In contrast with the relatively stable period from 1867 until 1930, the last half-century has been marked by rapid expansion of and diversification in the functions of the state, by considerable dissatisfaction with the division of powers, and by a growing incongruity between the de facto division of powers and the scheme formally enshrined in sections 91 through 95. The fifth section of the paper attempts to explain the changes in the division of powers by reference to the activities and initiatives of provincial and federal governments, the private sector and the courts, as well as the expansion of state activities. The sixth section examines the consequences of the evolving division of powers for governments, for economic and other organized interests, for the effectiveness of the state and for democratic responsible government. The seventh section considers the need for reform in the light of present realities and, more cautiously, with reference to possible trends in the future role of the state. The brief concluding section suggests how the division of powers might be revised should this be considered feasible.

Conceptual Frameworks

Even a casual reading of sections 91 through 95 of the Constitution Act, 1867 suggests the remarkable heterogeneity of the subjects that required specification in the federal division of powers. Broad and abstract categories of legislative enactments seem jumbled together with those that are narrow, concrete and specific. Heads of power that might be used to legitimize the most sweeping interventions in the civil society may be contrasted with those that pertain exclusively to the internal housekeeping of the government itself. How can one sensibly compare "Property and Civil Rights" or "The Regulation of Trade and Commerce" with "Marine Hospitals," "Public and Reformatory Prisons" or "Beacons, Buoys, Lighthouses and Sable Island"? A precondition for any serious analysis of the division of powers must be to make some order out of this chaotic picture.

Probably the most familiar categorization of legislative powers is that which divides them into "economic" and "sociocultural" areas of jurisdiction. It is sometimes asserted that Canada's federal Constitution was designed to place most of the economic powers in the hands of Parliament while conferring on the provincial legislatures the powers over sociocultural matters. This is at best an oversimplification, since only Parliament can legislate matters concerning Indians, naturalization and aliens, and marriage and divorce, while the legislatures have jurisdiction over public lands, local works and undertakings, and the incorporation of companies with provincial objects. Nonetheless, it is undeniable that most of the economic powers were given to Parliament; and it is interesting that in 1972 a parliamentary joint committee on the Constitution proposed a reallocation of powers that would strengthen the primacy of Parliament over economic legislation, and of the provincial legislatures over sociocultural matters.[4]

Despite its apparent popularity, the categorization is not very useful. "Social" programs, such as the Canada and Quebec Pension Plans, can have a significant impact on the economy, while "economic" initiatives, such as manpower training or regional development schemes, have social implications as well. Powers such as taxation or the criminal law can be used for both social and economic purposes.

Perhaps in an effort to overcome these difficulties, other classificatory schemes have been devised. For example, Lyon and Atkey, in their textbook on constitutional law, classify legislative powers as pertaining to power, well-being, rectitude, wealth, respect, enlightenment, skill or affection.[5] Peter Leslie classifies powers according to whether they relate to categories of people (e.g., Indians), objects of policy (e.g., agriculture), instruments of policy (e.g., taxation) or purposes of policy (e.g., peace, order and good government).[6] A simpler classification might distinguish powers related to concrete objects (e.g., public lands or works and undertakings) from powers related to abstractions (e.g., property and civil rights or trade and commerce).

In this paper a different classification will be used, one that distinguishes four basic types of government initiatives, as follows:

1. powers to tax;
2. powers to regulate;
3. powers to spend; and
4. powers to provide services.

Although this classification has not, to the author's knowledge, been used before, it has been selected not for the sake of novelty but because of its usefulness in calling attention to some of the issues involved in the division of powers. It will be suggested that the characteristics of these different forms of intervention cause them to affect intergovernmental relations and federalism in different ways, and that, in the revising of the division of powers, each initiative should be dealt with separately. Before proceeding, however, it is necessary to define the four categories, which is most conveniently done by illustrating them with reference to the existing constitutional division of powers. An examination of the ways in which the four categories were dealt with by the Fathers of Confederation will also facilitate a subsequent discussion of the difficulties that have arisen from the existing division and the possible direction of reform.

Powers to Tax

The most obvious category is perhaps "powers to tax." Taxation is mainly an instrumental power, providing the state with the revenue needed to perform its various functions. It can also serve other purposes; for example, it can provide financial incentives or disincentives to various kinds of behaviour. A high tariff discourages the consumption of imported goods, and a high tax on tobacco might discourage smoking. It is, however, mainly as a source of revenue that taxation is vitally important to the state, and indeed a precondition for all its other activities. Former premier Maurice Duplessis of Quebec was fond of asserting that "the power to tax is the power to govern," and few would dispute the truth of the observation.

Canada's federal Constitution gives Parliament the power to raise money "by any Mode or System of Taxation": section 91(3). The provincial legislatures are given the power of "Direct Taxation within the Province in order to the raising of a Revenue for Provincial Purposes": section 92(2) and the power to issue licences "in order to the raising of a Revenue for Provincial, Local or Municipal Purposes": section 92(9). The new section 92A, added to the Constitution in 1982, allows the provinces to impose indirect as well as direct taxation in respect of mineral resources, forest resources and hydro-electric power, provided that such taxation does not discriminate between consumption within the province and consumption in other parts of Canada. Although a royalty is not, strictly speaking, a tax, it should also be noted that the provinces can impose royalties in return for the right to extract minerals, section 109, and charges for the sale of timber from Crown lands, section 92(5). Finally, section 125 provides that neither level of government can tax the other level. With the growth of state enterprises and Crown corporations at both levels, this provision is of far more practical importance than it appeared to be in 1867.

Powers to Regulate

"Powers to regulate" comprise a more complex category, and are dealt with at much greater length in Canada's federal Constitution. Subjects that can be regulated by Parliament or its agencies include Trade and Commerce: section 91(2); Navigation and Shipping, 91(10); Quarantine, 91(11); Fisheries, 91(12); Ferries, 91(13); Banking, 91(15); Savings Banks, 91(16); Weights and Measures, 91(17); Bills of Exchange and Promissory Notes,

91(18); Interest, 91(19); Legal Tender, 91(20); Bankruptcy and Insolvency, 91(21); Indians,91(24); Interprovincial or international works and undertakings and other works declared to be for the general advantages of Canada, 92(10); Agriculture, 95; and Immigration, 95. Jurisdiction over the criminal law, 91(27) confers, in addition to the specific powers, a very broad general power to regulate.

Provincial powers to regulate, although much less numerous, are substantial. They include powers over Hospitals, Asylums, Charities and Eleemosynary Institutions, 92(7); Local Works and Undertakings, 92(10); The Solemnization of Marriage, 92(12); Property and Civil Rights, 92(13); and local or private matters generally, 92(16). The provinces share with the federal government the power to regulate agriculture and immigration, although federal legislation is paramount. Provincial regulatory powers are reinforced by the power to impose fines, penalties or imprisonment for enforcing any law relating to the enumerated areas of provincial jurisdiction, 92(15).

Powers to regulate can be divided into a number of subcategories. There are broadly defined and general regulatory powers such as the federal powers over Trade and Commerce and the Criminal Law, or the provincial powers over Property and Civil Rights and "Matters of a merely local or private Nature." Somewhat more specific powers are those directed toward particular sectors of the economy, such as Fisheries, 91(12); Banking, 91(15) and 91(16); Transportation, 91(10), 91(13), and 92(10); and Agriculture, 95. There are two regulatory powers related to particular categories of persons: Indians, 91(24), and Aliens, 91(25). Finally, there are powers to regulate specific activities or situations such as Weights and Measures 91(17); Bills of Exchange and Promissory Notes, 91(18); Interest, 91(19); or Bankruptcy and Insolvency 91(21).

Powers to confer recognition or status are an aspect of regulatory powers and are shared between the two levels of government. Parliament can provide for the incorporation of banks, section 91(15); Patents, 91(22); Copyrights, 91(23); Naturalization, 91(25); and Marriage and Divorce, 91(26). The provincial legislatures can provide for "The Incorporation of Companies with Provincial Objects," 91(11). The courts have ruled that Parliament can also incorporate by virtue of its general power to make laws for the peace, order and good government of Canada.

Powers to Spend

"Powers to spend" do not seem to be explicitly limited by the federal Constitution, and there has been controversy over what limitations, if any, should exist, particularly in relation to the powers of Parliament. At the very minimum, each level of government can obviously spend in relation to the matters over which it has specific jurisdiction; for example, both levels can spend in relation to agriculture. Usually, Parliament's power over "The Public Debt and Property" is considered to confer a very broad, and perhaps unlimited, spending power. In practice, both levels of government have made a variety of subsidies and payments to individuals and organizations, as well as to other governments, and they have acted as though the power to spend were virtually unlimited.

Powers to Provide Services

The final category consists of "powers to provide services." Although the service-providing functions of the state were far less developed in 1867 than they became subsequently, a considerable number of service-providing powers are specifically assigned by Canada's federal Constitution. Services to be provided by the federal level of government include Postal Service, section 91(5); The Census and Statistics, 91(6); Militia, Military and Naval Service and Defence, 91(7); Beacons, Buoys, Lighthouses, 91(9); Quarantine and Marine Hospitals, 91(11); Currency and Coinage, 91(14); and Penitentiaries, 91(28). Subsequent amendments added unemployment insurance, pensions and survivors' benefits, although, in relation to the last two items, provincial legislation has paramountcy over federal. Services to be provided by the provincial governments include Public and Reformatory Prisons, section 92(6); Hospitals, Asylums, Charities and Eleemosynary Institutions, 92(7); Municipal Institutions, 92(8); The Administration of Justice, 92(14); and Education, section 93.

It may be noted that some of the enumerated heads of jurisdiction in Canada's federal Constitution include both a regulatory power and a power to provide services, with the choice apparently left to the discretion of Parliament or the legislature. For example, jurisdiction over education includes both the power to regulate the curriculum of private schools and the power to provide education through a system of public schools. The same may be said of the provincial power over "Hospitals, Asylums, Charities and Eleemosynary Institutions." Although it is phrased so as to suggest that the provinces themselves would provide such services, in practice, until long after Confederation, they did little more than regulate them. Generally, governments seem to have moved from regulating activities in their traditional areas to providing services directly, while their regulatory involvement has extended into new fields of activity. This tendency will be discussed later as one aspect of the changing role of the state in modern society.

Techniques for Distributing Powers

The specification of legislative powers in a federal constitution is not as simple a matter in practice as it may first appear. Before proceeding to distribute the legislative powers, constitution makers must make a number of basic decisions. How many lists of powers should there be, and is it necessary to specify the powers of both levels of government? Should powers be exclusive or concurrent? (If the latter, which level of government should enjoy paramountcy in the event of conflict?) Where should the residual power be located? Should all provinces or states have the same powers? Should delegation of powers from one level to another be permitted? Should the enumerated subjects of jurisdiction be broad or narrow? The different federal constitutions in the world, past and present, have found varying answers to these questions.

The Constitution Act, 1867, lists the legislative powers of Parliament in section 91, those of the provincial legislatures in section 92, and those shared by both (agricultural and immigration) in section 95. As though this were not complex enough, section 93 provides that education is a provincial field but with a federal power to legislate in certain circumstances, while section 94 enables Ontario, Nova Scotia and New Brunswick to delegate to Parliament their legislative power over property and civil rights. Later amendments added new shared powers over pensions and survivors' benefits (section 94A) and natural resources (section 92A). As a final source of confusion, Parliament's powers to legislate about interprovincial or international works and undertakings, and to declare that other works within a province are for the general advantage of Canada, appear as exceptions to the provincial powers listed in section 92, rather than in section 91 — where it would have been logical to list them.

Compared with this complicated arrangement, the constitution of the United States is extremely simple. Article I, Section 8, lists the powers of Congress; and Article I, Section 10, lists certain matters about which the states may not legislate, including some of the same subjects listed in Section 8. There is no list of legislative powers for the state legislatures, on the theory that, unless the constitution provided otherwise, they retained the powers which they had had before the constitution came into effect. The Australian constitution is similar in form. Sections 51 and 52 list the powers of the national parliament while Sections 114 and 115 prohibit the states from adopting certain kinds of legislation, but there is no list of the legislative powers of the states.

Two more recently drafted constitutions organize the division of powers in different ways. The constitution of India somewhat resembles that of Canada in that it has a Union List (enumerating the powers of the national parliament), a concurrent list and a state list. These lists all are much longer than their Canadian equivalents, with 97 fields of jurisdiction enumerated on the Union List, 47 on the concurrent list, and 66 on the state list. The Basic Law of the Federal Republic of Germany has a list of exclusive powers for the Bundestag as well as a list of concurrent powers shared by the two levels of government, but there is no list of exclusive powers for the states. In addition, the Basic Law contains a feature not found in other federal constitutions: a short list of subjects about which the Bundestag can enact guidelines or general principles for legislation by the states, although these matters otherwise remain under the jurisdiction of the states. Subjects treated in this way include post-secondary education, the media, the environment and regional planning.

The question of whether powers should be exclusive or concurrent also varies from constitution to constitution. Sections 91 and 92 of the Constitution Act, 1867, as well as the comparable sections in the constitution of India, are, in theory, watertight compartments whose contents do not overlap one another, and each section is the exclusive preserve of the level of government to which it is assigned. In Australia, by contrast, the states are allowed to legislate to almost all the subjects assigned to the national parliament, provided their enactments do not conflict with those of parliament. This is theoretically true in the United States, although a careful reading of Article I, Section 8, in conjunction with Article I, Section 10, suggests that most of the powers assigned to Congress in the former section are really exclusive. In the Basic Law of the Federal Republic of Germany, the list of concurrent powers is about twice as long as the list of exclusive federal powers. Canada's Constitution is almost unique in the scarcity of concurrent fields of jurisdiction.

Where power to legislate in a particular field is concurrent, or shared between two levels of government, the almost unvarying practice is to specify that, in the event of any incompatibility, enactments of the national legislative body will take precedence over those of the provinces or states. In the Basic Law of the Federal Republic of Germany, this rule is somewhat qualified by a statement to the effect that the Bundestag can only legislate in concurrent fields if the states cannot act effectively, if action by states would harm the interests of other states, or if national action is required to preserve national unity. These conditions, however, are so broad that they impose no real restriction on federal power. Section 94A of Canada's federal Constitution, which concerns pensions and survivors' benefits, is unique in stating that provincial legislation takes precedence over federal legislation in those areas.

The location of the residual power — the power to legislate concerning matters not specifically assigned to one or the other level — also varies among federal constitutions. The most usual practice is to place such power in the hands of the provinces or states, but the constitution of India assigns the residual power to the national parliament. In Canada the wording of the preambular paragraph of section 91 suggests that the intention was to place the residual power in the hands of Parliament, but the Judicial Committee of the Privy Council was generally reluctant to interpret it in this way, preferring to fit new subjects of public policy into one of the enumerated provincial powers, such as "Property and Civil Rights." More recently, a leading constitutional lawyer has suggested that the Constitution Act, 1867, really contains two residual clauses, with the last subsection of section 92 — "Generally, all Matters of a merely local or private Nature in the Province" — sharing this status with the preamble of section 91.[7] The significance of a residual power in practice depends not only on the preferences of the judiciary, but on the comprehensiveness of the listing of specified powers. If the lists are lengthy and comprehensive, as in India, there will be few new subjects that have to be assigned with the aid of the residual clause.

We may assume that the assignment of the residual power to one or the other level of government indicates a preference on the part of the constitution makers for maximizing the power of that level in relation to the other level. Certainly in both Canada and India the intention to create a highly centralized version of federalism is clear from the record. In the other constitutions, however, it is less apparent that there was a generally shared intention to emphasize the autonomy of the individual states. If there was, it was to no avail, for in practice there are very few limits to the legislative powers of the West German Bundestag and the United States Congress. The real reasons that residual powers are assigned to one or the other level seem to be historical. In India, the central government already existed when the constitution was adopted (and even before independence); in Australia, there was no central government until the constitution came into effect; and in Germany, the central government and state structure had been dissolved after the country's unconditional surrender to the Allies. The United States had rudimentary institutions at the centre dating from 1778, nine years before the drafting of the constitution, but Thomas Jefferson and probably most other Americans at the time believed that the thirteen states were individually sovereign and independent. Canada had a common government from 1841 onward for what are now Quebec and Ontario, and it was the provincial governments in those two provinces, rather than the central government, that had to be brought into existence by Confederation. The situation was the reverse for Nova Scotia and New Brunswick; those provinces already had their own institutions before 1867 but had not previously been part of Canada.

Although it is normal for all provinces or states within a federation to have the same legislative powers, this is not always the case. In India there were originally three categories of states, each having different degrees of autonomy. (These distinctions were abolished when the states were reorganized along linguistic lines in 1956.) In Australia one state, Western Australia, was given the special right to impose customs duties on imports from other states for a transitional period of five to seven years after federation. Canadian federalism has a number of such anomalies. Section 94 of the Constitution Act, 1867, allowing Parliament to legislate for the uniformity of laws relating to property and civil rights with the consent of the provinces concerned, applies to all the original provinces except Quebec. Section 124, which was repealed six years after Confederation, gave New Brunswick a special right to impose export duties on lumber. Manitoba, Saskatchewan and Alberta were all denied ownership of public lands and resources when they acquired provincial status, and section 92(5) did not apply to them until 1930. The constitutional protection accorded the French language and denominational schools has varied substantially from one province to another. Section 23(1)(a) of the Constitution Act, 1982, will take effect in Quebec only when that province gives its consent. The new amending formula in the same act, with its provision for provinces to opt out of amendments that would otherwise reduce their powers, leaves open the possibility that substantial variations in legislative powers, from one province to another, may eventually exist.

The division of powers in a federal constitution could be made more flexible by allowing one level of government to delegate its powers to the other, but in practice this device is not common. It was proposed in the Fulton and Favreau amending formulas of the 1960s, but was never implemented. The Supreme Court of Canada has ruled that Parliament and the legislatures, under the existing Constitution, cannot delegate legislative powers to one another, but that they can delegate powers to administrative boards or commissions established by the other level of government.[8] This device has been used for agricultural marketing and for the regulation of highway transport.

Criteria for Distributing Legislative Powers

Despite the many differences among federal constitutions, and the social, cultural and economic differences among the countries to which they pertain, there is a surprising degree of similarity in the divisions of legislative powers, both in theory and in practice. In nearly all federations, the national legislative body is responsible for defence, trade and commerce, customs and excise taxes, the currency and the financial system, postal service, copyrights, weights and measures, social insurance programs, and transportation by rail, air and water. In nearly all federations, the provinces or states are responsible for education, social institutions, health, highways, municipal affairs, renewable resources, regional planning and the environment. Jurisdiction over labour and industrial relations is usually divided, although in most federations the central government plays a stronger role than in Canada. Only with respect to two important fields — criminal law, and the power to implement treaties — is there a lack of consistency among federations. The criminal law is a federal power in Canada, Switzerland and India, but a state power in the United States, Australia and the Federal Republic of Germany. The power to implement treaties belongs to the national legislative body in the United States, Switzerland, Australia and India, but is shared with the provinces in Canada and with the states in the Federal Republic of Germany.

To some extent this uniformity can be explained by the fact that constitution makers have deliberately modelled their efforts on previously existing constitutions, particularly on the constitution of the United States, which serves as the prototype of modern federalism. The uniformity also suggests, however, that similar criteria have been used to assign powers in the various constitutions, leading to similar results.

It would seem that powers can be distributed in a federal constitution according to five criteria, which are not mutually exclusive. In practice, all five were probably taken into account in the drafting of most federal constitutions. These five criteria are:

1. avoidance of externalities;
2. capacity to act effectively;
3. simplicity and accountability;
4. spatial distribution of policy preferences; and
5. concern for subnational communitarian identities.

Avoidance of Externalities

Avoidance of externalities means that provinces or other component units within a federation should not be assigned powers that would enable them to affect the interests of people residing outside their own boundaries. That this was a major concern of the Fathers of Confederation is evident from a reading of the Constitution Act, 1867. Eight of the sixteen subsections of section 92 include the qualifying phrase "in the Province" or "within the Province," and, in fact, the word "province" or "provincial" occurs in every subsection, leaving no doubt that provincial governments and legislatures would be rigidly confined to the jurisdiction affecting only their own territories and populations. The prohibition of indirect taxation was also intended to serve the same purpose; an "indirect" tax was then understood to mean a tax that could be passed on by the person taxed to someone else — and thus to someone residing outside the province.

Parliament, on the other hand, was given powers over matters affecting interests or activities in two or more provinces, such as interprovincial transportation; the banking system, which must move capital freely between the provinces; trade and commerce, which implies the movement of commodities; and fisheries (fish are notorious for their disregard of provincial or even national boundaries). Parliament could also assume jurisdiction over "works" within a province if it believed them to be for "the general Advantage of Canada." (John A. Macdonald illustrated the need for this provision by referring to the Welland Canal, which was located within Ontario but was of obvious interest to Quebec as part of the St. Lawrence waterway.) Additional safeguards against externalities were provided by the lieutenant governor's power to reserve provincial legislation, the federal government's power to disallow it, and Parliament's power to ignore provincial powers if their exercise would obstruct the implementation of imperial treaties.

From the standpoint of avoiding externalities, the Constitution is no longer as effective today as it once was. The powers of reservation and disallowance are now too controversial to be used, and Canada's independence has deprived section 132, dealing with imperial treaties, of any practical consequence. Of greater significance, however, is the fact that a more advanced, interdependent economy, a more mobile population, and modern means of transport and communication have created many more types of externalities. Provinces now create externalities when they regulate the trading in securities that are purchased by residents of other provinces; when they speed up or slow down the extraction of their energy resources; when they reduce or increase the operating grants of universities whose graduates do not necessarily remain within the province; or when they seek to regulate the relations between corporations and unions whose operations transcend the provincial boundary. Given the vested interests and the emotions that have grown up around the provinces since Confederation, resolving these problems will be no easy task.

Capacity to Act Effectively

There are a number of different aspects to the second criterion, the capacity to act effectively. Provincial governments might be unable to exercise a power effectively because they lack the necessary financial resources or because there are economies of scale that make it more efficient for one government to do so than for ten governments. It would obviously be foolish, for example, if each of the ten provinces had its own military forces. For the same reason, some provinces do not even have their own police forces, preferring to hire the services of the federal police force on a contract basis. Provinces might be unable to act effectively for less obvious reasons as well. For example, provincial regulation of environmental standards or labour conditions might prove futile if the regulated industry could simply move to a province whose regulations were less onerous. To avoid being penalized for their high standards by a flight of jobs and investment, provinces might prefer to have uniform regulations imposed by the federal government.

The criterion of capacity to act effectively does not necessarily suggest placing all powers in the hands of the federal government, however. For one thing, the federal government and administration, and particularly Parliament, could not act effectively if they were overloaded with too many tasks and responsibilities. The transfer of responsibility for decisions that create no significant externalities to the provincial governments and legislatures leaves Parliament and the federal government with more time and administrative resources to perform the functions they perform best. Also, for many types of decisions, the more effective government may be one that is smaller, less cumbersome, closer to the grass roots and able to adapt its policies to local needs and conditions. It would make no sense if decisions about the installation of sewers or street lights in Edmonton were made in Ottawa. Few Canadians would wish to emulate the minister of education under Napoleon III, who boasted that he could look at his watch and know what page of what book every school child in France was reading at that moment.

Simplicity and Accountability

Simplicity and accountability are perhaps the easiest criteria to understand but the most difficult to realize. To apply them, a federal constitution should minimize the overlap between the powers and responsibilities of different levels of government. Ideally, each government should be able to make policies and exercise powers in its own spheres of activity, without having to pay any attention to the activities of other governments. Thus, if one power is assigned to the provincial level of government, then closely related powers should also be assigned to that level. Responsibilities for particular functions should not be shared, either in theory or fact. Governments should not have to coordinate their activities, or to consult one another about related activities, or to make their policies jointly through a process of intergovernmental negotiation. Each government would be accountable only to its own electorate, and each voter would know precisely which government deserves the credit or blame for a particular output of public policy. There are many practical reasons why this ideal cannot readily be achieved, or why simplicity and accountability must be sacrificed for the sake of other criteria, but simplicity and accountability are nonetheless worth pursuing and should not be neglected.

The Fathers of Confederation probably believed that they had achieved a high degree of simplicity and accountability by placing federal and provincial powers in exclusive, watertight compartments, but they consciously violated the principle by including under section 93 such anomalous provisions as disallowance, reservation, and the possibility of remedial legislation. They allowed some unnecessary overlapping between categories such as "Prisons" and "Penitentiaries" or "Marriage and Divorce" and "The Solemnization of Marriage." They provided for shared powers over agriculture and immigration, perhaps because they could not agree among themselves as to which level of government should have those powers. Over time, many more areas of overlapping have developed through the vagueness of broad powers like "Property and Civil Rights," through the exercise of undefined spending powers, and through the competitive occupation, by both levels, of new fields of jurisdiction.

Spatial Distribution of Policy Preferences

The spatial distribution of policy preferences as a criterion for the division of powers can be illustrated by a simple example. Imagine a hypothetical country with two regions. In one, 90 percent of the population believe that motorists should be required to wear seat belts; in the other, 90 percent believe that freedom of choice is more important than safety. Assuming that the two regions are equal in population, any decision on this issue by the national government would automatically displease half the voters. If regional governments were allowed to make the decision, each would presumably respond to the wishes of the majority in its region, and only 10 percent of the voters would be dissatisfied.

The Fathers of Confederation were well aware of this criterion, and they governed themselves accordingly. In predominantly Catholic Quebec, prevailing opinions about education, about the operation of charities and hospitals, and about who should have the right to perform a marriage ceremony were known to differ from opinions in other parts of the country. Therefore, these subjects were placed under provincial jurisdiction so that the majority in Quebec, as well as majorities elsewhere, could receive the kinds of policies that they preferred.

In Canada today there are many more fields of public policy, and thus many more potential differences of opinion, than there were in 1867. (Public opinion polls also make it much easier to measure the differences today.) However, opinion on most kinds of issues seems to be surprisingly uniform across the country. Where there are pronounced interprovincial differences of opinion, they tend to be on issues such as the price of oil, the preferential recruitment of bilingual people for the public service, equalization payments, or the tariff protection of secondary industry. These issues, however, have a special character that explains the pattern of opinions in relation to them. While issues such as seat belt legislation are properly described as conflicts of taste, issues such as those listed above are really conflicts of claim between regions.[9] That is to say, giving the people of one region what they want will automatically deprive people in another region of benefits, regardless of the level of government that makes the decision. It is therefore not necessarily appropriate to place such decisions under provincial jurisdiction. Indeed, provided that decision-making procedures in the federal government are equitable and fair, it may be more appropriate to place them under federal jurisdiction.

Concern for Subnational Communitarian Identities

This leads us, finally, to the most difficult and dangerous criterion: concern for subnational communitarian identities. If a group of people have a strong sense of collective identity and mutual attachment and if one of the provincial governments is identified with that group in the minds of its members, then such a body may simply demand that the provincial government be given or retain a wide range of powers, regardless of any of the other criteria discussed above. Such sentiments are difficult to measure, and there is disagreement about their importance in present-day Canada, but they obviously cannot be dismissed.

Recent Evolution of the Division of Powers

In any federal constitution, the formal division of powers provides no more than a starting point for a continuous process of distributing powers between the two levels of government. New problems arise to which governments must react, and new objects of public policy are invented or discovered. Groups who attempt to persuade governments to take initiatives on their behalf rarely allow the formal division of powers to dictate their choice as to which level of government will be the principal target of their representations. Governments themselves seek to expand their authority and to increase their popularity with little concern for the formal boundaries of their jurisdiction. In any event, the roles of the formal heads of power listed in the constitution are soon found to be imprecise, incomplete and overlapping. In a sense, the formal division of powers begins to become obsolete almost as soon as it is enacted.

In discussing the recent evolution of the division of powers, therefore, one must be concerned not only with formal amendments and with judicial interpretations of the written constitution, but with the largely unplanned and uncoordinated expansion of activity by both levels of government in the era of the interventionist state. It is appropriate to begin with the Depression of 1929–39 because, prior to that time, the functions of the state and their distribution between the federal and provincial levels of government had remained substantially congruent with the arrangements made in 1867. Over the last half-century, however, changes have been far more extensive. The somewhat chaotic division of powers that has emerged de facto almost defies concise description, and it certainly bears little resemblance to the terms of the federal Constitution.

There is probably little point in attempting to compare the actual division of powers today (or at any other time) with the formal division of powers enacted in 1867, for the two are not strictly comparable. A "power" that exists on paper arguably has no reality until it is used and until the courts have had the opportunity to rule on whether it was used legitimately. Its meaning may be unclear until confirmed by actual experience, particularly if it is couched in such broad and general term as "Property and Civil Rights" or "The Regulation of Trade and Commerce." A power formally conferred may in practice be unused or unusable, a notable example being Parliament's alleged power to protect the educational rights of religious minorities through remedial legislation. Alternatively, a significant constitutional power to deal with some new subject of concern may be discovered by reference to a section that was drafted with quite different purposes in mind.

Formal changes in the division of powers have been few, although it is interesting to note that there have been four since 1940, in contrast to the total absence of such changes in the first seventy-three years of Canadian federalism. In 1940, by a constitutional amendment, Parliament gained the powers to provide unemployment insurance. It gained power to legislate concerning old age pensions in 1951 and concerning supplementary benefits in 1964, although provincial legislation in relation to these fields has paramountcy over federal legislation, a peculiarity that was apparently the price paid for Quebec's consent to both amendments. The amendments of 1940, 1951 and 1964, which facilitated federal assumption of responsibility for income support programs, were all necessitated by the 1937 decision of the Judicial Committee of the Privy Council in the Employment and Social Insurance Act reference, a decision that struck down an early federal initiative in this area. It cannot be said, however, that the gains of federal power through the amendments represented a loss of provincial power in any real sense, since the provinces had never effectively occupied the fields in question and were perhaps never in a position to do so. This is a reminder of the significant fact that the division of powers is not, in practice, always a zero-sum game. Both levels of government have expanded their power more at the expense of the private sector than at the expense of each other.

The fourth and most recent formal amendment to the division of powers is the lengthy and complex provision concerning natural resources, which now appears as section 92A of the Constitution Act, 1867. Included as part of the package of constitutional changes that took effect in 1982, it increases provincial powers to legislate concerning mineral, forest and hydro-electric resources traded interprovincially, and for the first time gives the provincial legislatures a limited right to impose indirect taxation. Because federal paramountcy in relation to the regulation of trade and commerce is explicitly retained by the terms of section 92A, it does not appear that Parliament's powers have been reduced by this amendment, so this amendment also illustrates the non-zero-sum character of the division of powers.

Informal changes in the division of powers are of course much less easy to identify and measure than are formal changes, although they have been considerably more important and extensive. Although no claims are made for the precision of the method, some indication of the scope and direction of changes in the concerns of the federal and provincial levels of government can be seen by comparing the lists of ministerial portfolios in the cabinets of Canada and a medium-sized province (Alberta) for the years 1934, 1959 and 1984.[10] The overall impression gained from this exercise is one of expanding government activity at both levels, particularly in the years since 1959. Moreover, the size of cabinets has increased at almost exactly the same rate in both jurisdictions. The federal cabinet increased from 16 members in 1934 to 21 in 1959, and to 37 in 1984. The Alberta cabinet increased from 11 members in 1934 to 15 in 1959, and to 27 in 1984. The extensive overlapping of de facto powers and responsibilities between the two levels is also suggested by the fact that many federal and provincial ministers hold similar titles, a tendency that becomes more pronounced as the cabinets expand.

Looking first at the federal level, the changes between 1934 and 1959 seem related mainly to the expansion of Canada's international role and status, rather than to a redistribution of power internally. Portfolios added to the cabinet in this period include External Affairs (an office occupied by the prime minister until 1946), Veterans Affairs, Citizenship and Immigration, Defence Production, and the position of associate minister of National Defence. In addition, the Department of Mines and Resources was divided into two new departments: Mines and Technical Surveys, and Northern Affairs and National Resources. Two other departments gained new names, reflecting the expansion of federal activities into new fields. Railways and Canals became Transport, thus incorporating the new field of civil aviation, and Pensions and National Health became National Health and Welfare.

In the Alberta government, changes during the 1934–59 period were even less extensive. The Department of Lands and Mines was divided into two successor departments: Mines and Minerals, and Lands and Forests. The three new departments created were Highways, Labour, and Public Welfare, none of which suggested an expansion of provincial jurisdiction at the expense of the federal government.

Between 1959 and 1984, changes at both levels were far more extensive, with both cabinets nearly doubling in size. At the federal level, the positions of postmaster general and associate minister of National Defence disappeared, but these changes implied no erosion of federal powers and responsibilities. Defence Production was replaced by a Ministry of Industry with a broader mandate. Citizenship and Immigration became Employment and Immigration. Entirely new portfolios included Energy, Communications, Supply and Services, Science and Technology, Fitness and Amateur Sport, Consumer Affairs and Environment. Ministries of State for Economic and Social Development were also added, the list reflecting the new dimensions and priorities of government activity. Junior ministries were added, too, with responsibility for specific client groups such as women, youth, multiculturalism and small business.

Changes in the Alberta cabinet were remarkably similar, suggesting a competitive expansion of the two levels of government into the same fields of activity. Mines and Minerals was replaced by Energy and Natural Resources; and Highways became Transportation, the result of provincial involvement in the field of civil aviation. While the office of provincial secretary disappeared, new portfolios were added, paralleling some of the new portfolios in Ottawa; for example, Consumer and Corporate Affairs, Manpower, Environment, Tourism and Small Business, and Recreation. Advanced Education was separated from Education; Personnel Administration, Housing, and Workers' Health, Safety and Compensation appeared for the first time. Unabashed incursions into federal areas of jurisdiction were indicated by the emergence of portfolios for International Trade, Native Affairs, and Federal and Intergovernmental Affairs, the last of which conducts extensive dealings with foreign governments as well as other Canadian governments.

Both levels of government have frequently accused each other of intruding on areas of jurisdiction that are supposedly beyond the scope of their powers. The report of Quebec's Tremblay Commission in 1956 and the lists of alleged federal "intrusions" collected by the Western Premiers' Task Force on Constitutional Trends in the 1970s are examples of provincial perceptions in this regard, while former prime minister Trudeau responded to provincial claims by accusing the provincial governments of trespassing on federal areas of jursidiction and "balkanizing" the country without regard for the national interest. Given the emotion and the vested interests that surround both sets of claims, it is not easy to evaluate them with any semblance of impartiality; and it is also not always clear what standards of evaluation should be used. If the intentions of Sir John A. Macdonald are the relevant criterion, it is clear that the provinces have become too powerful, but Sir John might also have been astonished could he have known of some of the activities in which the federal government is now engaged. If the written text of the Constitution Act, 1867, is the appropriate criterion, one is faced with the problem of deciding the meaning of the words in the document, a task that can be performed with varying results, as the history of judicial interpretation bears witness. Moreover, the different perceptions of the two sides of this controversy rely on different evidence; the situation suggests the blind men in the poem, who reach varying conclusions about the elephant by touching different parts of its anatomy. If a federal "intrusion" in one area is matched against a provincial "intrusion" in another, who is to decide which outweighs the other in importance? Finally, and perhaps most significantly, there is the problem of those government activities that were simply not envisaged at all in 1867. Federal enthusiasts tend to assign all such matters to the residual category of "Laws for the Peace, Order and Good Government of Canada," and thus they believe that only the federal government should be involved in them. Provincialists — although in recent years they have tended not to base their arguments on the written Constitution — seem implicitly to believe that these new activities are "Matters of a merely local or private Nature," or perhaps that they pertain to "Property and Civil Rights."

It would seem that there have been some intrusions by both levels of government into areas of policy that belong to the other level. The federal government has a long history of limited involvement in the forest, mining and petroleum industries, all based on resources that are owned by the provinces. Since the early 1970s, intervention in the petroleum industry has become increasingly pronounced, to the point where that industry has become one of the major preoccupations of the federal government. The governments of the petroleum-producing provinces have viewed this trend with considerable resentment and suspicion, as have many of the people who reside in them. In fairness, however, it must be noted that the uncertain global situation with regard to petroleum over the last decade has arguably made it a subject directly related to the "Peace, Order and Good Government of Canada."

The federal government has also been involved in various aspects of education. From 1952 until 1967, direct federal grants were made to universities, although since 1967 the federal government has made its contributions through the intermediary of the provincial governments, and since 1977 it has virtually abandoned any control over how its contributions are spent. At the same time, the federal government continues to subsidize research in the universities and second-language education in the schools. Federal involvement in manpower training programs, which the provinces tend to view as a part of education, has been extensive since 1960.

Public health has been another area of federal concern for several decades. Conditional grants for various health programs began in 1948 and those for hospital insurance began a decade later. The replacement of conditional grants for medical insurance, with the Established Programs Financing arrangements in 1977, lessened federal influence over the health and hospital sector; but the Canada Health Act, introduced in Parliament in 1983, indicated the federal government's renewed desire to become involved.

These instances of federal involvement in provincial fields must be balanced, however, against the evidence of federal self-denial in other areas. The declaratory power of Parliament under section 92(10)(c) has not been used since 1961, and the regulation of highway transportation has been left to the provincial governments, even though the Judicial Committee of the Privy Council determined in 1954 that international and interprovincial "undertakings" by truck or bus fell under federal jurisdiction. Family allowances, a purely federal program when they were first introduced — and one upheld by the Supreme Court of Canada — have been administered since 1974 in collaboration with the provincial governments, which are now permitted to vary the schedule of payments depending upon the age of children or the number of children in a family.

In addition, the provincial governments, through their own initiative, have become involved in many areas of federal jurisdiction. Most of the larger provinces are active in the area of international trade and commerce, with government departments and agencies dedicated to this purpose, visits made abroad by premiers and ministers, and networks of permanent missions established in foreign capitals and commercial centres. The larger provinces also assert the right to deal directly with foreign governments on a variety of issues, with Quebec and Alberta having embryonic foreign ministries and quasi-diplomatic activities, much as Canada itself did before the Statute of Westminster. Fisheries is another area of federal jurisdiction in which some provinces, particularly Newfoundland, are very active. The western provinces and Quebec are also intruding on the federal jurisdiction over "Indians, and Lands reserved for the Indians," a development that is viewed with disfavour by the Indians themselves. Eight of the ten provinces have full-time officials dedicated to the field of civil aviation, which the Judicial Committee of the Privy Council assigned to exclusive federal jursidiction in 1932. Alberta operates a network of savings banks in the guise of "Treasury Branches," and appears to ignore the federal jurisdiction over this field of activity. Ontario and Quebec are both active in the field of television broadcasting, for which they claim authority because of the allegedly educational nature of the programs, although all broadcasting was placed under exclusive federal jurisdiction by the Judicial Committee of the Privy Council in 1932.

In areas of government activity that are entirely new, so that the federal Constitution does not specifically assign them to either level of government, the general rule is for both levels of government to be involved, either cooperatively or competitively. There are a few exceptions, such as atomic energy, over which Parliament assumed jurisdiction by using its declaratory power, and civil aviation and broadcasting, both of which the Judicial Committee of the Privy Council placed under the rubric of "Peace, Order and Good Government" during its brief and untypical display of enthusiasm for the federal power. In general, however, the law and the courts have provided little guidance for the assignment of new fields of public policy, and the result has been to leave such fields open to initiatives by either level of government.

These grey areas of the federal Constitution are both numerous and heterogeneous, so that few generalizations about them may be possible. In terms of the typology outlined earlier, they include regulation, spending and the provision of services. Some of the more important of these areas of policy are the following.

Science policy   This includes the encouragement and subsidization of research. The federal government pioneered in this field by establishing the National Research Council as early as 1917, but the expression "science policy" was rarely heard prior to the 1960s, when a Senate committee, chaired by Maurice Lamontagne, was established to report on the subject. Subsequent initiatives included establishment of the Science Council of Canada and of the Ministry of State for Science and Technology. Several provincial governments are also interested in the field, no doubt in part because, in practice, the distinction between research and education is difficult to draw. Alberta, for example, has been using its resource revenues to encourage both medical research and research into oil sands technology within the province.

Housing   This has been an area of government activity since the Bennett government secured the adoption by Parliament of the Dominion Housing Act in 1935. Canada Mortgage and Housing Corporation (CMHC) is a major federal Crown corporation, with a budget in excess of one billion dollars annually. It provides mortgage loans, insures mortgage loans provided by the private sector, and makes funds available for public and cooperative housing projects. There are also other federal programs related to housing, such as grants for the rehabilitation of older residences. The provinces are also extensively involved in housing, particularly with respect to the public housing that provincial housing corporations build with funds borrowed from CMHC; also, several provinces regulate rents in the private sector. Generally, housing appears to be more an area of cooperation than an area of conflict between Canadian governments. There is, however, considerable suspicion among provincial governments regarding direct federal-municipal relations, although such relations are very limited in Canada, especially when compared with those that exist in the United States.

Anti-discrimination measures   Beginning with Saskatchewan in 1946, all Canadian governments have now adopted legislation prohibiting discrimination on such grounds as race, sex and religion. Provincial jurisdiction over property and civil rights appears to give the provinces broader jurisdiction than the federal government has in this area. Beginning in 1985 the Equality Rights provision of the new Charter of Rights and Freedoms will impose greater uniformity in this field, although some of the provincial statutes will continue to protect against forms of discrimination not specifically referred to in the Charter.

Medical insurance   Hospital insurance and physicians' fee insurance were introduced first in Saskatchewan and then subsidized by the federal government, after which the other provinces introduced similar programs, with varying degrees of enthusiasm. The two programs, originally separate, are now integrated in all provinces. Although popular with the public, medical insurance has been the subject of considerable conflict between the federal government and the more conservative provincial governments. Nonetheless, something resembling the present arrangements, with the provinces operating their programs under federal supervision and with federal funds, will probably last for the foreseeable future.

Youth policy   Quebec established a Ministry of Youth in 1946, while the federal government has had a portfolio for this field of policy only for the last few years. Both levels of government have shown sporadic interest in the field over the years, punctuated by occasional dramatic initiatives such as the federal government's creation of the Company of Young Canadians in 1966 and the Opportunities for Youth Program five years later. There does not seem to have been much intergovernmental conflict in this area.

Cultural policy   Federal support of cultural activities dates from the Royal Commission on the Arts, Letters and Sciences, which in 1951 recommended an active federal role in this area. Some of the provinces, particularly Quebec, had already become involved, and the legitimacy of federal preoccupation with this area was contested by Quebec's Tremblay Commission in 1956. In recent years all governments have become increasingly active in the field, to the accompaniment of much turgid rhetoric about national or provincial "identities" and "cultures." The federal government and governments of certain provinces in recent years have made frequent reference to "multiculturalism" and the encouragement of cultural diversity as goals of their cultural policies. Both levels of government would appear to be competing for the support and allegiance of those who either produce or consume cultural activities. However, the cultural policies of governments do not seem to have contributed directly to intergovernmental conflict, at least not to any significant extent.

Regional development policies   In a sense, governments have always been concerned with the spatial distribution of economic activity, but regional policies at the federal level were haphazard at best until the Agricultural and Rural Development Act was adopted in 1961. Federal interest in the field reached its height during the years in which the Department of Regional Economic Expansion (DREE) was in existence, 1968 to 1982. Until 1973, DREE programs were largely competitive with, or at least uncoordinated with, those of the provincial governments. After that year, emphasis was placed on the joint funding and administration of specific programs in the context of General Development Agreements with the provincial governments. Provincial interest in regional development appears to have developed slightly earlier than federal interest, first appearing in slowly growing provinces such as Newfoundland, Nova Scotia and Manitoba, which in the late 1950s became concerned over the increasing concentration of population and economic activity in Ontario. Shortly afterward both Ontario and Quebec began to implement policies designed to stimulate economic activity in the peripheral northern and eastern regions of their respective provinces. The provinces west of Manitoba, although generally prosperous, have at times apparently sought to redirect economic activity toward their peripheral and rural areas and to counteract the centralization of population and economic activity in their major cities. Thus, most governments have pursued regional policies of one kind or another, and with mixed results. One can argue that such policies have been unnecessarily costly as a result of intergovernmental competition, and even that they have cancelled one another out to some extent.

Regulation of foreign direct investment   This is mainly an area of federal concern, particularly since the adoption of the Foreign Investment Review Act (FIRA) in 1973, but some provinces have expressed an interest here, either negatively or positively. Only New Brunswick, Newfoundland and Nova Scotia have been consistently hostile to any restrictions on foreign direct investment. Quebec, Ontario, British Columbia and Saskatchewan have occasionally imposed restrictions of their own. Predictions made prior to the enactment of FIRA, that this would become an area of constitutional controversy and litigation have not materialized.

Industrial strategies   Closely related to science policy, regional policy and foreign investment policy is the much discussed, but to date rather insubstantial, field of industrial strategy. In the broadest sense, industrial strategy appeared at a very early state, reflected in the protective tariff at the federal level and in the "manufacturing conditions" imposed by certain provinces on the export of unprocessed resources, particularly timber cut on Crown lands. In the more specific modern sense, industrial strategy means the promotion of internationally competitive manufacturing industries through a combination of subsidization, export promotion, mixtures of state and private ownership, and corporatist planning on the French or Japanese model. To date, federal involvement has been largely limited to specific industries such as aircraft, electronics and nuclear reactors. Quebec and Ontario, the provinces most directly interested, have discussed moves toward creating industrial strategies, but have progressed even less rapidly than has the federal government.

Environmental policies   Both levels of governent have attempted to control the quality of the environment and to regulate pollution. Some clarification and improvement of the constitutional framework for such policies appear to be required. In 1975 the Supreme Court of Canada ruled that a Manitoba statute dealing with water pollution intruded on federal jurisdiction, despite the fact that the federal government itself argued in favour of upholding the Manitoba statute.

Consumer protection   The federal government and most provinces now have departments of consumer and corporate affairs that seek to regulate various kinds of business activity in the interests of the consumer and also to provide consumers with advice and assistance in protecting their interests, both individually and collectively. The political popularity of such policy is understandable, but the competitive enactments of two levels of government, in a context of uncertainty over their respective powers, may produce confusion and a mutual frustration that has economic costs and that benefits neither business nor the consumer. In recent years, federal enactments concerning the labelling of beer and the grading of apples have both been struck down by the Supreme Court of Canada on the grounds that they trespassed on provincial jurisdiction.

To summarize the present de facto division of powers, it is useful to refer to the categorization mentioned earlier: taxing, regulating, spending, and providing services. Table 3-1 shows the share of various types of revenue that went to the central government in 1979–80. It can be seen that the only sources monopolized by the central government are those related to international movements of goods or capital. Local governments and school boards monopolize the field of real estate taxes, while provincial governments have a monopoly on health insurance premiums and a virtual monopoly on natural resource revenues and licence and permit fees. The remaining sources of revenue are shared; provincial governments take the larger share of sales taxes (particularly those on motor fuel), and the federal government takes the larger share of social insurance premiums, corporation tax and personal income tax. However, the federal share of corporation tax and personal income tax has declined sharply; in 1969–70 it was 76.7 percent and 72.6 percent, respectively, versus 69.6 percent and 61.0 percent in 1979–80. Succession duties and estate taxes, once an important source of revenue, have disappeared, while the 19th century distinction between direct and indirect taxation has become almost meaningless.

TABLE 3-1   Share Going to Federal Government by Source of Revenue, 1979–80

Source	Percent
Customs Duties	100.0
Oil Export Charge and Petroleum Levy	100.0
Income Tax on Interest and Dividends Sent Abroad	100.0
Universal Pension Plan Levies	74.0
Corporation Tax	69.6
Other Social Insurance Levies	63.1
Personal Income Tax	61.0
Sale of Goods and Services	48.2
Sales Taxes (Except Motor Fuel)	47.1
Other Revenue from Own Sources	37.8
Return on Investment	37.7
Miscellaneous Taxes	34.4
Motor Fuel Taxes	19.1
Privileges, Licences, Permits	3.7
Natural Resource Revenue	0.5
Health Insurance Premiums and Taxes	0.0
Other Business Taxes	0.0
Property Taxes	0.0

Source: Canadian Tax Foundation, *The National Finances*, 1982–83, p. 29.

Regulatory powers and activities have multiplied at both levels of government. In accordance with the terms of the Constitution Act, 1867, the federal government regulates most imports (through the Tariff Board and the Anti-Dumping Tribunal), exports of certain commodities (through the National Energy Board), as well as railways, water carriers, banks and savings banks. Through judicial decision, it has acquired and now exercises regulatory powers over airlines and broadcasting. The federal government regulates the major telephone system in Central Canada as an interprovincial work or undertaking, while other telephone systems and utilities are regulated by the provinces. The provinces regulate highway transport, as Parliament has delegated its authority over interprovincial and international undertakings of this nature. The provinces regulate the industries exploiting their natural resources and also regulate such traditional provincial areas of concern as horse racing, the professions and the sale of alcoholic beverages in restaurants or bars. Censorship of films and other media is also a provincial power. Industrial relations, except in a few federally regulated industries, and stock exchanges are regulated by the provinces. Among the newer areas of concern, as noted earlier, foreign direct investment is mainly regulated by the federal government, human rights mainly by the provinces, and responsibility for the environment and the protection of consumers appears to be shared by both levels. Rent regulation, which might be seen as an aspect of consumer protection, is an undertaking of some provinces. Quebec, through its language charter, regulates the language of work in business and industry, which may in some sense be an aspect of industrial relations.

Spending powers have developed in a way that is even less obviously related to the formal Constitution, a fact that is understandable because the federal government has traditionally claimed the right to spend in areas outside its formal jurisdiction. Table 3-2 shows the federal government's share of spending in various categories, as accounted for in 1979–80. (It excludes the general purpose federal grants such as equalization payments.) Defence and foreign affairs are the only categories apparently monopolized by the federal government, and even the latter is questionable in view of the quasi-diplomatic activities undertaken by certain provinces. No category is totally monopolized by the provincial governments, but the provinces are clearly dominant in their traditional fields of education and health (albeit subsidized through EPF) and, to a somewhat lesser extent, in the protection of persons and property. The federal government accounts for most spending on the economy, apart from transportation where, as Harold Innis noted, its dominant position did not survive the transition from railways to highways.[11]

The distribution of spending on some of the less traditional fields of government activity is less predictable. The federal government appears heavily dominant in scientific research, while the provinces are almost equally dominant in recreation and culture. Housing is mainly federal, but regional planning is mainly provincial. Social services are mainly federal, but the provincial governments account for most spending on the environment.

TABLE 3-2 Share Spent by Federal by Category of Spending, 1979-80

Category	Percent
Defence	100.0
Foreign Affairs	100.0
Research Establishments	95.2
Labour, Employment, Immigration	84.2
Social Services	66.5
Housing	61.6
Resource Conservation and Industrial Development	59.0
Transfers to Own Enterprises	54.9
Debt Charges	49.5
General Services	37.6
Transport and Communications	34.7
Protection of Persons and Property	22.4
Recreation and Culture	17.5
Regional Planning and Development	12.9
Environment	9.8
Health	2.4
Education	1.9
Other Spending	1.8

Source: Canadian Tax Foundation, *The National Finances*, 1982–83, p. 29.

Powers to provide services are clearly much more important today than they were in 1867, although they were apparently not negligible then either. Both the federal and provincial levels of government continue to provide the kinds of services outlined in relevant provisions of sections 91, 92 and 93 of the Constitution Act, 1867. They also provide various other kinds of services, through government departments and through various other agencies such as Crown corporations, state enterprises, independent commissions and marketing boards. Both levels of government are heavily involved in the transportation of persons and of goods by road, rail, air and water. Most of the provinces exercise a virtual monopoly over the generation and sale of electricity, and all do so over the sale of alcoholic beverages. Three provinces operate their own telephone systems. All eleven governments are involved in the marketing of agricultural produce. Most provide services of various kinds to business enterprises, such as assistance in exporting their products. Specific industries such as mining and fishing benefit from services designed to fit their needs. People involved in cultural activities, such as painters and musicians, benefit from other types of services, which are also provided by both federal and provincial governments.

The municipal level of government, frequently ignored in constitutional discussions, is exceedingly important in the provision of public services. Municipalities provide water purification, sewage and garbage disposal, public transportation, snow removal, parks, libraries, health clinics, police and fire protection, and a variety of other services. Some operate utilities such as electric power or telephone service. The constitutional subservience of municipalities to the provinces, and the municipalities' lack of financial independence, hardly do justice to their real importance.

Explanations for the Recent Evolution

Judicial Interpretation

In seeking explanations for the way in which the division of powers has evolved, attention often focusses on the judiciary and its interpretations of the formal Constitution. Judicial review, like the division of powers itself, is often viewed as a necessary condition of federalism. A.V. Dicey, while acknowledging that judicial review of national legislation did not exist in federal Switzerland, identified federalism in general with conservatism and legalism, characteristics which he attributed to the power exercised by the judiciary.[12] A once highly influential school of thought about Canadian federalism attributed the growth in provincial power — and the frustration of Sir John A. Macdonald's hopes for a quasi-unitary state — to the interpretations of the division of powers by the Judicial Committee of the Privy Council.[13] The belief that the Judicial Committee had both disregarded the intentions of the founders and ignored the real needs of the country for effective government contributed to the abolition in 1949 of appeals from Canadian courts to that tribunal. Abolition of appeals, however, did not end the controversy over judicial review. Since 1949, and especially in the last decade, supporters of provincial autonomy have argued that the Supreme Court of Canada has excessively curtailed provincial legislative powers and enlarged those of Parliament.

Judicial review has undoubtedly contributed to the defining of the powers of both Parliament and the provincial legislatures, particularly so with regard to taxing and regulating powers. Powers to spend, to provide services and to confer status or recognition have not been subjected to much restriction by the courts. This is partly because these powers are more vaguely defined by the Constitution than are the taxing or regulating powers, and partly because individuals and corporations are less likely to litigate against governments that do them favours than against those that tax them or prohibit them from doing what they wish.

Parliament's taxing powers appear to be virtually unlimited, except that its power to earmark special funds for purposes of social insurance or income support was definitely established only after the constitutional amendments of 1940, 1951 and 1964. The legislatures have been constrained by the familiar, although somewhat questionable, distinction between direct and indirect taxation. The judiciary decided as early as 1887 that corporation taxes could be imposed by the provinces, and retail sales taxes were declared to be "direct" in 1943. Business taxes that directly increase the price of commodities, however, or that have a prohibitive impact on activities falling under federal jurisdiction, are likely to be struck down by the courts. In general, the evolution of Canadian public finance has been far more influenced by economic trends than by judicial decisions.

The regulatory powers of Parliament have been a popular subject for consideration by the judiciary, frequently with controversial results. At times the courts have interpreted the general power to make laws "for the Peace, Order and Good Government of Canada" broadly as a residual power, while at other times they have viewed it narrowly as being, in the absence of an "emergency" situation, subordinate to the enumerated powers of the provincial legislatures. Two of Parliament's enumerated regulatory powers have also been considered frequently by the courts, namely "The Regulation of Trade and Commerce," 91(2) and "The Criminal Law," 91(27). The former has, on the whole, been viewed more restrictively than has the comparable power of Congress under the constitution of the United States. On the other hand, the criminal law power has sometimes been interpreted broadly enough to legitimize its use for the regulation of economic activity.

In strict theory, the judiciary, in making decisions, cannot either enlarge or restrict the regulatory powers of Parliament; it merely discovers the powers already inherent in the Constitution and applies them to specific situations. In practice, however, this may not be the case. Some decisions have the effect of enlarging or restricting a regulatory power because Parliament's role is perceived differently after the decision, in a way that affects the subsequent behaviour of both government and the private sector. Thus, the Judicial Committee of the Privy Council ruled in 1916 that Parliament lacked a general power to regulate the insurance industry; in 1922 that it could not regulate hoarding or control prices in peacetime; in 1925 that it could not regulate labour-management relations except in the industries explicitly placed under federal jurisdiction; in 1937 that it could not regulate the marketing of agricultural products consumed within the province of origin; and in the same year that it could not implement a treaty that purported to regulate the conditions of labour.[14] On the other hand, the Judicial Committee declared in 1915 that Parliament could incorporate companies by virtue of the preamble to section 91.[15] In 1931 it decided that Parliament could use its criminal law power to regulate combines and mergers in industry, and in 1932 that it could regulate the new fields of aeronautics and broadcasting.[16]

The Supreme Court of Canada after 1949 appeared more permissive than the Judicial Committee in defining Parliament's regulatory powers, but there were no really dramatic departures from the previous trends of interpretation. Since about 1975, the Supreme Court has become somewhat more restrictive in its approach, and portions of some acts of Parliament have been declared ultra vires. The overall impact of the Court on the evolution of federal government activity, however, would seem to be relatively insignificant.

The regulatory powers of the provincial legislatures have also received extensive consideration from the courts and, before that, from the Judicial Committee of the Privy Council. Although often criticized for its narrow interpretations of Parliament's powers, the Judicial Committee frequently did protect those powers against trespassing by the provinces, particularly with respect to the regulation of interprovincial works or undertakings, or of corporations chartered by Parliament. The Supreme Court since 1949 has had similar concerns and has also been wary of provincial enactments that regulate trade and commerce.

Judicial review of provincial legislation has at times been controversial, particularly since the abolition of appeals to the Judicial Committee of the Privy Council, an event that caused misgivings on the part of some provincial governments. In the 1950s, several Quebec enactments relating to civil liberties were struck down by the Supreme Court on the grounds that they related to criminal law.[17] In 1966, the Court ruled that Quebec could not regulate the minimum wage in an interprovincial utility.[18] In the 1970s the Court struck down Quebec's effort to license cable television operators and attempts by Manitoba and Saskatchewan to regulate the trade and commerce in livestock, oil and potash.[19] On the other hand, the Court has upheld a number of new and controversial regulatory initiatives on nonresident ownership of land and Quebec's regulation of television advertising directed at children.[20]

Powers to spend have received relatively little consideration from the courts, but the Supreme Court in 1957 upheld the validity of federal spending on family allowances.[21] The provinces, as a leading constitutional law textbook aptly observes, "have never recognized any limits on their spending power and have often spent money for purposes outside their legislative competence."[22]

The courts have also had little to say about powers to provide services and have imposed few if any restrictions. It might be noted that several provinces have agencies providing railway or airline transportation, and that the federal government operates certain schools and hospitals as a by-product of its responsibilities for Indians and for national defence.

From 1949 on, and perhaps from even before then, the courts, on balance, do not seem to have had a decisive influence on the evolution of the de facto division of powers. Some of their decisions dealt with relatively minor matters, while others were fairly obvious inferences from the division of powers as previously understood. Some of the more controversial decisions were circumvented by constitutional amendment, delegation or intergovernmental agreement, or simply by redrafting the legislation to achieve the same objective in a somewhat different way. The more fundamental cause of change must apparently be found in the reasons that lie behind the expanding activities of the state, a phenomenon obviously not confined to Canada, and in the reasons that explain why new kinds of state activity emerged in Canada at one level of government sooner than at the other.

Expanding State Activity

The impact of expanding state activity on Canadian federalism has been noted by various observers, including the Rowell-Sirois Commission in 1939 and F.R. Scott in 1945. Both noted that a formal division of powers, dating from an era of laissez-faire in the economic and especially in the social spheres of activity, had to be adapted to an era of much greater intervention by governmental authorities. Scott also noted the impact of Canada's then-new international status as an independent actor on its federal system.[23] Yet the transformation since 1939 — and especially since 1945 — in the role of the state, and particularly in the amount of public expenditure, has been even more dramatic than in the first seven decades following Confederation.

At least seven major factors have contributed to the growth in the functions and activities of the state, all, with one possible exception, contributing to growth at both levels of government. The first factor, and the one that constitutes the possible exception, is the impact of the two world wars, which accustomed Canadians to a more active, powerful and interventionist state than they might otherwise have accepted and at the same time accustomed politicians and public officials to the exercise of more power than they might otherwise have enjoyed.

It is arguable that this impact of the world wars was felt only at the federal level of government, but it is not impossible that there were some effects on the provincial level as well. The wartime activities of provincial governments have been ignored by Canadian historians, and the conventional wisdom that they were insignificant may require revision. In any event, the rising popular expectations concerning the appropriate level of state intervention (and of taxation) may ultimately have benefited the postwar provincial governments to some extent.

Even without war, most or all of the growth in state activities would probably have taken place, for six reasons.

1. Politicians have impelled the state to make expenditures and to provide services in an effort to gain the support of voters.
2. Bureaucracies have encouraged the expansion of state activities in an effort to maintain and enhance their own importance, power, prestige and access to funds.

3. Programs have been devised to reinforce the legitimacy of the state in the eyes of a population that is increasingly heterogeneous, rootless and uncertain in its loyalties.
4. Urbanization and related social changes have increased the dependence of the population on services and programs that only the state can provide.
5. The externalities created by modern capitalism, such as pollution, technological unemployment, or the sudden rise and fall of whole communities associated with the extraction of non-renewable resources, have had to be dealt with by the state, since private enterprises accept no responsibility for the consequences of their own actions.
6. The increasing proliferation of special interest groups has caused a corresponding proliferation in the number of demands that the state intervene in support of particular group interests, whether or not this benefits, or is desired by, the society as a whole.

Electoral Politics

The first of these factors, state activities and expenditures designed to attract votes, has been a familiar Canadian phenomenon for nearly two centuries, and indeed was commented upon by Lord Durham in his report. The traditional "pork barrel" approach, for example improving the roads in a marginal constituency prior to an election, is by no means extinct, but it has been supplemented by more sophisticated and far-reaching programs directed toward whole sectors of the population, not necessarily defined in terms of location. The federal commitment to family allowances in 1942, Ontario's involvement in commercial aviation in 1971, and Alberta's program to subsidize interest payments on residential mortgages in 1982 are all good examples of buying votes with the taxpayers' money, whatever may be the merits of the programs concerned. Interestingly, the Canadian public's perception that the benefits must be paid for by the society, and are not a free gift from the politicians who promise them, appears to have made little or no progress since the days of "Duplessis donne à sa province." Part of the explanation, of course, is that the costs are spread thinly over the entire population while the benefits, in most cases, are concentrated and thus have more impact.

This factor has its chief impact on the spending and service-providing functions of the state. As discussed earlier, the formal division of powers between federal and provincial governments in relation to these functions is somewhat vague, and the courts have been permissive in their attitude toward initiatives by both levels of government. Both levels are in practice free to provide whatever expenditures and services appear to be dictated by electoral considerations, although the financial resources of a government in relation to its existing commitments may impose some constraints. Political circumstances might increase the probability that one level of government, rather than the other, will act. For example, a more competitive party system may produce a greater tendency to spend public funds for electoral gain.

Bureaucratic Self-Interest

Tendencies to self-expansion on the part of the bureaucracy have sometimes been cited as an explanation for the growth of the state, and the theory initially appears plausible. The reluctance of any bureaucracy to dissolve itself may well explain the persistence of state activities and programs once they have begun, and the resulting cumulative effect of expansionist pressures, but it is perhaps less convincing to argue that the bureaucracy generates the initial pressures that lead to state activities expanding in the first place. Robert Presthus in his empirical study of Canadian elites found that bureaucrats had distinctly less favourable attitudes toward state intervention (which he termed "economic liberalism") than did elected politicians or directors of interest groups.[24] The conservatism of bureaucrats in this regard, while particularly pronounced at the provincial level, was evident also at the federal. It may in fact be that bureaucracies are motivated less by a desire to expand than by a resistance to any change in their established routines, and a change that leads to expansion may be almost as threatening as one that leads to contraction. In any event, new programs or initiatives by government often lead to the creation of a new bureaucracy (whose personnel may be drawn in part from existing ones) rather than the expansion of bureaucratic structures already in place.

Insofar as bureaucratic tendencies to self-expansion are a factor, they will affect mainly the regulatory and service-providing powers of the state and, perhaps to some extent, the taxing powers. Spending programs, particularly if the money is provided with "no strings attached," do not typically require much bureaucratic manpower. The regulatory powers, and to a lesser extent the service-providing powers, are quite explicitly divided by Canada's formal Constitution, so there may be less randomness in determining which level of government will develop a new regulatory or service-providing function. Also, it is presumably the government that already operates similar or related programs, and thus has an existing bureaucracy with an interest in the field, which is likely to face bureaucratic pressures to provide a particular new program or service. It should also be noted that regulatory programs, and the bureaucracies that run them, are conducive to federal-provincial conflict; Christopher Armstrong's study of relations between the federal and Ontario governments over the regulation of insurance companies may be cited as an example.[25]

Legitimation

The desire to reinforce the legitimacy of the state in the eyes of the population is a very important factor that has led to the expansion of state activities in recent decades. In contrast to the situation at the time of Confederation, the population has largely been cut loose from the traditional attachments to the church, the extended family, the locality and the client-patron relationship with local notables, all of which gave stability to the Canada of Macdonald and Cartier. In addition, the population is far better educated and better informed than in the past, and is bombarded by influences from the printed and electronic media, many — or most — of which originate in a foreign country, the United States. In fact the permeability of Canada to ideological influences from an external source probably has no parallel in the world. Furthermore, the Canadian population is relatively heterogeneous, with two official and countless unofficial languages and with almost one-sixth of the population having been born outside of Canada. The problem of legitimation is reinforced by class conflicts that, contrary to the conventional wisdom, are at least as pronounced as those in other liberal democracies, judging by the length, duration and frequent bitterness of strikes in both the public and private sectors.

Efforts to promote legitimation will, like efforts to win elections, result mainly in the use of two types of powers: powers to spend and powers to provide services. Spending that contributes to legitimation may confer tangible benefits on a large proportion of the population (e.g., family allowances) or on a small and narrowly defined target group (e.g., support for amateur sport). It also includes spending on propaganda or on ceremonies designed to strengthen loyalty and attachment to the state. Legitimation may also be promoted by the use of powers to confer recognition or status (e.g., membership in the Order of Canada) and even, indirectly, by the use of some regulatory powers. The regulation of broadcasting to require a minimum quota of Canadian content is an example of an effort along these lines, although it is possibly counterproductive because of the resentment caused and the increased incentive to watch American channels that results.

Legitimation is an important activity for both the federal and provincial levels of government, and an important aspect of legitimation in Canada is the competition between the two levels. Each level seeks to mobilize support among the population for its battles against the other level and uses all the techniques of legitimation to this end. Louis St. Laurent was concerned as early as 1945 that the federal government become more "visible" in Quebec to counter the attraction of Quebec nationalism, represented at that time by the Union Nationale.[26] Since 1968 this has been a major federal priority, and the Quebec government has responded in kind. Other provincial governments, particularly those engaged in conflicts with the federal government over natural resources, have also made legitimation a priority in recent years. Thus the total expenditure on legitimation in Canada is undoubtedly greater than it would be in a unitary state.

Competitive legitimation between levels of government is probably the best explanation for the recent plethora of government activities, programs and propaganda campaigns directed at specific target groups such as women, immigrants, ethnic minorities, artists, academics or fitness buffs. It also explains the existence of the Canadian Charter of Rights and Freedoms, and of the human rights codes in the provinces. It can even account for such apparently disparate phenomena as the televising of the House of Commons debates, Pope John Paul's visit to Canada in September 1984, and the massive celebrations of the seventy-fifth anniversaries of Alberta and Saskatchewan.

Urbanization and Industrialization

Another factor contributing to the expansion of state activity in recent decades is the social change associated with urbanization and industrialization. The main impact of this is the lessening of the independence of the individual and the family, and the resulting need for social insurance and income support programs, or what is generally known as the welfare state. This change has greatly increased the spending and service-providing functions of the state in all industrialized countries. In Canada it has affected mainly the federal level of government, which provides pensions, unemployment insurance and family allowances, and which subsidizes the provision of public assistance and health insurance by the provinces.[27] However, the provinces are the direct providers of some jointly funded services, and Quebec has its own contributory pension plan. Changes in the division of powers in this area have not been entirely informal, but have led to constitutional amendments in 1940, 1951 and 1964.

Corporate Capitalism

The externalities created by corporate capitalism are another, and according to some observers the most significant, factor contributing to the growth of the state. The profit-making activity of the private sector is possible only through extensive direct and indirect assistance from the state. This includes direct subsidies of various kinds; hidden subsidies built into the tax system; and the provision of services required by business — services that range from the training of the labour force and the conducting of research in government research establishments, to the provision of energy, transportation and other inputs whose costs are underwritten, to some degree, by the state. In turn, the profitable activities of the private sector have social costs such as environmental pollution, occupational threats to health and safety, and the stresses associated with the rise and fall of one-industry towns like Schefferville and Fort McMurray. These costs are largely assumed by the state as well. The total cost to the state of all this activity is staggering, even excluding the many "tax expenditures" that never appear on the expenditure side of the ledger. To take only one example, the 1982–83 estimates for the federal department of Energy, Mines and Resources approached eight billion dollars, more than the annual total of all federal expenditure only 20 years previously, and this did not include spending by the Crown corporation, Petro-Canada.[28]

Government activities that assist accumulation in the private sector are to be found among all four of the categories of powers discussed above, and are carried on by the federal and provincial, not to mention the municipal, levels of government. Tax expenditures are impossible without taxing powers; regulatory activities are frequently intended, in whole or in part, to assist the regulated industry (air carriers being a case in point); spending on direct subsidies is directed toward almost every sector of the economy; and a wide range of services is offered to business through government departments and Crown corporations.

In all federations this type of activity is shared by the different levels of government, but Canada is unusual, and perhaps unique, in the importance of the role played by the provincial level. Some unusual provisions of the Constitution Act, 1867, notably the provincial ownership of natural resources under section 109, contributed to this situation, and the thrust of judicial interpretation in the Haldane era (1912–28) should perhaps not be neglected. The main reasons for provincial prominence in accumulation-related activities, however, are almost certainly of an informal nature, and are related to the economic and social underpinnings of the federal state. For example, the regional division of labour in Canada and the varying resource endowments of the provinces have produced specialized provincial economies: forestry in British Columbia, petroleum in Alberta, agriculture in Saskatchewan and so forth. A provincial government is likely to be more sensitive to the needs of an industry that plays a dominant role in its provincial economy than is a federal government which presides over a far more diversified economy. It is also possible that the historic preoccupation of the federal government with transportation and finance made it less sympathetic than provincial governments to the needs of other sectors of the economy. For example, it was the Ontario government, rather than the federal government, that took over hydro-electricity from the private sector when manufacturing interests demanded such an initiative. In addition, the uneven development of the country makes federal economic policies an uneasy compromise between the needs of rapidly growing regions and those of stagnating or declining regions. Since in neither type of region are business interests fully satisfied with the results, businesses tend to turn to their provincial governments for policies more in tune with their own needs. Finally, it should be remembered that small or medium-sized firms with operations confined to a single province are still of very great importance in the Canadian economy, and such firms find it much easier to gain access to their provincial government than to the federal government.

Special Interest Groups

The final factor that may be called upon to explain the expansion of state activity is the demand by organized special interest groups for the state to act on their behalf. The vast majority of state activities and programs in all countries directly benefit only a specific target group of modest numerical size, but they are paid for by the entire population. Such activities are politically possible because the costs, being divided among a large population, are painless for each individual, while the benefits, being distributed among relatively few, are substantial enough for each participant that their loss would be resisted.[29] As society becomes richer, larger and more complex, organized groups and special interests of all kinds proliferate, each with its demands that the state do something on its behalf, and state activities proliferate accordingly. The empirical research of Robert Presthus, cited earlier in connection with the bureaucracy, may be cited again as evidence of the close link between organized group activity and the growth of the state. As Presthus describes it, "the larger outcome [of elite accommodation] is a relatively uncontrolled expansion of activities, without much qualitative differentiation among the competing claims of major social interests."[30]

One may hypothesize that most organized interests in Canada are relatively indifferent, at least to begin with, as to which level of government they would prefer to respond to their demands. Most of the major organized interest groups in fact operate at both levels and have a federal structure corresponding to that of the state itself. The choice of a level on which to concentrate their lobbying efforts is more likely to be influenced by pragmatic considerations than by respect for the supposedly watertight compartments of the Constitution. Certainly both the federal and provincial levels of government have been faced with numerous demands for intervention, and both have responded. It is probably impossible to quantify which has done so to the greatest extent, but one cannot doubt that untidiness in the de facto division of powers has resulted.

Some of the reasons why business interests often direct their attention to the provincial level have already been mentioned. For other types of organized interests — and Presthus has nine categories in addition to business — the reasons may be different. Physical proximity to the provincial capital may be a factor for groups with limited resources; the provincial capital is within four hours driving range for the vast majority of Canadians, while Ottawa may be half a continent away. Another factor is related to Canada's linguistic duality. The federal government must accommodate both anglophone and francophone interests, but it may as a result have difficulty in not falling between two stools. Many franco-phones have always perceived the federal government as too "English," and many anglophones, particularly in the West, increasingly perceive it as being too "French." Thus, unilingual interest groups and their leaders may feel more comfortable with a provincial government than with the federal government, and may direct their lobbying efforts accordingly.

New Areas of Public Policy

To conclude this lengthy discussion of explanations, Table 3-3 shows the two "new" areas of policy that led to formal changes in the division of powers, and the eleven others, identified earlier, that have grown up in the undefined no-man's land of jurisdiction. The columns are intended to suggest the first and second most important factors contributing to the emergence of each new field of policy. On the basis of this rather impres-sionistic survey, the present writer would conclude that legitimation, social change and externalities created by the private sector are the most impor-tant primary factors in the expansion of the state, although interest group activity and electoral politics play a role as well and are particularly impor-tant as secondary factors. Pressures to expand from within the bureaucracy seem to be of relatively little importance.

TABLE 3-3   New Fields of Public Policy With Primary and Secondary Factors Contributing to Their Emergence

Field	Primary Factor	Secondary Factor
Pensions	Social Change	Electoral Politics
Unemployment Insurance	Social Change	Legitimation
Science	Interest Group Demands	Bureaucratic Demands
Housing	Social Change	Electoral Politics
Human Rights	Legitimation	Interest Group Demands
Medical Insurance	Electoral Politics	Social Change
Youth	Legitimation	Electoral Politics
Culture	Legitimation	Interest Group Demands
Regional Development	Private Sector Externalities	Electoral Politics
Regulation of Foreign Direct Investment	Electoral Politics	Legitimation
Industrial Strategy	Interest Group Demands	Bureaucratic Demands
Environment	Private Sector Externalities	Interest Group Demands
Consumer Protection	Private Sector Externalities	Legitimation

Consequences of the Recent Evolution

To summarize the argument of the preceding sections, the recent evolution of the division of powers has been characterized mainly by an increase in the number of fields of state activity not explicitly provided for in the formal Constitution, and by the involvement of both levels of government in the majority of the new fields — and in some of the more traditional fields as well. Thus, most fields of jurisdiction are now shared, and very few are exclusive to a single level of government. This section will explore the consequences of this situation from the viewpoint of governments and of private interests, and in relation to the normative criteria of effectiveness, efficiency and democracy.

From the perspective of governments, the expansion of state activity has had costs as well as benefits, a not surprising conclusion if one accepts the view that the factors conducive to expansion have been largely beyond the control of governments themselves. While some of the disadvantages associated with expansion would also exist in a unitary state, they are more pronounced in a federal state, in which several governments are expanding simultaneously on the same territory.

One problem that seems to be increasingly serious is the imbalance between the revenues and the commitments of governments. The federal government appears to have entered into a chronic position of being able to finance only about three-quarters of its expenditures out of current revenues, and must borrow to cover the rest. This cannot continue indefinitely. At the provincial level, even the most prosperous provinces have been forced into a combination of tax increases and draconian efforts to cut costs, particularly in the fields of health and education. Both levels rely increasingly on the personal income tax to finance their activities, but that form of taxation is clearly approaching a saturation point, and the economic and political consequences of further increases cannot be contemplated with equanimity. The problem is no longer merely one of vertical balance, which could be solved by transferring provincial functions to the federal government (as the Rowell-Sirois Report recommended) or by transferring federal revenues to the provinces (as the provinces demanded, with considerable success, in the Diefenbaker-Pearson era). The fiscal crisis of the state now afflicts both levels of government, and there may well be no easy solution. However, the duplication of effort by two levels of government with overlapping and ill-defined responsibilities certainly exacerbates the situation.

Another consequence of the recent evolution of the division of powers is that governments are increasingly frustrated by the inefficacy of their policies, so that both voters and governments are losing faith in the very possibility of achieving collective goals through political action. While there may be many causes for this phenomenon, not all of them related to federalism, one reason for it must be the deadlock between and the mutual frustration of governments pursuing their different objectives in the same functional area of jurisdiction, so that the actions of one government oppose, countervail and frustrate the actions of another. The situation appears to be a common one in fields as diverse as industrial policy, regional policy, energy policy, transportation policy, communications policy and health policy. Obstacles exist at the best of times to the successful achievement by public policies of the goals for which they are designed. The additional burden of having the policies of governments frustrated by the analogous policies of other governments is a serious matter.

This mutual frustration contributes in turn to another consequence, namely increased conflict between provincial governments and the federal government. The phenomenon is not a new one, of course, as the relations between Macdonald, Mowat and Mercier a century ago attest. In their era, however, such conflict involved only a few issues and a few governments at any one time, had little or no effect on the lives of ordinary Canadians, and was closely related to partisan conflict in a two-party system, so that the tension was periodically reduced by a change of government at one or the other level. In the last 20 years, by contrast, it has become endemic and almost continuous, with occasional "common fronts" involving most or all of the provinces, with vast bureaucracies and propaganda machines on both sides mobilized as though for war, with ordinary taxpayers and consumers turned into the pawns of intergovernmental struggles, and with the survival of the federation itself often called into question. Moreover, an increasingly fractured party system provides no possibility of relief. Faith in the federal government, respect for the Constitution and, except possibly in Ontario, the sense of a common identity as Canadians, have been so seriously eroded by these developments that it is uncertain whether they can ever be restored.

For private interests that are taxed, regulated, subsidized or provided with services by governments, the recent evolution of the division of powers has a number of other consequences. On the one hand, private interests have benefited in some ways from the competition between two levels of government with overlapping jurisdictions. For example, an entrepreneur wishing to incorporate a firm has a choice between seeking a federal or a provincial charter, and may select the jurisdiction whose rules and procedures are convenient. A cultural organization seeking a subsidy can apply to one level of government if refused by the other, or it may be fortunate enough to receive subsidies from both. It is for this reason that public choice theorists, who draw the analogy between voters in the political system and consumers in the market economy, view intergovernmental competition and overlapping jurisdictions in a federal system as beneficial.[31]

On the other hand, competition and overlapping have less attractive consequences for the private sector as well. Dealing with two levels of government is more costly and time-consuming than dealing with only one. There may be considerble confusion and uncertainty as to which level of government is actually responsible for performing a particular function and which has the administrative capability and the legal authority to do so. Difficulty may also arise if conflicting rules, regulations or directives come from federal and provincial governments, so that following those provided by one level of government leads to conflict with the other. For example, some oil companies have become embroiled in conflict between the federal government and the government of Newfoundland, both of which claim the right to regulate drilling activities and to issue permits on the continental shelf. There are more general adverse consequences as well. For example, the cost of duplication of effort between levels of government is ultimately borne by the private sector through higher taxes. Policies that are incoherent or ineffective because they are frustrated or counteracted by the policies of the other level of government will presumably not benefit the private interests that they were designed to benefit and that may have demanded them in the first place.

The balance between the good and bad consequences of overlapping and intergovernmental competition is likely to vary depending, among other things, on the type of powers that are being used by the governments in question. Duplication of taxing powers raises the spectre of "double taxation" or the "tax jungle" with which the Rowell-Sirois Commission was concerned. Since the Second World War this problem has largely been avoided by intergovernmental agreement and the partial integration of the personal and corporate income taxes, although the decision by Alberta in 1981 to follow the example of Quebec and Ontario in collecting its own corporation tax suggests the possibility of a trend back to the tax jungle of the prewar years. For the mining and petroleum industries, problems of double taxation have already appeared on some occasions over the last ten or fifteen years, a difficulty exacerbated by different views among governments as to the relationship between royalties and taxes, insofar as the distinction still has any practical significance.

Duplication of regulatory powers, and uncertainty as to who can regulate what, are likely to pose even more serious problems. It is obviously not possible to adhere to the regulations of two governments attempting to regulate the same activity unless the regulations adopted by the two are identical, and in that unlikely event there would be little reason for both levels of government to remain in the field. Efforts by provincial governments to regulate portions of the broadcasting system, or by the federal government to bring caisses populaires under the legislative framework provided for the banks, have not made life easier for the private sector.

The consequences of duplication, overlapping and jurisdictional uncertainty in the spending and service-providing powers of goverments are, however, much more likely to be benign, apart from their financial costs to the taxpayer. A symphony orchestra or a research laboratory that receives a million dollars from each of two governments is obviously no worse off than if it had received two million dollars from only one government — even if the administrative costs of subsidizing music or research in this way are somewhat higher — and the orchestra or the laboratory may even benefit from not putting all its eggs in one basket. In fact, the enthusiasm of public choice theorists for intergovernmental competition is largely a result of the fact that they seem to concentrate their attentions on the spending and service-providing functions of government and to ignore the less pleasant subjects of taxation and regulation.

Even here, however, some caveats are in order. Services are not quite as simple a case as are subsidies. Competition between a federal and a provincial air carrier probably does no harm, but for the federal government to set up a parallel school system within a province or for a province to establish an agency competing with the Canada Wheat Board or the National Harbours Board would make little sense. Even subsidies may be used to manipulate private interests or to force them to take sides in intergovernmental controversies, as when former premier Duplessis ordered Quebec universities not to accept federal grants on pain of losing their provincial grants.

From the viewpoint of society as a whole, how can one assess the recent evolution of the division of powers in terms of efficiency, effectiveness and democracy? The last major effort to perform this task was that of the Rowell-Sirois Commission. Relying largely for its conclusions on a research monograph by Dr. J.A. Corry, the commission issued a stern warning against the evils of divided jurisdiction and a plea for the classic dual federalism of the 19th century, suitably brought up to date.[32] The warning was forgotten in the postwar enthusiasm for "cooperative federalism" and then in the almost continuous crisis that overtook the federal system from 1963 onward. Today, when the two levels of government are involved in a range of competing and overlapping activities that the commission could not possibly have imagined, the question perhaps poses itself with greater urgency than before.

Duplication of activities by two levels of government obviously has a financial cost related to the salaries and expenses of administrators performing parallel tasks, the upkeep of buildings in which to house these administrators, and so forth. Governments incur other costs in monitoring each other's activities or in coordinating their own activities with those of another government. Shared or cooperative activities may well depart from Weberian models of rational administration, as Corry argued, and competitive activities may simply duplicate each other to no purpose. Thus, the overall efficiency of the public sector has probably deteriorated as a result of the recent evolution of the division of powers.

Effectiveness is possibly more difficult to evaluate than efficiency, since the criteria are not self-evident. The symphony orchestra that receives two grants, to return to that example, will probably evaluate the effectiveness of public policy more positively than the financial institution or telephone company that faces two competing sets of regulations. For any type of public policy, more than one factor weighs in the balance. The policies of the federal government in most fields are probably more incoherent and slower to materialize than they would otherwise be because of the necessity to consult, inform or coordinate with the ten provincial governments. The complex contortions required to amend the Canada Pension Plan, as a result of provincial paramountcy in that field, provide an extreme example, but the snail's pace of policy making with respect to taxation, the price of oil and natural gas, the financing of the health insurance system, the conservation of renewable resources, or the phasing out of the Crow's Nest freight rates suggests that the problem is a general one. Some federal initiatives, such as the guaranteed annual income, the restructuring of the Atlantic fisheries, or the proposed industrial strategy, were abandoned entirely as a result of provincial obstruction. Even the final version of the package of constitutional amendments that took effect in 1982, after the federal government decided to negotiate a compromise with the dissident provinces, recalls the familiar definition of a camel as a horse designed by a committee. Yet while all of this may be viewed by some observers as evidence of the ineffectiveness of the present informal division of powers, others will argue that responsiveness to varying provincial views and perspectives is itself a valuable component of "effectiveness," given the regional diversity which, in their eyes, the provincial governments represent. While the present writer is less sympathetic than most of his colleagues to this line of argument, its popularity is perhaps reason enough for a nod in its direction.

The discussion of the division of powers from the standpoint of democracy can be brief, since most of the arguments resemble or parallel those that have already been discussed in some other connection. The measure of democracy is presumably the accuracy with which the wishes of the people are transformed into public policy. If one accepts the market model of the electoral process, overlapping and competing jurisdictions may increase the choices available to the voter-consumer — and the responsiveness to the voter's wishes of the governments that offer their wares in the political marketplace. Against this must be balanced the difficulty experienced by the voters in formulating their preferences and, above all, in organizing collectively to achieve them, if they are not certain about which level of government actually performs the function with which they are concerned. A government cannot easily be held responsible for its actions if it can plausibly blame their consequences, or their lack of consequences, on another level of government that is either competitively or cooperatively involved in the same field of activity. A government that modifies its own policies in order to achieve a compromise with the policies of another government (a practice rather self-righteously described by Premier Bill Bennett of British Columbia as "the Canadian way") cannot transform the wishes of its own electorate into policy as accurately as one that does not, unless the other government is more representative of the first government's electorate than is the first government itself. If the second government is in fact more representative, it can only be so by coincidence, and an unlikely one at that since it represents a different electorate, either larger or smaller as the case may be.

Problems with the Status Quo

The division of powers in the Constitution Act, 1867, has on balance not served Canada too badly, particularly when one takes into account the tremendous changes in technology, economic development and the role of the state that have occurred since it was drafted. However, some of the expressions used in the act may no longer have the same connotations that they did at the time, and should perhaps be replaced by more precise and meaningful terminology. An even more important requirement, however, is to make some explicit provision for the many new subjects of public policy that have evolved since 1867, and especially over the last half-century. Where these are not explicitly provided for in the written Constitution, they become the object either of arbitrary and unpredictable decisions by the judiciary or, more typically, of competitive involvement by both levels of government and the inevitable consequences of waste, confusion and conflict. The need is for a division of powers that will be as precise and meaningful in modern circumstances as the existing one was intended to be in the circumstances of the 19th century.

Since any changes that will be made should presumably be made with an eye to the needs of the future, and not merely to those of the present, it would be useful to be able to estimate how the role and function of the state will evolve over the next several decades. Unfortunately, this is no easy task. On the one hand, several circumstances that have contributed to the expansion of state activity seem likely to continue or even increase: more competitive electoral politics, the contest for legitimacy between the two levels of government, the inability of the private sector to generate profits without creating externalities and incurring costs for which the state must accept responsibility, and the proliferation of special interest groups. On the other hand, there are signs in the United States, and to some extent in Canada, of a growing resistance to taxation and regulation. The national governments in both the United States and the United Kingdom, more recently followed by the provincial government in British Columiba, have made dramatic efforts to reduce the extent of state intervention. It remains to be seen whether these represent a long-term reversal, or at least the termination, of what has been the major trend over most of the 20th century.

The prognosis does not become much clearer when the activities of the state are broken down into the categories used elsewhere in this paper.

With regard to taxation, it is difficult to believe that the personal income tax in Canada can increase much beyond present levels. On the other hand, new forms of taxation, such as the value-added tax (VAT) used in western Europe, may well be required to maintain even the present level of expenditures and services, let alone the additional expenditures and services that may be required in the future.

In the field of regulation, there is some evidence of a trend to reduce the activities of the state. Railway freight rates are now virtually unregulated in Canada, as is the trucking industry in the province of Alberta. Pressures to deregulate the air carriers increased sharply after deregulation was implemented in the United States, and in May 1984 the then minister of Transport announced that Canadian air transport would be deregulated, except in the North. Regulation of broadcasting is also unpopular except among the small and noisy elite that benefits from it directly. However, there are increasing demands for regulation in other areas, such as occupational health and safety, the use of tobacco and alcohol, traffic safety, pornography, and prostitution.

Spending and taxation are interdependent in the long run, however much governments may seek to postpone the evil day by borrowing. Hence, if taxation is approaching saturation point, which appears at least possible, the rate of increase in spending must eventually taper off as well. The last several years have seen major efforts at both the federal and provincial levels to restrain the growth of spending, with the brunt of such efforts being borne by health, education, and the salaries of public employees. These efforts must be balanced against, and are partly explained by, the increasing burden of tax expenditures, subsidies and services to shore up the private sector of the economy. In effect there has been not a reduction of spending, but a shift of spending from "social" to "economic" programs and initiatives. Unless the Canadian private sector demonstrates more independent vigour, initiative and good judgment than it has done recently, it is hard to foresee any reversal of the trend.

The service-providing functions of the state appear to be at least temporarily on the wane, as suggested by the recent vogue for "privatization." This has gone farthest in British Columbia, but the many suggestions to "privatize" federal Crown corporations, the sale by Alberta of Pacific Western Airlines, and the proposal by Quebec to turn over its liquor stores to employee cooperatives, are all further straws in the wind. These developments can be explained by two factors. In the case of profitable services, there seems to be a growing ideological belief, perhaps of U.S. origin, that they belong in the private sector. In the case of unprofitable services, governments increasingly view them, and particularly the salaries of their numerous employees, as an insupportable burden. On the other hand, electoral politics, intergovernmental competition for legitimacy and the demands of interest groups will continue to provide incentives for the provision of new kinds of services, which may at least counterbalance the losses through privatization.

All of this uncertainty makes even the identification of problems with the present division of powers, let alone the prescription of remedies, a hazardous and uncertain exercise. With this caveat, an effort will nonetheless be made, organized around the by now familiar categories of taxation, regulation, spending and the provision of services.

As far as the taxing power is concerned, a reasonable degree of harmony has been maintained for most of the time since the Second World War. Most forms of taxation are now shared between the federal and provincial governments, as shown by Table 3-1; and the practice of negotiating federal-provincial fiscal arrangements every five years has been quite effective and successful. There are, however, two problems connected with taxing powers that may suggest the need for constitutional revision.

The first problem concerns the restriction of the provinces to "direct" as opposed to "indirect" taxation. At the time of Confederation this distinction had been popularized by John Stuart Mill, but the distinction no longer appears as obvious today as it did then, and it has been treated in an inconsistent and unpredictable manner by the courts. It would seem desirable in a revised Constitution to abandon the terms "direct" and "indirect" and to declare more specifically which types of taxation should not be available to the provincial govenments. Since the principal if not the only justification for restricting provincial taxing powers is to prevent the provinces from interfering with the economic unity of the country, an amendment providing that the provincial governments cannot impose either tariffs or export taxes might suffice as a replacement for the present provision regarding "indirect" taxation.

The second problem concerns the unanticipated consequences of section 125, which declares that property belonging to Canada or to a province is not subject to taxation. In 1867 governments did not own much property, but today they own and operate a variety of commercial enterprises that are thus permitted to evade the taxes to which they would be liable, were they in private hands. Still worse is the fact that some Crown corporations, such as the Newfoundland and Labrador Petroleum Board, appear to be designed specifically and perhaps exclusively for the purpose of tax evasion. It seems desirable therefore that a revised section 125 should define more narrowly the kinds of "property" that are exempt from taxation, or the kinds of taxation from which government property is exempt.

Regulatory powers have required considerable interpretation, not to say embellishment, by the courts, and will continue to do so unless they are more explicitly and precisely provided for in the written Constitution. Most of the subjects now regulated by governments were not envisaged, or at any rate not regulated, in 1867, and are therefore not mentioned in the Constitution Act of that year. Apart from aviation and broadcasting, both of which were rather surprisingly allocated to exclusive federal jurisdiction during the brief interlude of common sense that followed Viscount Haldane's departure from the Judicial Committee of the Privy Council, all have had to be subsumed under the broad categories of "Property and Civil Rights," "Regulation of Trade and Commerce," or "Criminal Law," and consistency has not always been apparent in the judicial choices among those three categories.

The result of this lack of specificity has been to leave many activities and sectors of the economy in a constitutional limbo where they are jointly regulated by two levels of government, which is about the worst possible situation both from their point of view and from that of the national interest. Oddities and absurdities abound, such as the de facto regulation of nationwide trading in securities by one provincial government owing to the location of the major stock exchange in that province; the evasion by the federal government of its constitutional responsibility for highway transport between the provinces; the necessity of basing anti-combines legislation on the criminal law power, with the resulting presumption of innocence until proven guilty; and the almost total confusion in the area of legislation to protect the consumer. It may be recalled that in 1980 the federal government proposed adding competition policy and product standards to the list of federal powers, as well as specifying that the regulation of trade and commerce included interprovincial movements of services and capital as well as commodities. These suggestions were abandoned shortly afterward for lack of provincial support, but the problem of interprovincial economic barriers has not abated since that time. The fostering of such barriers, whether by the provinces or, as has happened in some cases, by the federal government itself, is self-defeating and reduces the well-being of Canadians generally.

An important area of regulatory jurisdiction that is not specifically assigned in the Constitution at present is jurisdiction over labour and industrial relations. The federal government became involved in this field early in the 20th century, but in 1925 the Judicial Committee of the Privy Council assigned most of the field to the provinces under the rubric of "Property and Civil Rights."[34] Federal jurisdiction still applies to interprovincial railways and airlines, banks and the stevedoring industry, but the Supreme Court has even ruled that workers engaged in constructing an international airport fall under provincial jurisdiction.[35] The scope of federal authority under the present Constitution appears unacceptably narrow for a modern industrial society. Labour has probably suffered as a result, not only because interprovincial competition for investment causes provincial legislation to favour the interests of management, but also because many provincial politicians come from small business backgrounds and appear hostile to the very idea of collective bargaining. A revised Constitution should specify, and define more broadly than the courts have done under the existing Constitution, those areas of the economy in which labour relations belongs under federal jurisdicion. Industries of national significance, and those that ship a large portion of the goods or commodities they produce outside of the province in which they are located, should definitely be included within the scope of federal authority, just as they have been in the United States through broad judicial construction of the commerce clause.

In general, therefore, the regulatory powers under the existing Constitution leave considerable room for improvement. The whole area of regulation should be sorted out and specified in accordance with modern realities, and with due regard for the general principle that matters affecting only one province should be regulated by that province while matters of national significance should be regulated nationally. Although implementation of this principle might mean some losses by the provincial governments of powers presently exercised by them, it might also make it possible as a quid pro quo to repeal the celebrated "declaratory power" in section 92(10)(c), which appears to cause some provincial governments so much anxiety at present.

As noted earlier, the spending powers of both provincial and federal governments are virtually unrestricted under the existing Constitution. This is not necessarily a problem, except from the standpoint of those who regard spending by any government as intrinsically evil. The unrestricted federal spending power, however, is frequently denounced by provincial governments who claim that it allows the federal government easy access into fields, such as health, education and welfare, which they consider to fall under their jurisdiction. Unfortunately, provincial governments rarely practise the self-restraint that they preach, and instead they spend their own funds on areas of federal jurisdiction, ranging from cultural and commercial diplomacy overseas to the purchase of equity in commercial airlines. From the perspective of the individual citizen, not predisposed toward either level of government, the pot calling the kettle black is an unattractive spectacle. On the other hand, the federal spending power, which David M. Cameron and J. Stefan Dupré have rightly called "the single most dynamic element of Canadian federalism," has unquestionably improved the quality of life for most Canadians.[36] Even though public expenditure on health, education and welfare appears to be currently unfashionable, the best way to deal with the spending power is probably to maintain the status quo, rather than imposing any new restrictions on either level of government.

Powers to provide services are also quite unrestricted, although some are exclusive to one or the other level of government. Apart from the somewhat illogical division of responsibility for penitentiaries (federal) from that for prisons (provincial), the existing allocation of specific responsibilities between the two levels is a sensible one and should be retained. Some of the types of services actually provided by governments, and not specifically mentioned in the written Constitution, might be formally allocated to the level of government that actually provides them. Finally, it might be desirable to recognize in the Constitution that many services are actually provided at the municipal level. Constitutional discussion tends to ignore local government and thus proceeds in an atmosphere of unreality, as though Canada were still a rural nation of farmers, foresters and fisherman.

Revising the Division of Powers

While the preceding pages have suggested the desirability of some reform, particularly in the allocation of regulatory powers, some readers may question whether a sufficiently strong case has been made to justify making this reform a high priority. Revising the division of powers would undoubtedly have costs as well as benefits, not only because of the time and effort diverted from other issues and problems but because of the conflict and ill-feeling, between governments and perhaps between residents of different regions, that might be generated by the process. Another consideration is the fact that the ill-advised amending formula that took effect in 1982, with its provision for provinces to "opt out" of any amendment that reduces provincial powers, would make the effective and uniform augmentation of federal powers extremely difficult. New federal powers that could be exercised in only seven, eight or nine provinces might in some cases be worse than no powers at all.

It is perhaps beyond the scope of this paper to weigh the costs of constitutional revision against the benefits. If the political authorities decide that the benefits are insignificant in relation to the costs, then presumably the present division of powers will be retained. As was suggested near the beginning of this paper, such a division has in some respects at least served the country quite well, however much it falls short of perfection. The suggestions offered in the final paragraphs of this paper, therefore, will be relevant only if it should be concluded that the benefits of revising the division of powers outweigh the costs.

In order to divide legislative powers appropriately in a new federal constitution for Canada, the first step should be to list all the powers that should be assigned, including those specified in the existing Constitution that are still relevant and all the new objects of public policy that have arisen since 1867. Wherever possible the very broad categories, such as "Property and Civil Rights" or "Trade and Commerce," should be broken down into more specific categories.

The second step, as an aid to dividing the powers between levels of government, should be to classify them into taxing powers, regulating powers, spending powers and service-providing powers. The division into these categories need not be made explicit in the new Constitution, although possibly it might be. However, the division into categories will be useful in assigning powers, because they should be dealt with in different ways.

Regulating powers, for example, should be made mutually exclusive — as nearly as possible — so as to minimize the number of disputes between governments over who should regulate what, and the number of cases where the regulated are uncertain about the level of government that has jurisdiction over them. On the other hand, taxing powers, powers to spend and powers to provide services can overlap without creating serious problems, and it may be desirable that they do so in many cases.

The third step is actually to divide the powers, not merely into federal and provincial powers, but into at least four categories: exclusive federal powers, concurrent powers with federal paramountcy, concurrent powers with provincial paramountcy, and exclusive provincial powers. Consideration should also be given to specifying some municipal powers, especially in the provision of services. These powers might be concurrent, as between municipal and provincial levels of government, with provincial paramountcy.

An additional question that may be addressed is whether Quebec should be given a slightly different allocation of powers from those of the other provincial governments. Although the idea of "special status" is no longer fashionable, some elements of it already exist in practice (notably the Quebec Pension Plan) and even in the formal Constitution (section 59 of the Constitution Act, 1982, pertaining to minority language educational rights). The question may arise, Should all provinces except Quebec agree to an amendment extending federal powers, given the opting-out clause in the amending formula? However, if special status in regard to any field of jurisdiction is given to Quebec, it should be for sound reasons based on a recognition of Quebec's special character, and not as an ill-considered response to a tactical situation. In some fields of jurisdiction, uniformity is important, and in general it would not be desirable to make Quebec's ties with the federal government any more tenuous than they are at present. In a few areas, however, a special status for Quebec might be appropriate. For example, post-secondary education might remain an exclusively provincial power in Quebec, while becoming a concurrent power with federal paramountcy in the other provinces.

Notes

This study was completed in December 1984.
1. A.V. Dicey, *Introduction to the Study of the Law of the Constitution*, 10th ed. (London: Macmillan, 1961), p. 151.
2. K.C. Wheare, *Federal Government*, 4th ed. (New York: Oxford University Press, 1964), p. 10.
3. W.H. Riker, *Federalism: Origin, Operation, Significance* (Boston: Little, Brown, 1964), p. 5.
4. Canada, 28th Parliament, 4th Session, Special Joint Committee on the Constitution of Canada, *Final Report* (Ottawa, 1972).

5. J.N. Lyon and R.G. Atkey, eds., *Canadian Constitutional Law in a Modern Perspective* (Toronto: University of Toronto Press, 1970), pp. 703–1154.

6. Peter M. Leslie, "Government Interaction in Policy Formation," Paper presented to the Canadian Political Science Association, Saskatoon, June 1, 1979, pp. 7–10.

7. W.R. Lederman, "Unity and Diversity in Canadian Federalism," *Canadian Bar Review* 53 (1975), pp. 597–620.

8. *A.-G. Nova Scotia v. A.-G. Canada* (1951), S.C.R. 31; and *P.E.I. Potato Marketing Board v. H.B. Willis* (1952), 2 S.C.R. 392.

9. Jack Mintz and Richard Simeon, "Conflict of Taste and Conflict of Claim in Federal Countries," Discussion Paper 13 (Kingston: Queen's University, Institute of Intergovernmental Relations, 1982).

10. Federal data are from the Official Records of Parliamentary Debates. Alberta data are from Ernest Mardon, *The Guide to the Alberta Legislative Assembly, 1905-83* (Lethbridge, privately printed, 1983).

11. "Confederation as an instrument of steam power has been compelled to face the implications of hydro-electric power and petroleum," Harold Innis, Essays in Canadian Economic History (Toronto: University of Toronto Press, 1956), p. 368.

12. Dicey, *Introduction to the Study of the Law of the Constitution*, pp. 171–80.

13. Frank R. Scott, *Essays on the Constitution* (Toronto: University of Toronto Press, 1977), passim. For a contrary view, see Alan C. Cairns, "The Judicial Committee and Its Critics," *Canadian Journal of Political Science* 4 (1971), pp. 301–45.

14. *A.-G. Canada v. A.-G. Alberta* (1916), 1 A.C. 589; in re the Board of Commerce Act (1922), 1 A.C. 191; *Toronto Electric Commissioners v. Snider* (1925), A.C. 396; *A.-G. British Columbia v. A.-G. Canada* (1937), A.C. 377; *A.-G. Canada v. A.-G. Ontario* (1937), A.C. 327.

15. *John Deere Plow Company v. Wharton* (1915), A.C. 330.

16. *Proprietary Articles Trade Association v. A.-G. Canada* (1931), A.C. 310; in re Regulation and Control of Aeronautics in Canada (1932), A.C. 54; in re Regulations and Control of Radio Communication in Canada (1932), A.C. 304.

17. *Saumur v. Quebec and A.-G. Quebec* (1953), S.C.R. 299; *Birks and Sons v. Montreal* (1955), S.C.R. 799; *Switzman v. Elbling and A.-G. Quebec* (1957), S.C.R. 285.

18. *Minimum Wage Commission v. Bell Telephone Company* (1966), S.C.R. 767.

19. *Public Service Board v. Dionne* (1978), 2 S.C.R. 191; *Burns Foods v. A.-G. Manitoba* (1975), 1 S.C.R. 494; *Canadian Industrial Gas and Oil v. Government of Saskatchewan* (1978), 2 S.C.R. 545; *Central Canada Potash Company and A.-G. Canada v. Government of Saskatchewan* (1979), 1 S.C.R. 42.

20. *Morgan v. A.-G. Prince Edward Island* (1976), 2 S.C.R. 349, and *A.-G. Quebec v. Kelloggs's Company of Canada* (1978), 2 S.C.R. 211.

21. *Angers v. M.N.R.* (1957), Ex. C.R. 83.

22. Peter Hogg, *Constitutional Law of Canada* (Toronto: Carswell, 1977), p. 72.

23. Frank R. Scott, "Constitutional Adaptations to Changing Functions of Government," in his *Essays on the Constitution*, pp. 142–56.

24. Robert Presthus, *Elite Accommodation in Canadian Politics* (Toronto: Macmillan, 1973), p. 299.

25. Christopher Armstrong, *The Politics of Federalism* (Toronto: University of Toronto Press, 1981).

26. R.M. Burns, *The Acceptable Mean: The Tax Rental Agreements, 1941-1962* (Toronto: Canadian Tax Foundation, 1980), pp. 46–47.

27. Keith Banting, *The Welfare State and Canadian Federalism* (Montreal: McGill-Queen's University Press, 1982).

28. Canadian Tax Foundation, *The National Finances, 1982-83* (Toronto: The Foundation, 1983), p. 217.

29. This is a major theme of Mancur Olson, *The Rise and Decline of Nations* (New Haven: Yale University Press, 1982). Olson attributes economic decline to the proliferation of special interest groups.

30. Presthus, *Elite Accommodation in Canadian Politics*, pp. 348–49.

31. For example, M.H. Sproule-Jones, *Public Choice and Federalism in Australia and Canada* (Canberra: Centre for Research on Federal Financial Relations, 1975).

32. Donald V. Smiley, ed., *The Rowell-Sirois Report*, Book I (Toronto: McClelland and Stewart for the Carleton Library, 1963), pp. 204–10.

33. On the neglected subject of state borrowing, see the unpublished dissertation by Robert L. Ascah, "Politics, Public Debt, and Debt Management" (Ph.D. diss., University of Alberta, 1983).

34. *Toronto Electric Commissioners v. Snider* (1925), A.C. 396.

35. *Construction Montcalm Inc. v. Minimum Wage Board* (1979) 1 S.C.R., 297.

36. David M. Cameron and J. Stefan Dupré, "The Financial Framework of Income Distribution and Social Services," in *Canada and the New Constitution*, edited by Stanley M. Beck and Ivan Bernier (Montreal: Institute for Research on Public Policy, 1983), pp. 333–99.

4

Federal-Provincial Relations and the Making of Public Policy in Canada:
A Review of Case Studies

FREDERICK J. FLETCHER AND
DONALD C. WALLACE

Introduction

General Objectives

It has for many years been commonplace in Canadian political discourse to attribute public policy failures to the federal system. It is commonly blamed for the failure of governments to deal with some pressing problem or, more recently, for the over-expansion of government. Inaction is blamed on the multiple veto points in the system and over-expansion on the competition among governments to respond to citizen demands. While some critics have blamed the system itself and advocated unitary government or, more commonly, secession, others have focussed on the alleged weaknesses of particular elements of the system. For example, various reformers have proposed such remedies as disentanglement of the division of powers, curtailment of the federal spending power, expansion of the list of concurrent powers, or changes in the mechanisms of federal-provincial relations. Although the rationales offered for these reforms are sometimes procedural, they more often reflect dissatisfaction with specific policy outcomes, often federal government policies.

In this study, we have attempted, through a survey of a sample of case studies of public policy, to assess the influence of the structures and processes of Canadian federalism on policy outcomes. The purpose of the project is to determine the circumstances under which federalism affects policy outcomes, the values which tend to be maximized or minimized in particular circumstances, the interests involved and the effectiveness of the process in managing conflict. In looking at the impact of the process of federal-provincial relations on the substance of policy, our focus has not been on the details of policy, but, rather, on the broad trends revealed in the case studies. While attempting to keep in mind issues related to democracy and community, we have taken a functionalist perspective, believing that governmental effectiveness is an overarching key issue for the Commission. Within the limits set by the available literature, we have tried to examine this issue in the terms suggested by Richard Simeon (1982–83, p. 155) when he observed that "the policy implications of alternative allocations of power lie at the heart of the functionalist perspective, yet studies of federalism have tended to neglect the linkage between interests, institutions and the content of public policy. . . ."

For a variety of reasons, the focus of federal-provincial relations appears to be changing. The fundamental questions raised by the independence movement in Quebec and the constitutional reform issue have been put aside, at least temporarily, and the focus has shifted to economic policy. The shift in focus from negotiating the terms of cost-sharing for the provision of social services to economic management and the promotion of economic development in hard times has left officials at both levels of government frustrated. The problems on the revised public agenda have proved to be intractable, and the history of the federal-provincial process provides few precedents for dealing with them. The eleven governments are in the process of building new relationships based on new issues. It seems, therefore, to be a good time to examine the process of federal-provincial interaction as it has evolved to date, with particular attention to its effectiveness in resolving disputes, its responsiveness to outside interests (especially in the economic sphere), its impact on public policy and its accountability to representative institutions. In particular, it is important to examine the conditions under which the system works most effectively and to try to determine whether the procedures developed in the past to deal with social issues, for example, can or should be applied now to economic issues.

The key questions guiding our research have been the following:

- Is the substance of public policy affected by the structure and operation of the federal system?
- Is there a crisis of federalism, as such, or are we experiencing rather a crisis of modern government?
- Should criticisms of the substance of policies be attributed instead to the process of decision making in the federal system?
- What factors in the federal-provincial bargaining process influence conflict management?
- Does the system itself promote conflict?
- What factors influence the access of non-governmental interests and the responsiveness of the process to their concerns?
- What types of interests appear to have most influence?
- How accountable are executives to legislative entities with respect to federal-provincial issues?
- Can differences by issue and jurisdiction be traced?

Approach:
Surveying the Literature

To fulfill these general objectives, we have examined the major texts in the field and prepared a thorough and careful review of existing case studies in a representative selection of public policy areas. Our search has gone beyond the literature in political science to related fields, most notably economics and law. We have examined a wide range of material focussing on public policy rather than federal-provincial relations as such. We have taken seriously Banting's observation (1982, p. 180) that "specialists in federal-provincial relations are not always well placed to evaluate the policy impact of institutions they study." We have, therefore, tried to find works that treat public policy as the "phenomenon to be explained" (ibid., p. 181) and to examine their findings with respect to the impact of federal-provincial processes. Our approach has been to identify the central propositions in the standard texts and then to examine them in the light of the findings in the case studies.

The major purpose of this paper is to examine the effectiveness of federalism as a system of policy making in meeting the expectations of citizens for a responsive and accountable process which deals with their concerns. The paper does not deal directly with the crises of community which have troubled the federal system over the past decade and more. While improvements in the public policy process might well help to ameliorate western alienation and reconcile Quebec to the system, the focus here is on non-crisis federal-provincial relations.

The literature in this area is frequently atheoretical and is generally not empirical or quantitative in approach. This state of affairs has required us to develop categories to impose upon the material and to infer propositions from studies not reported in propositional terms. The work thus has an unavoidable subjective element.

In addition, the case literature is uneven. There is considerable case-study material on such areas as fiscal relations and constitutional reform — omitted here because they have been studied rather thoroughly — as well as on pensions, health, social security, manpower and regional development. The federal-provincial process is less well studied in such areas as economic policy, communications and education, although recent works go some distance to fill these gaps. We have made particular efforts to find relevant works in the latter areas.

Focus and Scope of the Study

Our analysis focusses on policy area (and type), jurisdiction, and interests mobilized. Time has proved to be an important element in the analysis. For example, the case studies which we have consulted on Canadian intergovernmental relations in the past few years document the tremendous growth of spending empires at the federal and provincial levels and the growing interdependence and entanglement of policy-making structures. As well, these studies portray the institutionalization of the structures of intergovernmental relations, especially the specialized central agencies charged with the management of the process. In addition, we have seen the shift from functional to summit federalism and from multilateral to bilateral relations.

Overall, we have surveyed some 50 general works on federal-provincial relations and more than 100 case studies and commentaries on specific areas of intergovernmental policy making. The case studies were selected primarily on the basis of their attempts to link the substance of policy with the process of policy making. Time and resources did not permit a full-scale search of the literature, and we can only hope that our scanning has produced a representative body of material. We found that few case studies of this sort have been done in French, thus limiting our access to a Quebec perspective (though we have consulted a number of more general works).

In the analysis, we have concentrated on case studies in eight broad policy areas. These include some areas where federal jurisdiction is almost exclusive (communications policy) through various degrees of shared responsibility (transportation, economic policy, regional economic development, energy and natural resource development, social welfare) to areas which fall primarily under provincial jurisdiction (education, health).

We have used the case study literature to focus on the impact of the particular array of structures, interests mobilized, issue area and type, and jurisdiction on specific policy outcomes. This has made the analysis complex, not only because the mix of variables is complex, but also because it changes over time. Arranging the factors in simple dependent-independent variable relationships proved to be impossible, and we have, instead, tried to discuss broad trends. In addition, we have found that the impact of jurisdiction and federal-provincial mechanisms (the federalism variables) rarely influence public policy in a simple or direct way. Rather, they have impact in combination with or through other factors. Nevertheless, we have tried to grapple with the issues in as systematic a manner as possible. We have grouped our analyses under three broad headings:

- the impact of federalism on public policy;
- conflict management; and
- federalism and democratic values.

Our analysis leads us to confirm certain of the main arguments in the literature. The system is not for the most part decisive and tends to be incapable of rendering decisions in certain controversial areas. The actual federal-provincial negotiations are usually inaccessible to relevant non-governmental interests, so that the deliberations often fail to canvas all relevant viewpoints, except insofar as the governments are in touch with their constituencies. As an instrument of conflict management, the system is only moderately successful, but it does work well under certain circumstances. The case studies provide some guidance in identifying these conditions and suggesting reforms that might make the process more decisive and more responsive, as well as more able to manage conflict.[1]

In an attempt to go beyond the descriptive and to suggest some of the main elements in the analysis to follow, we have identified four major controversies in the literature with respect to the impact of federalism on public policy upon which our analysis permits us to comment.

General Critique of Federalism: Four Debates

CONSERVATIVE OR INNOVATIVE?

First, there is the debate between those who contend that federalism has a conservative bias, permitting strong interest groups to use the multiple veto points in the system to block government action to assist the weak (Mallory,1954; pp. 53–56, chap. 3) and those who view divided jurisdiction as permitting innovation at the provincial level, often followed by emulation (Trudeau, 1968, pp. 124–50). The innovation thesis is supplemented by the argument, offered by Trudeau and supported by the public choice theorists, that one level or the other will provide a particular service if there is sufficient citizen demand.

On the basis of a careful study of the income security case, Banting (1982, pp. 73–76) concluded that federalism has both a conservative and an expansionist dynamic. This view is supported by the findings reported in a wide range of case studies. With respect to the innovation thesis, he makes the point that it fails to take fully into account the limiting effects of regional disparity and interprovincial economic competition. No doubt, this applies especially to the costly social programs in which he was interested. On the other hand, competition for the credit that goes with expanding popular programs (pensions, family allowances) or in occupying jurisdictional grey areas (regulation of communications, aspects of the economy and some social services, for example) promotes the expansion of government activity. By the 1970s, at least, the conservative effect of multiple veto points had been largely overcome by the erosion of jurisdictional boundaries through federal-provincial collaboration and federal use of the spending power. The changes in public expectations resulting from the increased level of government activity dating from the Depression were among the forces which moved federalism away from the individualism, legalism and laissez-faire non-interventionism with which it had been associated (Corry, 1958, pp. 95–98).

On the other hand, the innovation thesis, which was derived largely from the hospital insurance and medicare case, seemed to have limited application. Increased interdependence, flowing from improved transportation and communications, accompanied by the emergence of nationwide corporations and a nationalizing of public and elite sentiment (ibid.),[2] had created a competitive environment which made local innovation difficult. In the social welfare area, innovation was discouraged by the need to keep tax levels competitive in the search for capital investment. Conversely, innovations in infrastructural support or subsidies to business were quickly matched, if not emulated, creating an unhealthy pattern of innovation-emulation (Tupper, 1982, chap. 7). Nevertheless, the potential remains for provinces to innovate when national majorities or vested interests block federal initiatives, but the limitations created by revenue shortfalls (despite equalization) and interprovincial competition are significant. The argument of the public choice theorists that the existence of independent governments competing for credit promotes innovation and enhances consumer choice (Sproule-Jones, 1975) founders on the realities of residence requirements, interprovincial competition and federal-provincial interdependence. Increasing federal government resistance to opting out with compensation and unconditional transfers was also, no doubt, a factor.

By the 1980s, therefore, it was possible to identify both a conservative pattern and an expansionist pattern. The conservative pattern, in which needed changes to various social programs, in areas such as social assistance, pensions and medicare, are blocked by the fact that substantial political resources must be expended to bring about change, is of considerable significance. The paralysis implied here is related only partly to federalism. It reflects not only the multiple veto points in the system and the erosion of trust in the system resulting from confrontational federal-provincial relationships in other areas, but also the shortfall in government revenues resulting from the worldwide recession and the decline in support among key elites for social service spending. (The latter development is, no doubt, related to increasing professional skepticism regarding the effectiveness of certain kinds of social spending [Leman, 1980, pp. 224–27]). The conflict of interest between those who would reform the system to expand services and those who would reform it to cut costs explains part of the immobilism and is essentially unrelated to federalism, though the interests are not evenly dispersed in regional terms. With respect to the impact of federalism, it can be said that it does raise the level of consensus needed to adjust existing programs or introduce new ones and permits private groups to block change (Banting, 1982, p. 174), especially where jurisdiction is shared or predominantly provincial. (This has given rise to unilateral federal action, where feasible, and attempts at bilateral agreements.) In addition, the operation of executive federalism insulates policy makers from public pressures, to a degree, and, therefore, from the expansionist pressures seen as inherent in democratic politics and from the cost-cutters in a neo-conservative era (ibid., pp. 114–15; Leman, 1980, p. 224).

The expansionist pattern derives not so much from the innovation-emulation model which operated in the health care area as from the increased competitiveness of governments in the 1970s (Cairns, 1979, pp. 188–89). The impact of the competition among governments to implement restraint programs remains to be seen. If restraint programs are viewed as a part of the competition to attract investment, the changes we have noted here in the federal dynamic may be related to a shift in emphasis from redistribution to capital accumulation by the governments in the system, a return to the anti-democratic intentions of some of the founders of federalism (Whitaker, 1983, pp. 36–37). If that is so, it is a movement that has no direct relationship to the federal system as such.

COMPETITIVE EXPANSIONISM

Second, we turn to a paradox in some recent literature: that inter-governmental competition has promoted government interventionism and yet led to a kind of functional paralysis (Cairns, 1979, pp. 175 and 189). The thesis here is that the inevitable competition among governments in an interdependent federalism to claim credit and avoid blame and to expand jurisdiction to the maximum (a kind of Parkinson's Law of federalism) leads to the expansion of services and, especially, inter-ventionist policies of economic subsidy and regulation. It is argued that the governments increasingly collide with one another and become entangled, while individuals and corporations get caught in the middle.

Much of the literature supporting this position tends to reflect a hostility to government intervention rather than analysis of federal-provincial relations. It does seem clear, however, that the jurisdictional situation in Canada, where each level of government has substantial economic powers, has led to conflict and a degree of competitive expansionism. In the social services and income support fields, the squeeze on government revenues in the past decade has curtailed expansionism. Indeed, many observers in the latter field are concerned not so much about expansion as contraction. The best available empirical evidence on the expansion of social services suggests that growth is related to centralization and that the existence of significant provincial jurisdiction delayed expansion of services.[3] In the economic field, intergovernmental cooperation has been hampered by the absence of incentives for governments to cooperate, the lack of well-developed shared programs to build on and the degree of regional mistrust in the system. Nevertheless, economists appear unable to demonstrate substantial negative effects except, perhaps, with respect to the bidding up of subsidies, tax breaks and other forms of assistance to industry.[4]

THE PARALYSIS THESIS

Third, we turn to a related proposition: that jurisdictional boundaries have become so blurred as a result of the development of cooperative federalism that governments try to be active in every area and paralysis has resulted (ibid., pp. 189–90). This is related to the traditional Quebec argument that federalism is a straitjacket preventing both of Canada's communities (in the form of the Quebec and federal governments) from fulfilling their objectives (Morin, 1976; Lévesque, 1977). The underlying assumption here, however, is that Quebec lacks jurisdiction in certain key areas.

The paralysis thesis is related to the view that there has been a decline in "constitutional morality" or respect for the spirit of the Constitution and that federal-provincial relations in the 1970s became a rather cynical competition for political power. Lacking the security of a settled jurisdiction, the argument runs, governments seek political support (Careless, 1977, p. 177). In fact, the end of the constitutional logjam and changes in various shared cost programs, as well as some innovations in restraint programs (British Columbia) and economic initiatives (Saskatchewan, Ontario), demonstrated that action was still possible. The failure to achieve concerted government action on the pressing economic problems of the 1980s probably relates more to the intractability of these problems (as shown by the difficulties faced by other countries) than to the federal system. It is also true, however, that intergovernmental mistrust, derived, in part, from attempts by both levels to expand their activities in the economic sphere and, in part, from spillovers on other issues, helped to block concerted action. The fact that jurisdiction was shared, not concurrent (with each level having substantial but limited capacity for action), was also a factor. The circumstances of the period, in which there was competition for support between Ottawa and a Quebec government which threatened the survival of the regime, clearly heightened intergovernmental mistrust. In general, there was an absence of incentives for cooperation. (In many areas, concurrent action might well have been preferable to contractual joint action in any case. Parallel programs, whether supported by shared jurisdiction or the openings left by concurrent jurisdiction, might well avoid the inflexibility of the contractual straitjacket while providing greater sensitivity to regional differences. The risk of countervailing policies might be mitigated by consultation.)

With respect to the Quebec argument, there is little doubt that Quebec government initiatives have been limited by the division of powers. This generalization applies over a wide range of activities, from language and education policies through the regulation of communications. On the other hand, it is also clear that the federal government has found its capacity to act in the constitutional area, among others, hampered by Quebec's political resources. In the end, however, it is not unreasonable to conclude that both governments have found ways and means to accomplish many, perhaps most, of their objectives. The pattern has been more one of delay and frustration than of paralysis. Regulation of communications is an area of considerable frustration for Quebec and a number of other provinces, yet there is little evidence that provincial jurisdiction would have served citizen needs better or, indeed, produced very different policies. The slow growth of Radio Quebec was more a matter of resources — and Quebec government priorities — than jurisdiction. In short, the central argument of the Parti Québécois that, as Simeon (1982-83, p. 154) summarizes it, "Quebec cannot achieve its own goals in economic, social or cultural policy so long as Ottawa controls so many of the levels of policy making," is undoubtedly true. However, the differences in substantive policy seem, to an external observer, to be, in many cases, minor or difficult to trace. Nevertheless, it is obviously true that federalism is one factor among many which limits the capacity of governments to make radical changes in the socio-economic order (Brunelle, 1982).

EQUITY VERSUS EFFICIENCY

Fourth, we examine a contention — widespread in recent years — that the federal system's emphasis on regional equity prevents concentration of resources and thereby hinders the pursuit of excellence (or in economic terms, international competitiveness). For example, the Conservative Party task force on technology and training argues that money is squandered "on ridiculous enterprises such as creating a microelectronic research centre in *every* Canadian province, which makes for good politics but lousy economics," in Jeffrey Simpson's paraphrase.[5] The tension is seen to be between "rational" allocations and political expedience.

Whether the argument is put in terms of efficiency or effectiveness, it seems plausible to argue that the primary problem is not so much federalism as regionalism. There can be little doubt of the correctness of the argument put by Cairns (1977) and others (Elkins and Simeon, 1980, pp. 290-99) that the existence of provincial governments with significant powers has mobilized interests in regional terms in ways that might not have occurred in a unitary system. In addition, the provincial governments have given voice to regional interests that might have gone unheard in a unitary system. It is also clear, however, that regional conflicts over the location of industrial development, port facilities, federal installations, and so forth, would be present in any system. Altering the division of powers to strengthen central jurisdiction would not make the issues go away, nor would it necessarily produce "better" policies. In the end, much depends upon the capacity of the federal government to summon the political will to make tough allocative decisions and to fashion compromises and tradeoffs to manage regional conflict.

Three Broad Concerns

This discussion of four controversies over the impact of federalism on public policy illustrates the complexity of the issue and the need to view federalism in the context of other factors. Its significance varies with jurisdiction, issue area, and so on. Federalism has clearly contributed to the political malaise of recent years, but it is by no means the major cause. In the section immediately following, we will try to specify its impact more clearly and explore the implications of that impact for the future of the system.

Having dealt with this, we then turn to our second broad concern: the effectiveness of the system in managing conflict. The conventional wisdom that consultation, trust relationships and an incremental approach to decision making are most conductive to effective conflict management found considerable support in the literature. We found that the federal system had evolved a number of ad hoc arrangements that had promise for improving conflict management if applied more systematically. Despite the problems posed for the system by intractable differences of economic interest and cultural preference, our survey suggests that there is substantial potential for effective conflict management.

In our third area of concern, federalism and democratic values, the case studies tend to support the conventional picture of the system as neither responsive nor accountable. This was particularly true in areas of shared jurisdiction. There were, however, important differences over time and by issue. It is important to note that there was evidence of a general responsiveness to public and professional preferences, especially when strongly held and transregional. We argue that, through some fairly simple reforms, responsiveness and accountability could be improved without seriously reducing decisiveness.

Finally, we attempt to suggest some promising directions for reform in the system, keeping in mind the need to balance decisiveness, responsiveness and accountability, while successfully managing conflict and coping with conflicting regional interests and concepts of community.

Divided Jurisdiction:
The Impact of Federalism on Policy Outcomes

Stating the Problem

To analyze the impact of federalism — the pattern of divided jurisdiction — on policy outcomes is a difficult task. It involves a speculative activity in which the analyst compares what did (or did not) happen with what might have happened under a system of central dominance or one of provincial dominance (Simeon, 1973, pp. 269ff.). The issue here is not so much the impact of federalism (as opposed to some other system) as it is the impact of any particular federal structure (as opposed to realistic alternative configurations). Some effects are direct, with a discernible impact on substantive policy outputs or on the implementation of programs. Others are indirect, creating conditions which influence policy. The task is not simply one of identifying winners and losers in the process. It involves also attention to the values reflected in policies chosen or rejected, as well as to the choice of policy instruments, the timing and scope of programs, and so on. While no definitive answers are possible, informed speculation based on a variety of cases can help us to understand the costs and benefits of the existing system and, therefore, suggest considerations relevant to reforms.

In many areas, the impact of federalism on policy derives indirectly from the regionalization of sentiment that federalism promotes. If Cairns and others are correct, that such attitudes are often mobilized by regional elites (or the very existence of provincial boundaries), then it is not unreasonable to trace such controversies as that over freight rates to the federal system.[6] Institutional arrangements which minimized regional sentiment, perhaps by involving provincial spokesmen in relevant decisions, might mitigate these sentiments and make the substantive issues easier to deal with. Joint regulatory boards (discussed in terms of conflict management, below) are one possible mechanism.

With respect to implementation, the case studies abound with allegations of rigidities, delays, duplication, high decision costs and other forms of waste associated with divided or shared jurisdiction. For example, until the shift from shared–cost programs to block grants in 1977, the provinces found it very difficult to coordinate the many health and welfare programs which they operated in contractual relationships with the federal government. Adjustments to changing conditions, adoption of cost-saving innovations and administrative reorganization of programs to increase efficiency were made difficult by the need to secure federal agreement. It was not so much that the federal government was intransigent as that achieving consensus among 11 governments was a slow process. (One irony here is that the needs test for social assistance was placed in the federal legislation in response to provincial pressures and subsequently became a barrier to provincial governments seeking innovative ways to assist the working poor.) The block grant solution promoted integration and flexibility at the expense of national standards (Hum, 1983, pp. 4–5).

In considering the propositions emerging from the literature, caution is required. Banting (1982, p. 4), for example, notes that institutions had less influence on income security policy than might have been expected and cautions analysts to guard "against attributing too much policy influence to institutions, or holding unrealistic expectations about the extent to which institutional engineering can solve policy problems." The tendency of Canadian politics to focus on federalism could easily lead analysts to exaggerate its significance. As Banting (ibid., p. 180) has pointed out:

> For over a generation now, federalism has been the most dramatic part of Canadian politics, full of conflict, tension and explosive potential. Furthermore, much of this drama has been played out on the public stage, unlike many other exciting battles that have remained fully cloaked in cabinet secrecy . . . . But drama and policy impact are decidedly different phenomena. To some extent, federal-provincial conflict has simply served to highlight certain policy areas, without increasing their substantive importance.

Nevertheless, our case studies make clear that both jurisdiction and the form of federal-provincial agreement — conditional versus unconditional grants, for example — make a difference in the timing and substance of public policy. Still, we do not believe there is a crisis of federalism at this level. The sense of crisis derives largely from issues which go far deeper than the processes by which our governments make decisions. In the eight policy areas we have examined (ranging from areas of primarily provincial jurisdiction to areas of federal predominance), there are many instances where it is plausible to attribute effects to the system itself. It must be noted, however, that significant effects can usually be attributed to a combination of factors, of which the federal system is only one.

Federalism:
Brake or Accelerator?

Does centralization of authority promote innovation, as some authors assume, or is decentralization of jurisdiction more likely to promote adjustment to changing conditions? It appears to depend upon the issue at hand. Birch, in his classic work (1955), argues that the complications of federalism inhibited the development of social legislation in Canada, delaying the emergence of the welfare state. Although noting that Canada has not lagged behind other non-federal states at the same level of industrial development, Banting agrees that social welfare programs developed fastest in centralized systems, noting that federal government involvement was a critical factor in Canada. Constitutional amendments to shift jurisdiction to the central government and the use of the spending power to create programs were key elements in the development of the Canadian welfare state. Provinces were and are inhibited by regional disparities in terms of government revenues and competition for investment from developing costly social programs. Banting's judgment is that the theory that federalism permits innovation in one unit that can then spread throughout the federation does not hold up under examination (1982, p. 174).

Other studies suggest, however, that there was a pattern of provincial innovation in the health care field. A number of programs began in one or two provinces and then were established in other provinces because the federal government, under pressure from the provinces with programs or from consumer groups, saw some electoral benefit in offering cost-sharing arrangements. Other provinces then introduced the programs, sometimes reluctantly, to get a share of the funds (and political credit). Hospital and medical insurance are the prime examples. These case studies (Taylor, 1978; Armitage, 1975; Weller and Manga, 1983) suggest that this pattern is most likely to occur when:

- jurisdiction is predominantly provincial or shared;
- there is significant public or professional demand for the program, across several regions;
- the federal government is seeking credit, as a result of either electoral or federal-provincial competition; and
- government revenues are growing.

These conditions are increasingly rare, so that this pattern is unlikely to recur in the years ahead. Province-led innovation is more likely to occur in low-cost fields (except with respect to industrial assistance). The health care case, therefore, is not generally applicable.

Major Cases:
Social and Economic Policy

Few case studies attempt explicitly to assess the impact of federalism on public policy. Among those which do are Simeon's (1973) study of the Canada-Quebec pension plan negotiations, Banting's (1982) overview of income security policy, Jenkin's (1983) study of industrial strategy and Tupper's (1982) examination of industrial assistance policy. These and related works by Thorburn (1984) and Brown and Eastman (1981) are discussed in some detail below. The other case studies we have consulted do not deal directly with the "counterfactual" possibilities of alternative federal arrangements. Nevertheless, many of them provide information that is of assistance in our attempt to assess the impact of federal organization.

Simeon (1973, p. 271) concluded that:

> The outcome of the pension plan negotiations . . . took the shape it did largely because of a certain pattern of federal-provincial interaction. It ensured that a particular set of interests — those of the provincial governments — was injected into the process.

In his view, had the federal government been able to pursue its initiative without regard for the provinces, the proposal would have been implemented more quickly, the policy process would have featured more parliamentary and interest group input and the pension plan would have been simpler. It would probably have emerged as a straightforward pay-as-you-go plan. Certainly, the investment funds for the provinces would not have been forthcoming, nor would they have gained tax points (ibid., pp. 269–71). It must be noted, of course, that the impact of parliamentary and national interest-group input is incalculable and might have produced consumer-oriented changes. One general conclusion that can be offered is that the process does give pride of place to the interest of governments and, potentially at least, to regionally concentrated interest groups.

Had the provinces been left to deal with the demand for pension reform, Simeon concludes, no plan like the Canada Pension Plan would have emerged. The matter was not a high priority for the provinces and was placed on the agenda by the federal government for electoral purposes: "Most provinces had neither the expertise nor the resources to establish a contributory pension plan" (ibid., p. 270). In addition, the populations of most provinces were too small to sustain it. The most likely outcome would have been increased regulation of private pension plans in some provinces. Of course, failure to act on the part of the federal government would undoubtedly have resulted in increased pressures from welfare-oriented lobby groups on the larger provincial governments.

Banting's fundamental conclusion, as noted above, is that while institutional arrangements have influenced certain aspects of income security, they have not determined its basic principles. With a unitary government, programs might have been introduced sooner or expanded faster and been administratively simpler. With a decentralized system, some programs might not exist and others would have taken a different form, but some form of income security would have been established: "Provincial fiscal limitations and the problems of mobility of capital and labour would have limited expenditures and produced a greater reliance on regulation of the private sector" (Banting, 1982, pp. 60–61).

Banting's arguments can be summarized briefly: the effects of provincial economic competition are such that federal involvement is necessary for the expansion of social programs; the centralization of control over income security after the 1930s (through constitutional amendments and shared-cost programs) produced a more expansive welfare state than would have occurred under provincial jurisdiction. Banting's view is that provincial fiscal limitations and differential wealth along with problems of mobility of capital and labour would have limited expenditures and created greater reliance on the private sector. His conclusion, therefore, is that the predominance of provincial jurisdiction which delayed the introduction of social programs would have limited their scope had federal involvement proved impossible. Indeed, he argues that divided jurisdiction has been a conservative force in welfare politics because it raises the level of consensus needed for new programs; it can result in an elaborate system of vetoes which restrains growth; and it permits the private sector to limit the scope of national programs by playing one level off against the other.[7] (It should be noted here that the inability of provinces to agree among themselves to mount joint or coordinated programs without federal involvement effectively restrains provincial initiative.)

All four of the economic policy studies noted above agree that federalism has contributed to Canada's economic difficulties. Jenkin's major concern is that the federal system has prevented a coordinated approach to industrial strategy, with attendant costs related to countervailing policies and spillovers from one province to another (1983, pp. 26, 170ff.). Thorburn (1984, p. 242) supports this view, arguing that federal-provincial competition has weakened Canada's international economic influence and hindered the development of trust between government and the private sector:

> We have developed a relationship of deadlock in federal-provincial relations that has set the pace for other relations, especially between business and government. This has prevented us from agreeing on our economic goals. . . . This failure to order our affairs rationally according to plan at the highest level has had most serious consequences: our economy has become balkanized and our politics confrontational, leading us to dissipate our top decision-making resources on struggles of allocation between regions, provinces, industries and so on, instead of building consensus around an agreed-upon program of development.

Brown and Eastman (1981) too found very real limits to consultation between the public and private sectors, deriving, in part, from federal-provincial conflict over critical jurisdictional issues. It was their judgment (p. 189) that "it is much easier to operate a public/private consultative process in a unitary state." They observed that economic interests felt at risk as rival governments sought their support and that the number of actors posed a problem.

Tupper, in his (1982) study of industrial assistance policies, found (p. 83) that "federalism, by 'institutionalizing regionalism,' makes difficult, if not impossible, the pursuit of federal policies which are indifferent to the spatial distribution of industry." This regionalization fosters interprovincial competition for job-creating investment as well as making it "difficult for the federal government to formulate policies acceptable to all regions" (ibid., p. 82). These conditions tend to weaken all governments in dealing with business interests, both domestic and foreign, and, therefore, weaken environmental safeguards and protection for labour. He noted, however, that factors other than federalism were involved and that "many of the 'economic critiques' of federalism are really statements of hostility toward the positive state or expressions of frustration with the complexity, slowness, and apparent irrationality of economic policy-making in a decidedly complex federation" (ibid., p. 91).

For those opposed to industrial planning, in favour of the encouragement of capital, or concerned about regional equity, the system clearly has virtues. For others, these consequences are extremely negative.

With respect to the broader implications of the federal-provincial process, it has been widely argued that the territorial nature of federalism fosters programs aimed at regional distribution and inhibits programs aimed at interpersonal redistribution.[8] After a careful analysis of available data, Banting (1982, p. 83) concluded that "federalism has not significantly altered Canadian redistributive goals, and has not diverted significant resources away from redistribution between individuals through the income security system." In his view, centralization of jurisdiction might well have expanded the welfare state and decentralization contracted it, but public and professional demand would have ensured that the basic principles applied. Decentralization of the income security function would, however, drastically reduce both the legitimacy and the economic management capacity of the federal government (ibid., p. 168).

Without challenging Banting's argument directly, Derek Hum (1983, pp. 3-10, 82-83) suggests that the Canada Assistance Plan (CAP) has a number of flaws and gaps which could be attributed to divided jurisdiction. Hum argues that the shared-cost contractual relationship between Ottawa and the provinces has prevented individual provinces from making adjustments to the CAP to extend services to the working poor and to deliver services more efficiently. (The irony is that the restrictive clauses were inserted at the insistence of some provinces.) Rand Dyck (1976) argues that the agreement to establish the CAP represented the highest attainment of cooperative federalism, but Hum regards it as severely flawed. The difference is that while Dyck is focussing on the process, Hum is primarily concerned with the values represented by the substance of the compromise that emerged from the federal-provincial process. Analytically, of course, the same problems of compromise can emerge out of departmental conflict in a unitary state. Indeed, Donald Savoie (1981a, pp. 152-53) and others (Jenkin 1983, pp. 170-71) argue that intradepartmental conflict in Ottawa is as important as intergovernmental disagreement in blocking the development of coordinated economic policies. The bilateral approach in vogue under the General Development Agreements led to special status for each province, with damaging spillovers for other provinces and no coordinated effort.

It seems clear from the case studies that shared jurisdiction limits the kinds of policies considered. As Banting (1982, pp. 77-78) suggests, there is an inescapable tension between the logic of planning and the logic of federalism which promotes incrementalism and limits the possible areas of agreement. For example, the inherent conflicts in the Canadian federal system have made agreement on matters of fiscal policy and economic development extremely difficult (Smiley, 1980, p. 185ff.). In particular, intergovernmental relations are underdeveloped in the industrial policy area because there is "an underlying conflict between the nature of the decisions required in industrial policy and the kinds of substantive collaboration possible within the intergovernmental framework" (Jenkin,

1983, p. 141). Perhaps the most important issue here is the extent to which this limitation is inherent in executive federalism itself or only in the form that emerged from the erection of the Canadian welfare state. This issue is covered in more detail in our discussion of conflict management.

It is interesting to note that case studies in such diverse areas as education, health, social welfare and energy policy suggest that interprovincial and federal-provincial disagreements have narrowed the range of policy alternatives that each level can realistically consider (Chandler and Chandler, 1979, p. 190; Leman, 1980, p. 283). This appears to be true not only in policy areas where jurisdiction is shared, but also in any field where a consensus is required for effective decisions, as, for example, under shared-cost programs.

The view that the process promotes attention to fiscal and jurisdictional issues rather than substantive concerns is very widespread. With respect to energy policy, for example, the focus on division of revenues has drawn attention away from substantive issues of development and taxation policy (Campbell et al., 1976). In the offshore minerals cases, substantial resources have been devoted to determining which level of government should make development policy rather than to what its central elements should be (Caplan, 1970; Laxer, 1983, p. 3). In the health field as well, the process has focussed on fiscal issues, rather than substantive concerns, such as the balance between preventive and curative medicine, thus rendering the system slow to react to new challenges (Weller and Manga, 1983). A similar pattern has been discerned in fisheries policy (McCorquodale, 1983) and education (Ivany, 1981, p. 111). This tendency to subordinate substantive concerns to issues of jurisdiction and revenue or expenditure is most prevalent in areas of shared jurisdiction or contractual joint programs. Where jurisdiction is exclusive, some observers argue, debate tends to have a more substantive focus. With respect to health care, for example, it has been argued that ideological issues are more often raised when jurisdiction is mainly provincial. When it is federal, regional or fiscal issues are most often at issue (Weller and Manga, 1983, pp. 240–41).

In areas of provincial jurisdiction with national implications, such as education or health, the barriers to effective national planning have been noted in several case studies. An Organization for Economic Co-operation and Development (OECD) study (1977, pp. 424–27; also Ivany and Manley-Casimir, 1981) argues that lack of national coordination in the education field can be blamed in part on the fact that the federal-provincial process focusses attention on cost-sharing and regional equity at the expense of agreement on objectives. The study argues that the predominance of provincial jurisdiction over education has been costly in terms of the country's capacity to compete in the international economy because a lack of national planning has slowed innovation while weakening national consciousness. While the potential exists for this weakness to be overcome by federal-provincial or interprovincial agreement, the record is not good.

The Politics of Regionalism

Several case studies note that the politics of regionalism (reinforced by provincial jurisdiction) creates a tension between regional equity and the pursuit of excellence or international competitiveness. In post-secondary education, for example, efforts have been dispersed, causing duplication of highly specialized facilities and the loss of momentum that results from the absence of a "critical mass" of specialists in a single centre of excellence (OECD, 1977, p. 421). Of course, such a pattern can also be discerned in areas of federal predominance such as broadcasting and funding of cultural activities. Regional considerations are also powerful in many unitary states, and efforts to centralize jurisdiction, even if politically feasible, might not change these patterns very much. (In any case, new communication technologies may well make the critical mass argument obsolete.)

There is, however, reason to believe that the uncertainties and delays resulting from the difficulties of rapid decision making inherent in executive federalism have had important indirect effects on policy. For example, in the energy and resource development areas, several cases demonstrate that federal-provincial conflict delayed development or slowed investment (Caplan, 1970, pp. 58–61; Tupper, 1982, pp. 82–83; Safarian, 1980, p. 19). Indeed, it has been argued that the uncertainty caused by such conflict over jurisdiction or policy slowed investment in related areas, such as high-energy manufacturing (Safarian, 1980, p. 19).

From a provincial perspective, the impact of patterns of jurisdiction is equally significant. On the negative side, there are many studies which argue that federal-provincial agreements are among the barriers to the development of a comprehensive program of integrated social services. This viewpoint is related to the argument that shared-cost programs distort provincial priorities. While this is undoubtedly true, many such programs were begun at the instigation of some provinces and many of the barriers to program adjustment stemmed from safeguards demanded by provinces in the first place. In addition, other factors, such as interdepartmental conflicts and the revenue squeeze of the past decade, are also factors in the failure of the system to develop more efficient and effective social service programs (Glaser, 1984, pp. 319–22; Leman, 1980, pp. 224–26). With respect to shared-cost programs, there is a tension between effective administration at the provincial level and the preservation of national standards. Such contractual relationships generally impede integration of programs and rapid adjustment to changing needs as a result of the rigidities noted above. The obvious solutions, unconditional block grants or transfer of tax sources to the provinces to provide more flexibility, lead to the erosion of national standards.

A number of case studies support the general proposition, derived from the origins of federalism itself, that provincial jurisdiction is a major factor in protecting regional interests. In areas of federal predominance, there are numerous examples of cases where federal agencies have been insensitive to regional concerns. For example, in terms of new telecommunications services, the inability of federal regulators to respond to provincial needs, e.g., for cultural development or socio-economic development, has delayed innovations and weakened provincial efforts to provide relevant services to smaller centres or the family farm (Fletcher and Fletcher, 1979; also Woodrow et al. 1980; Buchan et al., 1982). When one examines the Columbia River case, it seems clear that, without significant jurisdiction as a lever, the British Columbia government would have found it difficult to get a hearing for its vital interests (Swainson, 1979, pp. 357–58). Certainly, many Albertans feel that their interests would have been much less well served without the leverage of significant jurisdiction in the various energy negotiations.

In the economic policy sphere, the existence of provincial governments with significant economic jurisdiction has:

- fostered interprovincial competition for investment, which has, in turn, limited provincial tax rates; weakened the federal government's capacity to deal with foreign corporations; restricted environmental protection; and weakened labour laws (including health and safety protection for workers);
- limited the capacity of the federal government to reduce regional disparities;
- made economic planning difficult, thereby weakening the country's capacity to meet international competition;
- inhibited the development of trust between governments, preoccupied with dealing with one another, and the private sector, thereby reducing international competitiveness (though increasingly both levels are assisting with international trade);
- limited the policy choices open to both levels; and
- increased lobbying and monitoring costs and uncertainty, including the risk of being caught in an intergovernmental cross-fire.[9]

In some areas of predominantly federal jurisdiction, it seems clear that federal insensitivity to provincial concerns has fanned the flames of regionalism. It is Darling's view (1980, pp. 235–42) that exclusive federal jurisdiction over freight rates combined with strong regional sentiments and an unresponsive federal government to create a major federal-provincial issue. One can find similar examples in telecommunications and broadcasting policy. Federalism has certainly contributed to these differences, but the real issue is the substance of federal government policies.

In purely administrative terms, there is little doubt that divided jurisdiction leads to duplication, gaps in program coverage, conflicting regulations, buck-passing and so on, creating problems for citizens and conflicts between governments. However, the administrative problems created by divided jurisdiction are not unique to federal systems; all modern governments face problems of geographical and interdepartmental coordination. In a federal system, they are just more visible (Banting, 1982, p. 180).

Winners and Losers: Systematic Biases?

The proposition that federalism is likely to advantage some groups at the expense of others seems, in principle, highly plausible. In practice, however, systematic biases in the federal-provincial process as such are difficult to detect. This is especially true with complex issues involving multiple actors. In addition, those most affected often had little say in the process. Furthermore, since federal-provincial agreements frequently undergo incremental changes in operation, the short-term winners may not always be able to hold their gains over the longer term. Nevertheless, it is possible to report some judgments about the systematic biases of the federal-provincial process and to make some assessments based on the case studies.

At the most general level, it appears that, among interest groups, the winners (business and professional groups) and losers (the working poor) tend to be those one would expect from the general literature on the politics of liberal democracies (e.g., Presthus, 1973). The exception here is local industry, which appears to benefit from barriers to interprovincial trade and to gain from federal efforts to curry regional favour. The federal government appears to have lost some legitimacy in recent years, with the provinces taking more policy initiatives.

With respect to governments, the conventional wisdom appears to be that the federal government, in normal circumstances, has a decided edge in bargaining power. Its chief bargaining levers are usually identified as its relative wealth (in the context of the spending power) and the widely recognized need for national coordination in areas of provincial jurisdiction (such as education and highways). The federal government's constitutional authority (including residual and emergency powers) and its access to expertise are given less importance than in earlier periods. However, the growth of bilateralism means that the federal government does have a decided advantage derived from its expertise and fiscal resources in dealing with the poorer provinces. The wealthier provinces are more able to resist fiscal initiatives, primarily because they can forego the conditional grants, but also because they have more planning and political resources. Traditionally, the main bargaining lever for the provinces has been their jurisdiction in areas of political and social importance, such as education and social services. The wealthier provinces now compete effectively in both planning and mobilization of political support.[10]

In recent times, most observers would agree that the provinces have held their own. Smiley (1980, p. 254) has expressed concern that the capacity of the federal government to effect interprovincial and interpersonal redistribution has declined as a result of changes in the federal-provincial balance. Such a change would indicate that the richer provinces and social groups have been winners at the expense of those with fewer resources. In bilateral negotiations, the provinces seem likely to have significant influence when federal officials are "deconcentrated" and given responsibility for programs in a specific province (Savoie, 1981a, p. 142).

CANADIAN COMMON MARKET

The extent to which provincial interests have been able to secure the erection of impediments to the Canadian common market suggests that certain interests have been winners and others losers. Local producers, for example, clearly benefit from preferential purchasing policies, the operation of provincial marketing boards and liquor board pricing policies.

INDUSTRIAL STRATEGY

With respect to industrial strategy, Jenkin (1983, pp. 170–71) argues that the federal government has been losing power over industrial strategy and that its failure to achieve agreement with the provinces is a significant factor. However, as noted above, he attributes this failure to the federal government's inability to agree internally on the direction an industrial strategy should take. It is Jenkin's view that the provinces have been able to move into the vacuum to develop their own (partial) industrial strategies but that they suffer some costly spillover effects from the absence of a national strategy.

In the private sector, the interests who might gain from an industrial strategy, such as "high tech" industries and processors of natural resources, are losers. Those who oppose such a strategy — industries, perhaps, which might be phased out — are winners, at least in the short run. Perhaps those with good access to provincial governments are less concerned than those operating nationally.

A number of the richer provinces have industrial strategies. There is, in this development, the obvious risk of countervailing or competitive strategies. There is, as well, the probability that provincial autonomy weakens the capacity of the federal government to deal effectively with foreign capital (Stevenson, G., 1979, pp. 101, 242–44) and in international negotiations (Thorburn, 1984, pp. 242ff.). Thorburn (idem.) also takes the view that both levels of government have been hampered in dealing with the private sector by the absence of intergovernmental agreement.

PENSIONS

In his pension case, Simeon (1973, pp. 256–59) concludes that Ottawa gained its basic objective, i.e., a national contributory pension plan with the same provisions for all Canadians, but it also gave up a good deal, especially in turning funds over to the provinces and restricting its freedom of action by agreeing to a veto power on amendments for the provinces. While some federal program specialists felt that the plan was, in substance, better than Ottawa's original proposal, and while intergovernmental officials were glad to have headed off a serious clash with Quebec, the latter were concerned that the agreement had weakened the status of Ottawa and strengthened the provinces. Quebec was the clearest winner, obtaining its own plan (with the political visibility and recognition of special status which that entailed) and most of the substantive changes it wanted. Ontario gained least but saved face with the opting out and veto provisions. The other provinces obtained the fund, and most also welcomed the broader coverage. The Ottawa-Quebec compromise satisfied Ottawa's concern for national unity, Quebec's demand for special status and the other provinces' desire for funds. The income security lobby gained an important new program, while the private pension industry lost some of its market (though this does not seem to have been highly significant in the long term).

ENERGY POLICY

In other policy areas, there was disagreement regarding winners and losers. In the energy field, for example, some authors (Berry, 1974) felt that the petroleum industry and affiliated interest groups were losers in the negotiations of the 1970s; others, however, saw them as winners (Pratt, 1976; Laxer, 1983). Berry's view was that the federal government favoured consumer interests and, therefore, abandoned the industry (with which it had previously had good relations) and the producing provinces. Smiley (1976, pp. 71–72) suggests that votes are often more important to governments than corporate money. The federal government's commitment to equalization also tied it into assisting the consuming provinces. Pratt argues that the oil industry was able to use its economically strategic position and influence on the governments of the producing provinces to wring unjustified concessions from Ottawa in the Syncrude deal, with the taxpayers being the big losers. Laxer does not dispute Berry's view that the oil industry was a loser in the pricing negotiations of the early 1970s, as the negotiations came to focus on the division of revenues between the producing provinces and Ottawa, but he argues (1983) that it rebounded to be a big winner in the 1980s.

SOCIAL WELFARE POLICY

In the social welfare/income security field, the consensus is that business-type groups have been able to hold back the expansion of the welfare state (Armitage, 1975, pp. 69–73; Bryden, 1974; Hum, 1983; Van Loon, 1979).

As noted above, Banting suggests that the federal structure has had a conservative effect in this area. The critics argue that the federal system has permitted business groups to limit the role of the public sector (preserving a profitable place for private medical insurance and pensions, for example) and to restrict the degree of redistribution in the system (using some provincial governments as agents). While plausible, there is no compelling evidence to support this view. Indeed, Canada has developed a relatively progressive welfare state (Banting, 1982, chap. 6).

COMMUNICATIONS POLICY

The case studies of communications policy (Babe, 1974, pp. 186ff.; Murray 1983, pp. 142–45) also suggest that industry has a better chance of influencing the federal-provincial process than do consumer groups. The closed nature of the process favours groups with greater access and resources. This generalization holds also for the legal aid negotiations (Poel, 1983) and pensions. In these areas, however, public demand tends to have an important influence on politicians' behaviour. This factor has clearly influenced the development of income security programs (Banting, 1982, chap. 6) and social services generally, as well as encouraging the provision of accelerated coverage and broader choice in broadcasting (Murray, 1983, pp. 142–45). However, bureaucratic domination of the process, which tends to occur in certain technical areas (especially in bilateral negotiations), weakens political (and, therefore, public) input. Media attention is obviously a factor here. Certain minority groups, like the "working poor," have limited access in any case (Hum, 1983).

In the communications policy area, the stakes were high in the negotiations throughout the 1970s and early 1980s. The federal government was seeking a broad consensus on how to deal with the new communications technology in terms of meeting social needs, protecting Canadian broadcasters and the culture industries, and satisfying public demand. At the same time,the provinces wanted more regulatory control to meet public demand for more services and to promote various ideological positions. The cable industry wanted to open new markets and get permission to provide new services. The results were essentially a compromise — neither open skies nor full cultural protectionism — but the "freedom of choice" proponents made some advance: "Those who value local programming and regional and cultural diversity have been encouraged; those who see the broadcasting system as the unifying purveyor of a single Canadian culture, discouraged" (Murray, 1983, p. 138). The cable companies apparently won the mandate as Canada's defence against completely open skies, breaking the broadcasters' monopoly of influence over the Canadian Radio-television and Telecommunications Commission (CRTC). The provincial input might have been helpful to them, since some provinces give them more attention than the broadcasters, but the Department of Communications' input was also significant. The ultimate CRTC decisions determined who would get pay-TV and northern service licences. The public got some new services. The report was seen as a clear win for Ontario, which had wanted an opening up of competition. The key factors in winning approval for new services appear to have been the capacity to meet the compromise criteria which emerged from the process: new services, some protection of Canadian culture, national services in both official languages, and so on (ibid., p. 89). Having been given access to influence in a predominantly federal area of jurisdiction, the provinces gained some policy victories but lost the jurisdictional battle. The industry had to pay the costs of dealing with both levels (ibid., pp. 140–41). This case is typical of many, in the sense that assessing winners and losers is not easy.

EDUCATION POLICY

In the field of education, there is clear evidence that the form of federal-provincial arrangements can be important. For example, post-secondary institutions lost some autonomy and, probably, funding when the federal government agreed to provincial demands to provide unconditional funding. This gave provincial governments considerably greater leverage in dealing with post-secondary institutions (Stevenson, H., 1981, p. 18; Ivany, 1981, pp. 110–16). In theory, at least, however, it increased their accountability, since they were no longer able to play one level off against the other.

Bruce Doern (1977, p. 158) suggests that the process is more "professionally open" than "democratically open" and that, therefore, professional groups (lawyers, doctors) have a better chance of having their interests taken into account than consumers. It seems clear that provincial predominance in the health field has given physicians more influence than they might have had in dealing with the federal government. In Kwavnick's view (1972, p. 213), the Canadian Labour Congress is able to influence the process only when its demands are compatible with government policy, when its support can be used as a resource in the bargaining process.

It is a plausible thesis that interdependent federalism disadvantages groups with fewer resources — notably, consumers groups and unorganized workers — because of the costs of lobbying at both levels and the multiple veto points in the system (Brunelle, 1982). However, hard evidence of policy impact is difficult to come by. The broader assertion that the competing federal and provincial states provide support for a growing bourgeoisie with interests tied to the growth of state intervention is also appealing (Stevenson, G., 1981, p. 127; Cairns, 1979, pp. 184–85). However, recent tendencies for a reduction of state activity suggest that it may have been a developmental stage rather than a trend. A similarly plausible assertion, "that the working class have paid a very high price for provincial jurisdiction over industrial relations" as a result of the competition for investment (Stevenson, G., 1981, p. 129) is also hard to confirm or deny on the basis of the evidence available. It is, however, hard to dismiss the notion that interprovincial competition for investment and the dependence of many provinces on a few key industries (combined with a significant degree of provincial jurisdiction), has helped those industries to weaken government regulations or to gain assistance that might not have been forthcoming from a more distant and autonomous federal government. Labour and environmental groups often feel disadvantaged at the provincial level.

The Impact of Federalism: Assessing the Literature

In short, it seems clear that changes in jurisdiction and in the form of federal-provincial cooperation, from cost sharing to block grants, for example, often do advantage some groups over others. Certainly, federal jurisdiction encourages national organizations, whether lobby groups or business corporations, and discourages regional ones. This is easily demonstrated with respect to interest groups (Dawson, 1975; Kwavnick, 1975) and seems to be true also for businesses (for example, cable ventures and trucking). Provincial restrictions on professional affiliations and credentials are also significant. It may also be true that federal programs tend to be more redistributive than provincial programs (which, if true, may be a function of resources). In general, however, aside from questions of mobility and organization, clear-cut patterns are difficult to discern.

Some trends can be identified, however. It can be said that in recent years, the poorer provinces and classes have been relative losers, with the poorer provinces losing autonomy (except in certain bilateral situations) and the federal government losing capacity to establish national programs and to redistribute wealth. More generally, the federal government has lost some legitimacy. The barriers to the common market appear to benefit local industries and to weaken national ones, though there is some disagreement as to how significant this tendency is. Certainly, territorially organized groups seem to have some advantage in areas of significant provincial jurisdiction, especially those whose interests are important to the provincial economy. Consumer groups often appear to do better at the federal level. In general, however, the winners and losers seem to vary by issue, as well as by jurisdiction, and outcomes are also influenced by short-term political factors. Of course, in many cases, the preferences of the analyst are determining.[11]

In the end, the policy outcomes of federal-provincial interaction reflect the political will of the participants. Scott (1976) tells us that economic modelling gives us no definitive answer on most jurisdictional questions, leaving jurisdiction as a matter of politics and not economics. This presumably means that federal-provincial economic decisions will reflect considerations of equity more than those of efficiency, and, as Smiley (1976) reminds us, federalism is designed neither for efficiency nor for majority rule.

It must be noted throughout this analysis that, despite the problems of divided jurisdiction, our system has delivered many effective programs. Indeed, in telecommunications, jurisdiction has been effectively shared, and the resulting system is one of the best in the world (Schultz, 1982, p. 43). In this case, better federal-provincial coordination may be needed to cope with advancing technological change, so that attention to that process is fully justified. Indeed, many of the problems attributed to federalism in Canada are, in fact, present in non-federal systems as well and reflect difficulties that are endemic to modern industrial states.

In examining the relationship between interests mobilized and policy outcomes, we concluded that the structures of federalism have their greatest impact on policy outcomes when there are major regional differences in policy preference or economic interest. In such cases, provincial governments often have both electoral and economic incentives to represent regional interests, while federal officials must try to minimize negative electoral consequences by balancing the interests involved. As a consequence, policy issues where decisions appear to have differential territorial impact (that is, where winners and losers can easily be identified in territorial terms) are difficult to resolve through the federal-provincial process. Banting (1982, chap. 6) argues that territorial interests have not been favoured at the expense of class interest in income security policy, for example. However, it seems clear that economic policies have been sensitive to regional interests. The federal government's attempts to balance differing territorial interests, as in the energy and transportation cases, tend to leave most groups dissatisfied. As noted above, however, where there is a broad national consensus, federalism tends to influence the timing and precise structure of the programs developed but not their basic principles. It should be noted here that the federal structure does not create regional differences so much as it mobilizes them politically. This mobilization of regional sentiment occurs regardless of jurisdiction over the issue, as the activities of the provinces in areas of federal jurisdiction, such as communications policy, make clear. The political costs for the federal government of deciding in favour of the interests of one region to the disadvantage of another are as great in areas of its own jurisdiction as in those where provincial leverage is significant. The only notable difference is that decisions are more easily taken and enforced.

It seems clear that divided jurisdiction does tend to slow innovation and to reduce the scope of programs in many areas. In general, as Banting argues (ibid., p. 141), federalism is a conservative force, especially with respect to the creation and expansion of costly social programs, except where intergovernmental competition exists. Competition between Ottawa and the provinces (or a province) for visibility, legitimacy and jurisdiction can be seen as a major motive for a number of policy innovations. When one level of government creates new programs, the other level feels pressure to innovate in order to maintain its legitimacy or to support its jurisdictional claims. Banting (ibid., p. 174) argues that the provinces learned in the 1960s that "no government can defend disputed jurisdiction effectively unless it is prepared to utilize it aggressively." Similarly, fear of loss of significant contact with citizens (manifest in Ottawa from the mid-1960s on) led to new federal programs designed to develop new constituencies (Smiley, 1980, pp. 109–10; Careless, 1977, p. 206). Competition among the provinces for investment, however, can limit the development and expansion of social programs, even as it stimulates the creation of economic incentives and infrastructural development. Clearly, divided jurisdiction has made the creation of national industrial strategy more difficult and has led to an absence of effective action in certain policy areas.

Although there is considerable disagreement in the literature, the consensus seems to be that federalism does make a difference. Divided jurisdiction influences the scope, the structure, and the pace of introduction in a wide variety of fields. It effectively blocks certain kinds of policies where interregional consensus is not possible. Jurisdictional issues are given special attention in the system. Nevertheless, the system rarely frustrates the popular will, and structural tinkering will improve its operation only if other conditions are right. The effort is worthwhile, however, if it makes the normal operation of the federal-provincial process more effective.

As Banting suggests, federalism often appears more important than it is. Structural change, therefore, may not have the positive impact expected. No amount of constitutional engineering can alter the existence of deep-seated differences in regional economic interest and policy preference. Nevertheless, reforms can aim to reduce the barriers to effective decision making in areas without such differences and to facilitate the framing of issues in non-confrontational ways. While disentanglement of jurisdiction might have some benefits in minimizing the negative consequences of interdependence, and changes in central institutions might reduce regional feelings of powerlessness, there remains a range of policy issues that must be dealt with through intergovernmental negotiations.

Conflict Management

Stating the Problem

The literature on Canadian federalism contains many propositions related to conflict management in the system, most offered as general prescriptions for more harmonious intergovernmental relations. A careful examination of the various case studies, however, suggests that there are no panaceas. The most promising approaches to effective conflict management appear to vary according to the pattern of jurisdiction, the type of issue, and the nature of the conflict.

The central assumption of the analysis that follows is that intergovernmental conflict is inevitable in our system, and effective management of that conflict is absolutely essential for good government. At the same time, the high level of conflict in a number of visible areas of federal-provincial relations has not only increased the difficulty of operating the many vital cooperative programs; it has also posed a threat to the legitimacy of the system. As Harold D. Clarke and his colleagues (1984, p. 43) have put it: "Survey evidence strongly indicates that dissatisfaction with the operation of the federal system [during the 1970s] was not confined to provincial political elites attempting to enhance their power and prestige but extended to the general public as well." Their public opinion surveys show that large numbers of Canadians in every region believed that their region was disadvantaged by existing federal arrangements. Specific dissatisfaction was expressed with the way in which the system operated, and the data make it clear that more respondents were dissatisfied with the federal government (41 percent) than with the provincial governments (25 percent) (ibid., pp. 43–48, Figs. 2–3 and 2–4). This public response to intergovernmental conflict raises concerns about the effects of apparent federal-provincial deadlock on the legitimacy of the system in general and of the federal government in particular.

The importance of effective conflict management has increased as the federal system has evolved. The system has developed from one in which the federal government's greater expertise and resources allowed it to influence provincial policy in areas of provincial jurisdiction to one in which each level requires the cooperation of the other in a wide range of areas (Van Loon and Whittington, 1981, pp. 530–31). The postwar focus on social programs and highway construction, where federal fiscal resources and expertise, backed by public demand for progress and national standards, were matched against provincial jurisdiction, gradually gave way to broader fiscal and constitutional issues. It has become clear that the federal government can no longer regulate the economy by unilateral action because the provinces and municipalities control more than half of public-sector expenditures and do a great deal of independent borrowing. The federal government must, therefore, seek cooperation even in areas of its own jurisdiction. The provinces equally find themselves requiring federal cooperation and (usually) financial assistance as they embark on economic programs. As Smiley (1980, p. 92) has put it: "The ever-broadening scope of public decision brings into being new circumstances where federal and provincial objectives must somehow be harmonized if public policy is to be effective." A relevant current example is job creation. He goes on (p. 93):

Contemporary levels of taxation, along with the deliberate use of fiscal policy by the federal and provincial governments to secure employment, growth and price stability objectives, mean that there is an increasingly intense competition for tax sources and the expenditure policies of each level have direct and indirect consequences for the other.

The pattern of interdependence is clear and, as noted above, the costs of failure to manage conflict effectively are significant. The promotion of economic development, an increasing priority for all governments, is so multidimensional that failure to achieve effective federal-provincial cooperation would doom many efforts to failure, thwarted by countervailing or uncoordinated policies.

The 1970s were marked by increasing overlap of government activities: by federal involvement in areas of provincial jurisdiction (as in medical care); by unclear or shared jurisdiction (culture, communications, regulation of insurance, consumer protection, development and sale of natural resources); and by provincial concern with federal policies (banking, tariffs, transportation, broadcasting, monetary management) with respect to their own policies and as representatives of regional interests (ibid., pp. 93–94). These developments (along with the sovereignty issue in Quebec and the constitutional reform issue) placed unprecedented strains on the system of conflict management.

The Roots of Conflict

In examining the process of conflict management in the Canadian federal system, it will be helpful to try first to uncover the roots of conflict. The most fundamental are, of course, those reflecting the linguistic and regional-economic cleavages in the country. While these cleavages colour much federal-provincial interaction, most conflicts have a narrower focus. At the functional level of interaction, the stakes tend to be allocation of costs, control of expenditures, regulatory powers, or substantive priorities. The increasing involvement of Ottawa and most provinces in economic planning and regulation has created overlaps and conflict. At the political level, issues of jurisdiction, priorities among program options, ideology, the relative importance and status of governments, and electoral considerations (maximizing credit and minimizing blame) come into play.

In policy and process terms, the relatively high level of conflict in our system can be attributed to :

• the constitutional division of powers;
• some of the central attributes of executive federalism;
• the increase in interventionist policies at both levels of government, particularly in the larger provinces; and

- a shift in the focus of federal-provincial relations from social to economic issues (Simeon, 1973, chap. 2; Smiley, 1980, pp. 4–6; Banting, 1982, p. 139; Doern and Phidd, 1983, p. 132).

Let us briefly examine each of these in turn.

CONSTITUTIONAL DIVISION OF POWERS

First, the constitutional division of powers allocates significant exclusive powers to each level of government, with the result that in many areas incentives to cooperate are lacking. (A wider range of concurrent powers might provide such incentives, perhaps at the expense of responsiveness to external interests and accountability.) In areas such as energy policy, both levels of government have impressive constitutional resources. Indeed, this is true of economic policy in general. In addition, the relatively even balance of constitutional authority is matched by a similarly even balance of political power, so that it is difficult for either level to achieve policy dominance.

EXECUTIVE FEDERALISM

The processes of executive federalism have frequently been identified as a second major impediment to effective conflict management in the system and as generators of conflict themselves. The cooperative federalism which developed in the postwar period was marked by program-oriented negotiations among officials with similar professional and programmatic goals to resolve conflicts arising from the organizational imperatives of the different levels of government. Their interests cut across, rather than reinforced, jurisdictional rivalries. During the 1970s, this pattern of interaction was supplanted in significant ways by what Donald Smiley has called executive federalism. Executive federalism involved central agents and senior ministers negotiating more fundamental issues. The focus has tended to be on power and prestige and on protecting jurisdictional turf rather than on function (Smiley, 1980, chap. 4; Stevenson, G., 1979, pp. 198–200).[12]

As Smiley (1980, p. 91) has put it, "In the Canadian system of government the executive has a very wide discretion — freedom from effective control of the elected legislature, of party organizations and, in most circumstances, of private interest groups." This is compounded by the federal system: divided jurisdiction adds complexity, and the requirements of effective bargaining add to secrecy (federal-provincial documents are exempt from the access to information legislation at the federal level). The policy process is dominated by ministers and senior officials. Simeon (1973, p. 38) argues that the shift from functional (or cooperative) to executive federalism made agreements more difficult:

If it is assumed that political leaders . . . have fewer areas of common interest than officials concerned with particular programmes, then such channelling of disagreements to the political level should increase the level of conflict. The values of the central officials predominate over those of programme officials and the values of the two groups often differ.

Considerations of jurisdiction, institutional status and prestige mix in with substantive program issues. The essentially political nature of executive federalism is summed up by Smiley (1980, p. 116):

> In summary, the institutions and processes of executive federalism are disposed towards conflict rather than harmony. Federal-provincial summitry along with the related phenomenon of administrative rationalization has weakened the capacity of the system to make piece-meal and incremental adjustments according to the norms of scientific and professional groupings. Even more crucially, the pursuit of jurisdictional autonomy increasingly takes place outside a shared acceptance of constitutional and legal norms about the respective powers of the two orders of government.

INTERVENTIONIST POLICIES

Third on our list and perhaps the most important factor in the heightened level of conflict over the past 15 years has been an increase in interventionist policies at both levels of government. In particular, the great increase in provincial aspirations to manage their own economic and cultural developments inevitably has led to clashes of priorities and disputes over the allocation of costs and over revenues generated by natural resource development. In a very real way, the increased level of provincial government activity transformed regional grievances over the exercise of traditional federal tax and regulatory powers into federal-provincial issues. This was compounded by the fact that federal regulatory activities frequently demonstrated insensitivity to regional concerns (and to the particular aspirations of provincial governments). We found many examples of such insensitivity in the case literature in areas of predominantly federal jurisdiction, such as communication and aspects of transportation policy. Westmacott (1973, p. 463) has observed that:

> The consultative procedures and the channels of communication utilized by the federal government in its dealings with the provinces in areas of federal jurisdiction do in fact differ from the channels of communication and consultative procedures employed by the federal government in areas of provincial jurisdiction.

Neither level of government has been very willing to establish regularized consultation on matters within its own jurisdiction, despite widespread acknowledgment of spillover effects.

SHIFT FROM SOCIAL TO ECONOMIC ISSUES

Finally, the shift in the focus of federal-provincial relations from the issue of provision of social services to that of promotion of economic development also appears to have increased federal-provincial conflict. As Alan Cairns (1979, p. 190) has put it, increased provincial government activity in fiscal policy, economic growth (including provincial 'protectionism' and international economic relations) has led to a "competition of objectives capable of frustrating the aims of both levels of government in such fundamental policy areas as energy, resource development, foreign investment, full employment and inflation." Garth Stevenson (1979, p. 108) has summed up the limitations of federalism as an allocative mechanism: "Whether producers or consumers benefit from resource developments, whether industries are established in the East or in the West, whether jobs go to anglophones or francophones — these are not the types of questions to which cooperative federalism provides answers." As noted above, cooperative federalism led to agreements on education, medical care, welfare, and pensions, providing social benefits not readily achievable by other methods. It worked much less well as a mechanism for dealing with sharply regional issues, such as energy pricing (1973–74 and 1980) or diffuse constitutional issues (from Quebec's demands for a new deal to patriation of the Constitution), or for making policies to cope with intractable economic problems, such as stagflation.

It appears also that the introduction of social programs is easier than their subsequent adaptation and reform. It has proved difficult to adjust the pension plan and the Canada Assistance Plan to deal with unforeseen problems and new realities because the effort required to gain consensus is too great for the political rewards involved. The extent to which these problems are the result of the hostility and mistrust built up around the new issues or of inherent defects in the process is a vital question. As will be seen, the case literature suggests that both factors are involved.

Three Types of Conflict

In this analysis, it is important to distinguish three types of conflict:

1. those that are inherently territorial but not directly related to federalism;
2. those that derive from the federal system itself; and
3. those that are not inherently territorial but are mobilized or generated by the federal system.

Although all are related and may be present in any conflict, each has somewhat different implications for the conflict management process.[13]

GENERICALLY REGIONAL

First, regional conflicts which affect the federal system may be derived from regionally discriminatory policies or from locational decisions (or, indeed, from the failure of the federal government to intervene to influence private sector locational decisions). The federal government must choose locations for major facilities and, given its commitment to reducing regional disparities, is inevitably involved in the locational decisions of many industries. In addition, subsidies to particular industries often have regional implications, given the inevitably uneven distribution of such industries. Tariff protection for manufacturing and the Crow's Nest Pass freight rates are two historical examples. Oil pricing decisions also have clear regional significance. Language policies, though communal in motivation, have territorial implications because of the uneven distribution of francophones. Conflicts over issues of this sort would arise under any political system, and their articulation could take many forms.

SYSTEMICALLY GENERATED

In addition, federalism itself can create federal-provincial issues, as provincial leaders seek to mobilize regional grievances by identifying and highlighting differential regional issues. The existence of powerful sub-units helps to focus resentment and transform regional grievances into intergovernmental issues. Provincial leaders often seem to have the advantage over federal spokesmen in framing issues in regional rather than other, equally appropriate terms. Both levels of government often attempt to mobilize interest group activity in support of their respective positions. Provincial leaders naturally tend to favour groups that frame issues in regional terms. A number of observers have noted that there is sufficient economic and cultural complementarity among the regions to permit many issues now seen as regional to be framed in non-territorial terms. For those who wish to improve conflict management in the federal system, the problem is to develop counterweights to the strong political incentives for provincial leaders to see policies primarily in terms of their territorial impact (Jenkin, 1983, pp. 87–88; Darling, 1980, pp. 235–41).

GENUINE INTERGOVERNMENTAL CONFLICT

In addition, of course, there are real intergovernmental conflicts of interest. Some of these derive from differences in provincial fiscal capacities, which pit the have provinces against the have-not provinces and, often, against the federal government, given its commitment to equalization. Others, such as oil pricing, range producing provinces against consuming provinces. These are issues in which interests represented by particular governments are in conflict. A second class of issues, reckoned by some analysts to have special importance in federal-provincial conflicts, are those in which the governments themselves have directly conflicting interests. These include property rights (for example, the ownership and control of offshore minerals), taxing powers, revenue sharing, transfer payments and other policies which shift the cost of programs from one level to the other, as well as matters of jurisdiction. At a more general level, there have been increasing clashes over strategies for economic development and the appropriate role of government.

Perspective on the Problem

It would be unwise to assume, of course, that the federal-provincial arena is used only to resolve conflicts. Federal-provincial interactions may be initiated simply to ratify an agreement upon which consensus already exists, or a meeting may be called simply to exchange information. The federal government might also wish to persuade the provinces to act in certain ways within their jurisdiction, as with the public-sector restraint programs of recent years. In functional areas, governments may be involved in cooperation (where jurisdiction is shared) or coordination (where jurisdiction is joint or overlaps) (Careless, 1977, p. 187). As Murray (1983, p. 3) has put it, "There are many objectives in federal-provincial negotiations — to exchange information, to generate policy alternatives, to assess inter-jurisdictional consequences of policies, and to harmonize the exercise of jurisdiction by both levels of government."

Similarly, it would be quite misleading, as our case studies demonstrate, to take at face value the public perception that federal-provincial relations have been generally conflictual and ineffective over the past two decades. The case studies document a large number of agreements and on-going programs, as well as areas of conflict and immobilism. An examination of the statistics on federal-provincial interactions confirms the warning issued by Dupré and his colleagues (Dupré et al., 1973, p. 236; Jenkin, 1983, p. 104) that the rise of summit federalism, which dominates the public agenda, has not been accompanied by a decline in functional relations. Therefore, any serious examination of federalism and the policy process must take the full range of interactions into account. In particular, it is important to note that these functional relationships have made it possible for many of the country's important social, cultural and educational programs to continue effective operation at a time of apparent intergovernmental crisis. As Donald J. Savoie has recently noted (1984b, p. 13), there is a high rate of interaction among federal and provincial officials (about 1,000 meetings per year), and they are generally successful in operating joint programs harmoniously and in coordinating activities in their independent but overlapping spheres of responsibility. It is the hard political issues that generate so much visible conflict, obscuring the underpinning of cooperation.

How realistic is it to expect that the existing system can be restructured to meet current problems? Alan Cairns (1979, p. 193) has expressed some skepticism regarding the prospects for reforming the system:

> Whether it is even technically feasible to devise a federal system capable of containing strong governments at both levels, of facilitating effective administration by each level where possible, and effective joint policies where unavoidable, is open to question.

We are more optimistic than Cairns.

It is the thesis of this study that joint policies (or at least parallel ones) are unavoidable over a wide spectrum of government activity and that, given due attention to the particular characteristics of each policy area, mechanisms and approaches are available to manage intergovernmental conflict effectively. The case studies suggest a considerable range of possible reforms.

The principal task is to frame issues in ways conducive to solutions, bearing in mind that some conflicts are so fundamental that no institutional reforms will resolve them. Effective conflict management may well mean avoiding issues on occasion.

Areas of Conflict and the Range of Reforms

It seems clear from a careful evaluation of case literature that the most promising approaches to effective conflict management vary according to jurisdiction, issue area and interests mobilized. This observation can be illustrated by an examination of the case literature in various policy areas: communications, transportation, social welfare and health, energy and natural resources, and education policy. In addition, we look at the special problems posed by regulatory policy and general economic policy.

Careful examination of policy decisions in these areas suggests that:

- Federal responsiveness to regional interests is vital in areas of substantial federal jurisdiction.
- Agreement on general development strategies and recognition of jurisdictional boundaries are crucial in the energy and natural resources area (so that there is a framework for more specific negotiations).
- In areas of provincial jurisdiction, such as education, greater efforts must be made to coordinate policies.
- In the high-cost social welfare and health care programs, mechanisms must be sought to make shared-cost programs more flexible while preserving national standards.

In many cases, it appears that there is much to be gained from cross-delegation, the development of bilateralism in a multilateral framework and the creation of ministerial councils, with staff support, to promote continual consultation. These are directions for exploration. Regulation

and economic policy in general pose particular problems for intergovernmental conflict management.

COMMUNICATIONS POLICY

With respect to communications policy, a subject in which jurisdiction
is predominantly federal, there are several dimensions of conflict:

- Community: Quebec and some other provinces wish to use regulatory
  power over communications for province-building while the dominant
  position within the federal government is that nation-building must be
  primary.
- Economic-ideological: Several provinces want less regulation and more
  rapid innovation to promote new services for economic and ideological
  reasons.
- Private sector: Competition exists among service providers for regulatory
  benefits.

Despite extensive federal-provincial negotiation, most decisions have been
made by the federal regulator and the federal cabinet, often with little
obvious attention to provincial concerns.

There is general agreement among case studies in the area that a better
balance between federal and provincial interests must be worked out if
Canada is not to lag behind in the new information age. The proposals
with widest support are those recommending some sharing of jurisdiction
through delegation of federal authority to the provinces (or through constitutional amendment to create concurrent jurisdiction) and the creation
of joint or parallel regulatory boards. The central objective of these proposals is to ensure that each government recognizes the legitimate concerns of the other in an institutional context that promotes agreement,
while avoiding two-tiered regulation and providing mechanisms for
industry and consumer input.[14]

TRANSPORTATION POLICY

In the transportation field, jurisdiction is divided and there exists already
some delegation of federal authority to the provinces. Nevertheless, the
interprovincial nature of our major transport systems makes the federal
government a crucial player. The key here is the nature of the conflict.
It is complex with many competing interests, involving not only the
transportation industries but also producers and consumers of a wide range
of products. In addition, it is a touchstone for regional grievances, as a
result of the historic role of transportation in nation-building. These conflicts involve not only freight rates but also decisions regarding services
and facility location. When examined closely, the grievances have much
to do with federal insensitivity to regional interests and to the fact that

provincial governments are denied legitimacy, i.e., treated as just another interest group, in the federal decision-making process, despite the powerful impact of federal decisions on provincial economies (Darling, 1980, p. 240; Westmacott, 1973, p. 463; Norrie, 1976).

The division of powers as such is not a factor. Rather it is the regionalization of interests and sentiments that federalism encourages. As Darling (1980, p. 240) has put it with respect to freight rates: ". . . at the bottom of our regional problem lies, not regional economic disparity, but the brittle and unresponding nature of the federal branch of our government." The problem lies in an accumulation of grievances that has produced such a degree of mistrust that resolution in specific cases is much more difficult than the facts of the case would suggest.

Although there has been much successful intergovernmental collaboration in the transportation field, decisions have a high level of spillover, and it seems clear that continuous consultation, perhaps through a permanent intergovernmental body, and some regulatory sharing would be desirable. To cope with the ideological and psychological effects, it is essential that regional input be highly visible (ibid., pp. 239–40).[15]

SOCIAL WELFARE AND HEALTH POLICY

In the social welfare and health care fields, where provincial jurisdiction is the norm, the general pattern seems to be broad agreement among governments on policy goals (except that each level of government wants the other to pay a larger share of the cost) coupled with conflict over extent of programs and means of delivery. Widespread public support for such programs as income security and medicare has reduced regional differences and muted ideological ones. In the creation of these programs, officials tended to view "federal-provincial divergences in tax powers and spending responsibilities as institutional hurdles peculiar to federalism, to be somehow overcome in the orderly pursuit of national social welfare and income redistribution policies" (Hum, 1983, p. 9). Tension persists between national standards and local preferences, division of costs, political credit and blame. In recent years, the federal government has become increasingly concerned about cost control and gaining its share of credit. Wharf argues that social welfare programs are popular and that governments gain political advantage by developing and extending them and lose by cutting them (Wharf, 1981, p. 85).[16] The contractual relationship required by shared-cost programs has served well in the social welfare and health care fields, despite the rigidities created by the need for intergovernmental consensus when adjustments are needed and conflicts arise over allocation of costs. The frustrations and difficulties of cost control and accountability resulting from shared-cost programs should not be exaggerated. Experience in non-federal countries demonstrates that such problems are not unique to federal systems. In Canada, conflict has often been interdepartmental at the federal or provincial levels, rather than intergovernmental, and inter-governmental conflict has, since 1975, revolved primarily around fiscal issues (with some federal concern over political credit). The commitment to the principles of the programs has been strong at both levels (Banting, 1982, pp. 122, 144; Taylor, 1978, p. 426).

ENERGY AND NATURAL RESOURCES POLICY[17]

The intergovernmental politics of energy and natural resources has been complex and difficult over the past 15 years. Jurisdiction is shared and overlapping, with each level of government having powerful constitutional resources. The nature of the interests mobilized is significant. First, the regional dimension is clear, pitting the producing provinces against the consuming provinces. Both government revenues and private economic interests are so significantly affected that public sentiments have been aroused. Second, matters of principle (involving commitment to equalization and degree of government intervention, for example) were involved, as well as matters of economic interest. The latter (primarily the sharing of windfall profits and, in general, the sharing of economic rents) have been exacerbated by long-standing regional grievances. Finally, the federal-provincial negotiations regarding energy pricing were carried out in an atmosphere of crisis in the 1970s, with the result that public concern was high, bringing electoral considerations into the process.

Viewing the issue area more broadly, it is evident that the fundamental areas of conflict have been two: the sharing of resource revenues (involving not only Ottawa and the producing provinces, but also the consuming provinces, with their concern for pricing policies) and control of development strategies. Jurisdiction, often prominent in discussion of the issue, appears to have been incidental to these fundamental matters. The clash over development policies has involved such issues as the speed and financing of development, export policies, environmental issues and measures to ensure local purchasing and hiring. This conflict has surfaced in connection with such diverse issues as the Columbia River treaty, oil and gas pricing and development and mineral exploitation, including off-shore development. The producing provinces want to diversify, to garner the bulk of revenues for reinvestment in the province, while the federal government is concerned with regional disparities, national development policies, including balance of payments and job protection (energy production is much less labour intensive than energy-consuming manufacturing, for example), and its own revenue base. Export policies have also been a matter of contention. Practical problems (including the inability of the federal government to tax provincial Crown corporations and anomalies in the equalization formula) appear soluble (Courchene, 1976; Courchene and Melvin, 1980), but mechanisms must be found to coordinate development strategies.

In the 1970s, it became clear that energy policy had become central to a wide range of policy concerns, including industrial restructuring, procurement and transportation policy, resource rents, fiscal policy and equalization, trade and security matters, native peoples' rights, and environmental safety (Doern and Phidd, 1983, p. 484). Whereas Doern and Phidd believe conflict was exacerbated by the recognition that energy issues involved such a wide range of economic issues, Thur argues that the issue might have been more easily resolved had it been seen in its larger context (ibid., pp. 484–85; Thur, 1981, pp. 19–35). Perhaps the problem from a conflict-management point of view was the lack of mechanisms to develop a clear pattern of tradeoffs from which negotiators could choose.

Throughout the 1970s, the traditional mechanisms of ministerial and first ministers' conferences contributed little in any direct way to the resolution of energy and natural resources issues. In the end, most conflicts were either resolved through bilateral negotiations or pre-empted by unilateral actions (usually by the federal government). The offshore cases demonstrated that judicial review does not necessarily lead to final resolution. The conflicting interests of the provinces are such that multilateral negotiations appear to have little chance of success using current mechanisms.

EDUCATION POLICY

In the education field, jurisdiction is predominantly provincial, though the federal government has some incidental responsibilities. The conflict has revolved around the legitimacy of federal initiatives and cost-sharing in various shared-cost programs. The federal government has sought certain goals, such as minority language training and education in both official languages, plus a degree of integration between labour-market planning and vocational training. As well, it has sought to control costs and gain more political credit for its financial contributions. Although significant in the specific case of vocational training (Dupré et al., 1973, p. 94), these issues are not vital to the development of education as a whole. The larger issues in the new technological age revolve around the development of coordinated strategies to promote the necessary research and program development at all levels, but especially at the post-secondary level, to maintain Canada's standard of living and position in the world. Intergovernmental conflicts in this area have been muted, in part because some of the most difficult issues, such as the tension between regional equity and efficiency in the development of new facilities and programs and of effective coordination, have yet to be addressed (Ivany, 1981, p. 102).

REGULATION

Several authors (e.g., Doern and Phidd, 1983, p. 85) who have looked at the conflict over regulatory powers make the point that this is a difficult area in which to achieve federal-provincial agreement. Smiley (1980, p. 102) argues that the increasing shift in emphasis after the mid-1970s from fiscal relations and shared-cost programs to regulatory matters (telecommunications, transportation, consumer protection, energy and the development of natural resources, control of environment) increased the level of conflict. "Circumstances specific to the regulatory function make such conflicts difficult to resolve." Jurisdiction tends to be divided (shared) and constitutional boundaries are often unclear. In contrast to shared-cost programs, federal funds cannot be used to induce provincial compliance, so that issues tend toward zero-sum games (winners and losers) without solutions that would serve the interests of both orders of governments (ibid., pp. 102–103). The federal regulatory agencies, which make many of the most contentious federal regulatory decisions, are often largely outside of federal cabinet control, making bargaining difficult, since key aspects are often not on the table (ibid., p. 103). The move toward a federal directive power and the advent of federal-provincial working groups to set guidelines for regulatory decisions, as in the case examined by Murray (1983), hold out some promise for ameliorating these difficulties. There is also room for sharing of regulatory authority (Fletcher and Fletcher, 1979, p. 185; Buchan et al., 1982, pp. 12–13; Westmacott and Phillips, 1979, p. 315).

Innovative approaches, such as joint task forces, may be the only way to cope with the difficulties posed by rapidly changing technologies which create jurisdictional uncertainty (Babe, 1974, p. 186; Woodrow, 1980, p. 76). Bilateral negotiations, which recognize explicitly the differences in situation and interests of the provinces, have promise. Bilateralism and responsiveness to provincial interests by the federal government were seen as having contributed to agreement in several cases. In his case study of the federal-provincial forest products strategy, Jenkin (1983, pp. 129–34) found that federal-provincial cooperation has been highly successful because:

- There are a number of mechanisms to promote federal-provincial dialogue.
- The policy area has been dominated in large measure by technical and professional considerations.
- Policies have been designed to meet differing regional needs.
- Mechanisms were established for consultation with the private sector.
- The federal government moved to prevent a competitive situation from emerging amongst the provinces.

- The federal government's approach was flexible and featured bilateral negotiations which offered compromises within broader multilateral programs. Bilateralism and flexibility were added to the traditional mix of functional federalism to produce a favourable outcome.

ECONOMIC POLICY

The making of broad economic policies appears to be even more intractable than regulatory issues. The record, according to Smiley (1980, pp. 185, 192), is clear: much intergovernmental talk and little intergovernmental action on economic development and fiscal matters. Among the problems is intergovernmental competition for revenues and for short-term economic benefits, which makes agreement on longer-term strategies difficult. Jenkin's (1983) study of the 1978 First Ministers' Conferences on the Economy concluded (pp. 125ff.) that the two meetings agreed on only minor issues for several reasons: the federal government had no clear objective (it had a diffuse agenda based on departmental inputs); the two main first ministers' conferences were open (televised nationally), raising public expectations and encouraging premiers to react to the home audience (discouraging compromises on regionally sensitive issues); and the existence of deep divisions over the content of economic and industrial policy. "In short, the achievements of the two conferences were limited by the need to reach a consensus in a group whose participants had very different economic interests" (ibid., p. 128). It seems clear that where there are deep regional differences of economic interest, no amount of tinkering with the process of intergovernmental negotiations is likely to produce results.

The fact is that differences in the economic interests of the provinces have become very clear, and provincial officials nearly always represent identifiable economic interests in such negotiations. Jenkin (ibid., pp. 86–96) notes the emergence of provincial economic strategies but argues that these are not necessarily incompatible. The problem is to find ways of structuring the issues so that limited agreements (or broader agreements with tradeoffs) are possible. However, the case studies we have examined suggest that intergovernmental collaboration works best when dealing with well-organized, highly specific, technical subject areas, with negotiations conducted on an incremental basis, using agreements on specific subjects to build consensus on a wider basis (ibid., p. 105). Industrial strategy, however, deals with grand designs in areas of high conflict. In general terms, it appears that there are two ways to reduce such issues to manageable proportions: either to limit the issues by defining the conflict in the narrowest possible terms and seeking to reach larger goals incrementally, or to limit the players by reducing the number of governments involved by dealing bilaterally or regionally. Because the number of interests represented is thus limited, the latter approach permits a broader range of issues to be dealt with than is generally possible in multilateral meetings. Federal leadership is cited in several studies as a crucial ingredient and some have suggested that the biggest impediment to progress in this area is internal conflict within the federal government (Smiley, 1980, p. 109).

The case studies presented by Jenkin (1983) and Savoie (1981a), among others, suggest that there may be ways to get around the incompatibility between the need for broad economic strategies and a system which works best when dealing incrementally with well-organized, highly specific, technical subject areas. Going beyond the obvious strategy of using agreements on specific subjects to build consensus on a wider basis, it may be possible to make progress by limiting the issues to be dealt with at the multilateral level to those which must be resolved to arrive at a broad consensus, leaving more detailed questions to be dealt with in bilateral negotiations. Bilateral negotiations within national programs with broad acceptance might permit the development of national policies which recognize regional differences. The bilateral negotiations permit tradeoffs not possible in multilateral bargaining. It appears that such negotiations work best when non-governmental groups are consulted in the bilateral negotiations and when there is adequate political oversight. The proposed pattern calls for a ministerial council, with adequate support staff, to monitor the overall agreement and, at the bilateral level, a clear line of ministerial responsibility to ensure that the bilateral negotiations have a political component. Some benefits might accrue from a formalized pattern of consultation with affected non-governmental groups, e.g., public hearings or advisory boards.

It seems clear that the objective must be effective national strategies sensitive to regional differences. Given the fact that provincial governments are concerned primarily with internal economic development (Brown and Eastman, 1981, p. 187), measures to involve them in national planning are likely to pay dividends. As Simeon (1979, p. 42) has suggested, the most promising approach appears to be a collaborative one, in which the interdependence of governments is explicitly recognized and continual consultation is the norm. Progress toward a national economic strategy appears most likely when: the federal and provincial governments treat one another as partners (Brown and Eastman, 1981, p. 186); the governments have a common data base and understanding of the central problems (Thorburn, 1984, pp. 212–17); and governments are aware of the potential effects of their decisions on the private sector (Brown and Eastman, 1981, p. 189). In many sectors, business fears the negative effects of uncoordinated provincial development strategies (ibid., p. 187). These concerns lead almost inevitably to proposals for a new set of intergovernmental institutions designed to provide a common data base and continual consultation, such as a council of ministers (Simeon, 1979, p. 42) or a federal-provincial planning body (Thorburn, 1984, pp. 212–17). In our view, the exact form of the mechanism is less important than that it meet certain requirements:

- that it have expert staff to synthesize federal and provincial economic data;
- that it be supported by all governments involved;
- that it have a mandate to maintain continuous liaison with business and labour; and
- that it have certain public reporting functions so that policy development has broadly based input.[18]

The key to success, however, is resolution of jurisdictional disputes and consensus among first ministers on general policy directions (Brown and Eastman, 1981, p. 188). Such backing would permit the intergovernmental process to iron out details and to establish multilateral and bilateral processes to deal with regional differences. Effective mechanisms for private-sector input could be established to ensure all viewpoints were canvassed. The existence of strong regional interests, competing provincial development strategies and dependence on outside economic forces makes detailed national economic planning unlikely (Simeon, 1979, pp. 42–43), but progress does seem possible. Excessive expectations should be avoided, however, since institutional change can only create opportunities. Real progress requires political will.

Toward More Effective Conflict Management

Conflict management has been the primary focus of many of the commentaries and case studies of federal-provincial relations, and propositions regarding effective conflict management abound. In order to examine these propositions as systematically as possible, we have divided them into two categories: those related to procedural factors internal to the federal-provincial process and those intrinsic to the issue but external to the process. As will be seen, the external factors tend to determine the appropriate approach to conflict resolution.

EXTERNAL FACTORS:
ISSUES AND INTERESTS

The external factors which appear to have most influence on the capacity of federal-provincial negotiators to reach agreement tend to fall into one of two categories: the type of issue and the nature of the interests mobilized. With respect to type of issue, we can observe that agreements are most likely to be reached when the issues are: relatively uncontroversial and of common concern to all or most governments; framed in ways which permit splitting the difference and avoiding winners and losers; and specific and limited in scope. Thus negotiations involving the provision of services have proved easier to conclude than those involving regulation, since it is easier to split the difference in terms of cost-sharing than in terms of jurisdiction. In terms of conflict management, there are clear benefits from attempting to narrow issues to manageable proportions and to framing them in terms of sharing.

With respect to interests mobilized, matters are less clear cut. For the many routine intergovernmental interactions that make the system work, even in times of crisis, it seems clear that lack of publicity facilitates agreement. When such an interaction attracts attention and becomes controversial, the political concerns of the governments are engaged, as well as other interests, and agreement is often made more difficult. On the other hand, the existence of widespread public and/or media demand for action appears to facilitate agreement. As long as there are no major regional differences in policy preference, such external pressures tend to bring issues into focus and facilitate agreement. The impact of politicization or publicity, therefore, depends upon the specific pattern of interests mobilized. (Publicity surrounding actual negotiating sessions appears to promote symbolic combat and impede compromise.) The issues which pose most difficulty are: those upon which there are major differences in cultural or economic interest among the provinces; those with a high level of symbolic content, such as language of education or western freight rates (especially if there are probable electoral implications); and those which touch fundamental questions of ideology, community, or regime support.

Certain other issues, such as fiscal policy and economic development (and especially industrial strategy), are extremely difficult to resolve in the federal-provincial arena because they require both long-term planning and coordinated program design covering many sectors. In addition, they deal with matters where there are deep regional divisions. In short, there is an inescapable tension between the logic of planning and the logic of federalism, which deals most effectively with specific, short-term issues (Banting, 1982, pp. 77–78). The inherent conflicts in the Canadian federal system have made agreement on matters of fiscal policy and economic development extremely difficult (Smiley, 1980, pp. 185ff.). Intergovernmental relations are underdeveloped in the industrial policy area precisely because there is "an underlying conflict between the nature of the decisions required in industrial policy and the kinds of substantive collaboration possible within the intergovernmental framework" (Jenkin, 1983, p. 141). Nevertheless, as will be seen, there are mechanisms which might help the system to overcome these difficulties.

The logic of federalism reflects its origins in a period of limited government (Corry, 1958, pp. 95–125). The intergovernmental mechanisms which evolved in the post-1945 period were designed to cope with the relatively moderate forms of government activism reflected in the development of the welfare state, from federal government leadership through exhortation to expenditure programs (shared-cost arrangements). Adapting the scale of intervention proposed by Allan Tupper and Bruce Doern (1981, pp. 16–18), we can say that the growth of regulatory activity and of public ownership (at both levels of government) marked a major increase in the degree of government intervention and involved a quantum increase in intergovernmental conflict. Similarly, economic planning on the Quebec model is notably more interventionist than Keynesian economic management. If increased intergovernmental conflict is a serious threat to the system, governments might be faced with the choice of pulling back to a more limited form of government or developing considerably more powerful mechanisms of intergovernmental coordination.

INTERNAL FACTORS:
NEGOTIATORS, APPROACHES, MECHANISMS

With respect to factors internal to the federal-provincial system, the conditions which encourage effective conflict management tend to involve: the characteristics of the negotiators; approaches to negotiations; and mechanisms of interaction.

In general, the case studies suggest that the process is most likely to be harmonious when: the negotiators share professional norms and commitments which allow policy issues to be framed as technical questions; the officials and ministers from different jurisdictions have come to trust one another through routine contact; and the negotiators are able to view themselves as allies (supporting a particular program or opposing their respective central agencies) rather than as competitors for credit. Conversely, negotiations are likely to be more difficult when federal and provincial officials view themselves as serving different clienteles or promoting different "grand designs" in a policy area. Problems such as these are more likely to occur, some studies suggest, when federal and provincial officials are specialists in different fields (Dupré et al., 1973, pp. 90, 200, 220). It has also been suggested that the emergence of the intergovernmental affairs manager has reduced the influence of program specialists and resulted in more interactions being viewed in a broader context, diminishing the chance of agreement and bringing more issues to the political level (Smiley, 1980, pp. 97–98).

The approaches to intergovernmental negotiations adopted by the practitioners are also important. Certain tactics are clearly less conducive to effective conflict management than others. Three factors seem to have marked many successful negotiations: the existence of a clearly defined and stated objective supported by all key units of the initiating government (usually the federal government); consultation at the early stages of proposal development; and flexibility in negotiations (Jenkin, 1983, pp. 104–105). Even where there is considerable disagreement about program structure, cost-sharing and other central issues, the existence of a shared commitment to resolve the issue generally leads to an agreement. While the general literature suggests that the emergence of rational planning at both levels of government has promoted distinctive approaches to common problems and increased the likelihood of disagreement, early consultation and the involvement of program specialists appear to facilitate compromise. The case studies also suggest that an incremental approach (seeking resolution of specific issues rather than more general disagreements) is effective.

The case studies suggest also that various mechanisms can promote attitudes and approaches conducive to harmonious relationships. Of particular promise are institutional arrangements which promote continuous liaison among ministers and officials. Properly structured, they can encourage the development of common vocabulary and perspectives, thereby facilitating agreement. The development of formal and informal networks promotes the kind of mutual understanding and trust that can resist the spillover effects of difficulties in other areas. This is particularly important because the federal-provincial arena is unlikely ever to be free from conflict surrounding some of the more intractable intergovernmental issues.

Contractual shared-cost programs, despite all of their difficulties of adjustment to changing conditions, do promote functional cooperation by providing financial incentives for program officials to overcome their differences in order to obtain adequate funding from both levels for their programs. They also appear to insulate the programs to a degree from external pressures, promoting stability of services at the expense of flexibility and accountability.

BILATERALISM

The increasing use of bilateral negotiations has obvious benefits in certain cases. For example, bilateral interactions provide an escape from the complexities of multilateral negotiations by reducing the number of actors and therefore the number of interests to be accommodated. They permit a focus on specific issues of interest to both parties, reducing the prospect that provincial governments with little involvement in the specific subject matter will bring in other issues of more interest to them. In addition, by reducing the number of participants, bilateral meetings permit tradeoffs between the two governments on a broader range of issues than can be handled easily in multilateral negotiations. It is also true that bilateral relationships are generally unpublicized, reducing the likelihood of extraneous political factors entering the picture (Van Loon and Whittington, 1981, p. 547).

In general, the willingness of governments to compromise depends in part on the interest mobilized. In many cases, it appears that governments are constrained by the divided loyalties of their constituents (Simeon, 1973, pp. 233–39). This is true even of Quebec, except on those issues where a social consensus for change exists (such as language policy). Where there is a strong sense of regional grievance, the limitations on provincial intransigence are considerably less than on issues where there are no strong regional differences.

Smiley (1980, p. 104) suggests that though the provinces have become increasingly less inhibited about presenting a united front to Ottawa over the past decade, they have not often taken the next step of shutting Ottawa out of areas of provincial jurisdiction by forging agreements amongst themselves. Smiley does not follow this line of reasoning very far, but it is worth considering the reasons for the failure of the provinces to go further into the business of negotiating reciprocal agreements on benefits or of developing common standards and procedures on matters of regulation and licensing. Most successful examples of such agreements have come about under federal government rubrics or on a regional basis. The importance of federal transfer payments in our system is certainly one reason. Another appears to be the uneven level of bureaucratic development amongst the provinces. Inability to agree is certainly a factor, though not a major one, since what is most notable is the lack of attention to this option.

Careful examination of the case studies suggests that although the political will to cooperate is crucial to the success of all negotiations, there is room for new approaches. One such approach is the integration of bilateralism within a multilateral framework, maintaining both national standards and sensitivity to regional differences. The willingness of the federal government to respond flexibly to provincial initiatives is important, since provincial involvement in economic and social intervention is not likely to recede greatly, even in the present period of restraint. The provinces might find themselves able to move forward in areas now blocked by pursuing agreements for cooperative or reciprocal action in areas of provincial jurisdiction. Such action might precipitate federal involvement.

SUMMIT FEDERALISM

While federal-provincial interaction takes place at all levels within the public services, it has long been accepted that policy questions defined as important must in the end be dealt with at the top political level. For the most important questions, the first ministers much decide. The centralization of executive decision making in the offices of prime ministers and premiers is perhaps even more pronounced in the federal-provincial arena than elsewhere. Simeon (1973, p. 144) noted the ambivalent impact of summit federalism more than a decade ago. In some cases, this "may make for easier resolution of conflicts because the political heads can make firm commitments [on behalf] of their own governments, but it may also mean that conflicts become much more sharply defined and therefore more intractable." The growing centrality of federal-provincial issues in the political system has led to an increase in reliance on first ministers' conferences.

Issues tend to rise to the summit because they are difficult to resolve or involve high stakes. They tend to reflect either the long-term economic or cultural interests of the provinces or matters of central concern to governments: jurisdiction, revenue, fiscal control, legitimacy, electoral success and so on. Public attention or politicization can also be a factor. In addition, some essentially technical issues have come to the summit (at least to ministerial conferences) as central agencies have struggled to exert control over program officials or to ensure that broader issues were considered in program-oriented interactions. Once issues have reached the summit, the interests of governments play a major role, reducing the possibility that an issue can be framed in purely technical terms.

While first ministers' conferences and ministerial conferences do provide an opportunity for the development of good relations at the top levels, trust networks are more likely to develop among officials, even at the summit level, given their greater continuity in office. In addition, they are more able than their principals to focus on the federal-provincial issues, being relatively less encumbered by the wide range of political problems facing first ministers. First ministers, in particular, must participate in several simultaneous games (ibid., p. 130) in order to retain their authority within cabinet and caucus. In particular, given the frequency of elections in Canada, at least one of the eleven leaders is likely to be focussing on the electoral game at any given time.

It must be noted, of course, that failure to reach agreement on many issues in the 1970s was not simply a function of the greater involvement of summit decision makers. Garth Stevenson (1979, pp. 196–97) has argued that functional or cooperative federalism is unable to "deal very successfully with conflicts that originate outside the government or bureaucratic milieu and that result from more fundamental antagonisms . . . ." The high level of disagreement in the 1970s, he suggests, resulted from the emergence of fundamental issues and not from the shift from functional to executive federalism. That shift, he argues (ibid., pp. 199–200), was a result of the emergence of difficult issues. In fact, of course, summit negotiations have some major agreements to their credit.

As with most public policy decisions, federal-provincial issues tend to be resolved through a series of negotiations at various levels and of various types, from bilateral to omnilateral. Summit federalism works most effectively, the cases suggest, when the issue comes to the summit with the issues clearly specified by previous negotiations at lower levels and with room for tradeoffs. Adequate preparation is clearly crucial, as is a degree of trust and a sense that to compromise is not to lose. The importance of regular meetings of ministers and of first ministers, both supported by secretariats, seems clear. The new rules developed during patriation, i.e., more public involvement and reduced emphasis on unanimity, may promote resolution of some of the less intractable issues. Bilateralism also holds promise as a mechanism for breaking deadlocks. Willingness to provide general direction to other bodies or to leave details for bilateral bargaining might also be helpful. However, the first ministers' conferences will still have to deal with the hard issues, and inability to achieve consensus should not be seen as a failure of the system.

INTERGOVERNMENTAL BODIES: SECRETARIAT AND COMMITTEES

With respect to facilitating agreement, there was widespread agreement that intergovernmental secretariats and other intergovernmental bodies could prove helpful. The discussion of secretariats revolved around the experience with the Canadian Council of Resource and Environment Ministers (CCREM). While permanent support staff for federal-provincial bodies can be viewed as subject to federal government dominance (vitiating some of the advantages), the CCREM provides a model for an independent body. The CCREM is a private corporation whose board of directors consists of federal and provincial cabinet ministers, with the presidency of the Council rotating annually among the member governments. The staff works for CCREM and not any member government (Van Loon and Whittington, 1981, pp. 540–41). Jenkin (1983, pp. 122–23) takes the view that intergovernmental cooperation is encouraged by the existence of permanent secretariats capable of providing continuous and fairly intensive bureaucratic support. In his examination of the CCREM, he found that it kept issues on the agenda, fostered common perspectives and vocabulary and helped to develop a cooperative network of officials and ministers. It worked well, in Jenkin's view, not only because of the structure, but also because the issues it dealt with were relatively non-controversial. As it became more involved with the public and with controversial issues, the political decision makers reduced its role.

Several case studies have examined special or ad hoc bilateral or multilateral intergovernmental bodies (or proposed them) and there is a general view that, under the right circumstances, they can effectively promote conflict management. Catherine Murray's case study (1983) examines a joint CRTC-DOC committee established to determine how the number and variety of television services to northern and remote communities could be improved in the context of satellite distribution and pay-TV. The committee was created in response to provincial demands for a greater role in policy development and to help the Department of Communications come to terms with the new communications technologies. The committee was the first attempt to establish a working group with federal and provincial input along with the usual public and industry input sought by the CRTC. It was made up of eight members, four chosen from nominees of eight participating provincial governments and four from the CRTC.

Murray (ibid., pp. 138ff.) concludes that the delegated committee structure is a useful model for combining federal-provincial and group consultation but that it is not a substitute for a broader resolution of the constitutional and political issues involved. The author suggests that joint federal-provincial task forces, with guidelines agreed upon through the federal-provincial process, and some regulatory involvement can be useful in dealing with situations where innovation is required. The combination provides for broad public input and policy grounded in the basic policy preferences of the governments involved.

In assessing the success of the committee in reaching a consensus, the author identifies these factors as significant: compromise was facilitated by bargaining *in camera* in an isolated atmosphere; the issue was broad enough to allow room for manoeuvre and a win-win situation; and it was perceived that there was strong public demand for action (ibid., p. 84). Timing is therefore important to success. Participants also perceived that the same urgency did not apply in other areas, such as telecommunications.

The CRTC was trying to respond to the fact that opposition to it often had a regional base, with provinces representing regional interests as well as seeking increased jurisdiction. "By building provincialism into the regulatory process itself, then perhaps the threat could be averted and the CRTC could avoid the total loss of its influence to the federal-provincial bargainers" (ibid., p. 138). But the CRTC can only succeed in this endeavour if there is a general intergovernmental agreement on basic policy directions and division of labour in the field. The joint delegation model can be used only within a context of agreement on the key issues of jurisdiction and general policy direction.

A number of other case studies propose joint federal-provincial committees for various special purposes. For example, McCorquodale proposes joint committees for planning implementation of fisheries policy (McCorquodale, 1983, p. 167). In looking at the operation of joint federal-provincial bilateral planning bodies in the context of the Canada–New Brunswick General Development Agreement, Savoie concluded that they facilitate harmonious relations but raise problems of accountability and interprovincial coordination. However, he believes that such bodies can be useful in program development and implementation if they operate within a national framework and adequate political oversight (1981a, pp. 151–67).

Assessment: Striving for Balance

In assessing conflict management in the Canadian federal system, it is essential to make some preliminary points. Even at the height of visible federal-provincial conflicts over energy pricing, offshore development, constitutional reform, and extra-billing by doctors, there was a great deal of effective intergovernmental collaboration, in all sectors of government activity. Nevertheless, competition and conflict are inevitable in Canada's federal system, even desirable in many cases to promote innovation and to air vital issues. However, failure to improve the information-sharing and collaborative processes may well have serious consequences for the economy and the legitimacy of the regime. In many areas, it will be necessary for governments to proceed with programs without intergovernmental consensus, but at least information must be shared, so that decisions are made in full knowledge of their spillover effects. In other areas, coordination or even collaboration may be necessary to the success of the enterprise. In particular, it is important to improve both the mechanisms for routine adjustments in an interdependent federal system and the operation of the forums for debating the hard political questions (which inevitably take on intergovernmental overtones). The appropriate goal is not the unrealistic one of establishing intergovernmental harmony but rather that of promoting effective conflict management.

MECHANISMS FOR COMMUNICATION

Norman Spector (1984, p. 46) has argued that our "distressing" record in resolving federal-provincial disputes can be traced not only to the difficult environment of intergovernmental relations, but also to "the virtual absence of intergovernmental machinery as such." Noting the limited role of the Intergovernmental Conference Secretariat, he suggests the creation of more sophisticated institutions based on an industrial relations model. His proposals include the establishment of a permanent federal-provincial advisory council to coordinate policies amongst the 11 first ministers, with a staff of fact-finding, conciliation and mediation officers to assist in resolving particular conflicts, and a special tribunal to adjudicate federal-provincial disputes, thus avoiding the winner-loser approach of the courts (ibid., pp. 44–46). While these recommendations are worthy of consideration, it is our view, based on the case studies of intergovernmental negotiations, that there is no simple institutional panacea. Requirements differ by issue area.

It would be easy to devise a paper empire of new intergovernmental agencies to facilitate conflict management, but it would not be very productive. Effective mechanisms must be developed to deal with particular problems. What we can do is to suggest a variety of possibilities which might be adopted as the need arises. In areas where one level has primary jurisdiction, a strong case can be made for institutionalized consultation, to facilitate the development of trust networks and full canvassing of the potential effects of decisions. In areas of shared, joint, or concurrent jurisdiction, especially where there is a great deal of interaction, councils of ministers and permanent intergovernmental secretariats are often warranted. They can provide needed data bases as well as developing trust and a shared framework for discussion. Such semi-permanent bodies can also promote consultation with the private sector. The Continuing Committee on Social Security made a major contribution to the development of the Canada Assistance Plan, for example. With respect to shared-cost programs, federal-provincial bodies with some rule-making authority would improve the flexibility of programs. Some shared-cost programs could be administered by private-sector bodies funded by both levels of government; for example, a federal-provincial student-aid program could be administered by a body representing the universities and colleges.

In the regulatory sphere, several models can be suggested. In areas of shared jurisdiction, joint agencies or parallel agencies with formalized mechanisms for consultation have potential. In areas of federal jurisdiction, it seems clear that better methods for provincial input are needed. For continuing liaison, provincial advisory bodies have some potential, especially if linked to ministerial councils. Special federal-provincial task forces to help both levels of government respond more quickly to technological change can be helpful, along the lines of the Therrien Committee.[19] Such task forces can facilitate industry and consumer input as well. Provincial governments must recognize the validity of federal input to provincial regulatory decisions, perhaps through federal observers. Interprovincial bodies with federal observers provide a precedent. All of these models would contribute to the development of trust networks, to framing issues in specific or technical terms, and to exchange of information.

Without a radical transformation of our political system, executive federalism will continue to be a major part of the Canadian policy-making process. A reduction in the level of government activism at both levels would undoubtedly reduce intergovernmental conflict; any major change, however, is unlikely. Similarly, a shift in focus from jurisdictional issues to substantive questions, a wish expressed in several case studies, can be achieved only partially through institutional change. However, the development of more continuous consultation at the functional level appears to hold promise for keeping issues narrow and manageable, while improved summit preparation may help to promote broad agreement on frameworks for substantive negotiations.

In particular, professionally staffed intergovernmental agencies can help to foster common perspectives and vocabulary, develop a cooperative network of officials and ministers, and keep issues on the agenda and frame them in a non-confrontational way. Politicians must generally focus on the short term; professional staffs, however, can take a longer view. The existence of such bodies might well lead to the development of client groups, which would provide not only for group input, but also help to provide pressure for action.

In general, the case studies suggest that the federal government can do much to promote consensus by providing well-informed leadership, demonstrating sensitivity to provincial concerns, and fostering the development of intergovernmental bodies. The most promising approaches appear to be a combination of the proposals to institutionalize the summit (by providing for regular conferences of first ministers and a strong secretariat) and the strategy of building consensus on the basis of narrower decisions through the development of more specialized bodies. Bilateral and regional negotiations within a multilateral framework approved by a summit conference seem to hold promise for effective conflict management and, in some cases, decisions that go beyond the incremental.

Federalism and Democratic Values

Stating the Problem

Much of the early literature on federalism attempted to assess its impact on such democratic values as participation, responsiveness, liberty and equality (Simeon, 1982–83, pp. 150ff.; Whitaker, 1983). More recently, analysts have become concerned about its influence on accountability. In this final section of our survey of case studies, we will examine the effect of various forms of intergovernmental decision making on responsiveness and accountability, two of the values most directly influenced by the process itself. We are concerned about the responsiveness of decision makers to relevant publics (represented by interest groups and identifiable constituencies) and to broad public preferences. With respect to accountability, executive federalism poses problems for both hierarchical accountability (of program officials to their respective governments) and democratic accountability (of decision makers to parliaments and legislatures).

Donald Smiley, the leading critic of executive federalism as practised in Canada, argues (1979, p. 107) that it "contributes to secret, non-participatory and non-accountable processes of government." The closed nature of federal-provincial decision making and the complexity of the issues raised make participation difficult. He continues (idem.):

> To the extent . . . that the actual locus of decision-making in respect to an increasing number of public matters has shifted from individual governments to intergovernmental groupings the effective accountability of executives both to their respective legislatures and to those whom they govern is weakened.

Responsiveness to Interest Groups

The responsiveness of decision makers in the federal-provincial process to interest groups and to public opinion has been the source of considerable speculation but a disproportionately small amount of research. In very general terms, the Canadian public policy process tends to be relatively closed. It appears that interest groups have seen their influence decline with the rise in importance of central agencies and rationalized decision making. The decline in autonomy of individual ministries having long-standing client relationships with interest groups has reduced group input.

The dominant view regarding access of interest groups to federal-provincial decision-making processes continues to reflect Simeon's findings. Based on three cases in the 1960s, Simeon (1973, p. 144) argued that:

> The machinery [of federal-provincial interaction] . . . limits the participation of interest groups in the bargaining process. Affected groups are not invited to participate or make their views known. The relative secrecy of debate means interest group leaders may often be unaware of developments in federal-provincial negotiations which might involve them.

He found that interest groups are often forgotten because governments tend to regard other governments as the crucial actors. Even when governments act as representatives of particular interests, those interests are likely to be sacrificed when the broader concerns of the participants, i.e., the governments, are involved (ibid., pp. 202–203).

These findings were challenged by Schultz (1980, pp. 170–73), on the basis of his case study of the trucking industry in the 1970s. He argues that there are circumstances in which interest groups are intimately involved in the entire process. He notes that interest groups are often involved in an exchange relationship with governments and that demands and supports flow in both directions. His view is that Simeon's limited access model is specific to particular conditions and that interest-group involvement varies with the type of issue involved.

A central assumption of much of the literature is that the institutional framework of federal-provincial interaction as such "influences the opportunities available to particular interests to shape policy decisions." In general, Banting (1982, p. 42) argues that:

> Because the institutional framework expands or contracts the circle of critical decision-makers, structures the nature of political competition, and specifies the form of representation of the wider public, it necessarily conditions the access of different political interests to policy-makers, smoothing the pathway of some and raising obstacles for others.

This is a plausible assumption, and the case studies we have examined suggest that access is influenced by such factors as jurisdiction, policy type, the nature of the interaction and interests mobilized. However, Smiley (1980, p. 152) sums up knowledge in this area on a cautionary note:

> In the state of our present knowledge we should be extremely cautious about making general statements about the relation between interest group activity and the processes of executive federalism. Some patterns of federal-provincial interaction, such as those related to the equalization of provincial revenues, appear to involve governments almost exclusively. In other circumstances,

for example . . . [regulatory issues], interest groups are much more influential. And in yet other situations, such as [energy pricing], the relative influence of interest groups in intergovernmental negotiations may change quickly and dramatically.

Without disputing the general proposition that the closed nature of executive federalism tends to insulate policy makers from public pressure, it is possible to identify factors which make access more likely. First, issues which have obvious and large-scale public impact or which touch the interests of large, powerful organized groups encourage consultation with interest groups, since politicians must be concerned about public reaction to the policies adopted (Simeon, 1973, pp. 155–56). Second, interest groups are likely to be invited into the federal-provincial process when their support is needed by one of the governments involved or when their cooperation is necessary for the success of a program (Schultz, 1980, pp. 157–59, 172ff.), and third, in some cases, usually technical matters, interest-group representatives have served as members of federal or provincial delegations (Simeon, 1973, p. 282; Schultz, 1980, p. 153). In general, interest groups are most likely to gain access to negotiators when they have well-established client relationships with one or more of the governments involved. As noted above, such relationships are exchange relationships in which groups tend to support the jurisdictional claims of the government to which they have the best access, while governments tend to represent the interests of their key clients whenever possible.

Governments themselves often seek to mobilize interest-group activity in support of their positions. External pressure can help a government to get an issue on the federal-provincial agenda or to frame an issue in a manner favourable to that government. For example, the federal government attempted to mobilize energy consumers and Canadian-owned producers in support of the National Energy Program, just as Alberta worked to mobilize regional and industry sentiments against it. Similar activities can be identified in the constitutional negotiations and in the conflict over Established Programs Financing. The tactical needs of governments thus influence access.

Interest Groups: Access and Influence

A related issue of considerable importance is the relative access and influence of particular interests. In the social welfare area, the proposition that federal institutions are especially attuned to territorially based claims and, therefore, favour regional redistribution over interpersonal redistribution is not sustained by the evidence, as Banting makes clear (Banting, 1982, p. 106). In other areas, there is some support for the notion that regionally concentrated economic interests have better access than less concentrated ones (as noted above), but access does not necessarily mean influence.

In the pension case, Simeon (1973, pp. 280–81) makes it very clear that interest groups had little influence: "In no case did interest groups have a significant effect on the outcome, once the issue had entered the federal-provincial arena." Nonetheless, he notes that interest groups were very active in the pension case: the pension industry, unions, and welfare groups. Indeed, the Ontario delegation at some meetings included group representatives (ibid., p. 282). The key argument in Simeon's case, however, is that when hard decisions had to be made, these interests were sacrificed to other values, e.g., access to the fund and national unity.

Schultz's study of trucking regulation (1980), on the other hand, revealed that interest groups were intimately involved at all stages and, indeed, played a vital role in the outcome as they switched allegiances between levels. Schultz argues (pp. 171ff.) that it is not surprising that groups lacked influence in the financial and constitutional reform cases discussed by Simeon, since these are "examples par excellence of government issues, of issues where the primary constituents . . . were the participants themselves." Subsequent events suggest that interest-group involvement in constitutional matters depends upon the actual constitutional issues at stake, the availability of access points, the militancy of affected groups and the degree of public attention.[20] For fiscal issues, access and influence depend in part on the awareness of influential groups of the impact of allocative decisions on their interests.

The mining industry's successful effort to block tax reform is another important example of interest-group influence. Bucovetsky (1975; Smiley, 1980, pp. 149–50) shows how the mining industries used their clout with the provincial governments to help defeat the Carter Commission's[21] proposals that their generous tax breaks be eliminated; he explains their influence in terms of their cohesion (the industry took a common position), their dominance in the communities in which they operate, and their presence in most provinces. As it happened, the tax reform confirmed their status as clients of the provincial governments and later made them vulnerable to provincial government decisions to raise provincial levies, in some cases radically.

In the energy field, Berry's finding that the petroleum industry was frozen out of the energy pricing negotiations of the early 1970s is not supported by the Syncrude case, in which an active lobby by the petroleum corporations involved got them much of what they wanted, nor is it supported by Laxer's findings in the late 1970s (Berry, 1974, pp. 634–35; Pratt, 1976, pp. 181–82; Laxer, 1983). Berry's finding, therefore, must reflect factors other than the clout of the industry and the structure of federal-provincial interaction. In fact, Berry argues (ibid., p. 634) that it was the combined influence of the crisis nature of the oil crunch and "the emergence of fundamental constitutional issues" that resulted in the exclusion of the industry. Jurisdictional disputes reinforce the governmental focus of federal-provincial negotiations. When the pressure for agreement is strong, for example, as a result of world crisis or popular demand, even normally powerful groups have limited influence. When the insurance companies were trying to block government-sponsored medical care insurance, they had good access at both levels, but were able to have only minor influence (Van Loon and Whittington, 1981, pp. 417-18).

Interest groups are probably disadvantaged whenever there are strong incentives for agreement. In his study of the Canada–New Brunswick General Development Agreement, Savoie found that officials of the two levels of government tried to keep information both from interest groups and from politicians in order to increase their own chances of gaining agreement in line with bureaucratic rationality. Officials at both levels felt that interest groups had little to contribute and that they tended to interfere with rational economic decision making. Where public consultations were held, they were held late in the process, when only details remained to be decided (Savoie, 1981a, pp. 105-106, 146-47). In fact, the joint planning committees featured in the GDA system are not structurally inimical to interest group input. Bilateral or regional federal-provincial bodies can include representatives of relevant groups or constitute advisory bodies to represent community and industry groups. Such structures could have real benefits for responsiveness and for legitimizing decisions (Van Loon and Whittington, 1981, p. 539). In addition, Savoie himself notes (1981a p. 142) that such bilateral negotiations tend to make the federal government more sensitive to regional concerns.

In the area of economic policy, the consensus of the case studies is that interest groups are usually frozen out of federal-provincial decision making, though governments often do represent particular interests in negotiations, especially in bilateral negotiations regarding industrial assistance. For electoral reasons, governments (especially the federal government) may speak for labour or consumer interests in particular cases, but corporate interests are more often expressed by provincial spokesmen. Many economic interest groups lack influence at the national level because they lack national cohesion, according to Jenkin (1983, p. 26). The nature of the economy means that they tend to be regionally oriented. More generally, Brown and Eastman concluded that neither business nor labour has found ways to participate consistently and effectively in federal-provincial processes (Brown and Eastman, 1981, p. 188). Governments are aware of the need for more consultation, they decided, but find it difficult to develop suitable means (ibid., p. 189).

The works on health and social welfare policy agree that the decision-making process is essentially closed, with civil servants having major influence. Glaser (1977, pp. 35ff.) observes that the secrecy surrounding intergovernmental interactions bars interest groups by making it difficult for them to keep up with proposals, let alone gain access. He notes that governments have tended not to consult advisory bodies, such as the Canada

Health Council, preferring to rely on in-house advisors or consultants. Banting (1982, p. 76), however, notes that the federal government has been more responsive to reformist groups than most provincial governments over the history of the development of income security. This tendency presumably reflects the quest of federal governments for electoral advantage and popular support for programs in areas of provincial jurisdiction.

Indeed, the conclusion drawn by Simeon from his 1960s cases that "there is little evidence that [federalism] has frustrated widespread public demand in recent years" (1973, p. 296), finds considerable support in more recent surveys of cases in the social welfare and health fields (e.g., Banting, 1982, p. 178; Taylor, 1978, p. 426). However, other studies have observed that in functional interactions, technical considerations can override responsiveness, and that the clash of grand designs in negotiations can produce a process which pays little attention to consumers (Dupré et al., 1973, p. 108). Dupré and his colleagues found in their case study on policy making with respect to adult occupational training that the clash of program "grand designs" and professional perspectives resulted in bargaining with little regard for those whom the programs were intended to benefit:

> The clash of these designs can be likened to a collision of ships at sea that results in both vessels remaining afloat and steaming off on their respective courses, taking water, displaying gaping holes in their superstructure, and relatively oblivious to the number of passengers and crew crushed by the impact. (ibid., p. 109)

A greater degree of political accountability might have increased concern for the consumer, though jurisdictional clash can have the same effect at the summit level as professional conflict at the operational level.

Catherine Murray, in her study of communications policy (1983, pp. 141–43), found a sharp contrast between the federal-provincial meetings and the public hearing tradition of the CRTC. The former were secretive and closed to interest groups, while the latter were open and accessible. Of course, major industry and cultural groups lobbied Ottawa and the provincial governments as well as appearing before CRTC bodies, but they were hampered in the case of the federal-provincial interaction by lack of information. Intervenors in the CRTC process were not given access to the federal-provincial guidelines underlying the hearings. Federal and provincial officials represented the views of identifiable interests in the negotiations but gave them little access and, in the crunch, focussed more on jurisdictional than substantive issues. Nevertheless, the innovative integration of the two processes is a promising one.

> The experience . . . demonstrates the benefits of balancing federal-provincial collaboration and consultation with interest groups. The public meetings served as a brake on the federal-provincial consensus guidelines, re-opening the question of the right to U.S. signals and of universal pay-TV. (ibid., pp. 144 – 45)

Although it is widely accepted that the structure of the Canadian federal system ensures that the interests of governments as governments tend to take precedence (Banting, 1982, p. 42), it is possible to identify conditions which hinder or promote the access or influence of interest groups. Several cases report that interest groups representing dominant interests in a province are, when united, able to recruit the provincial governments to act as their representatives in the federal-provincial arena (Bucovetsky, 1975, pp. 87–114). As with access, interest group influence is greater when the issue is technical and has identifiable impact on a particular group. Not surprisingly, there is reason to believe that interest groups that are ideologically in tune with one of the governments in the process are likely to have greater influence (Smiley, 1980, pp. 266–67). In general, the more governments an interest group can gain access to, the greater its influence. Therefore, the usual factors in interest group influence (cohesion, resources, contacts) are important in the federal-provincial arena (Presthus, 1973). A major question here is the appropriateness of measures to make access and influence more equal.

Federal-provincial negotiations place particular hurdles in the way of all interest groups. Among the conditions which limit interest group influence are the financial costs that federalism imposes on interest groups which must monitor and attempt to influence eleven governments, thereby putting a premium on funding; the political costs in terms of setting priorities and maintaining cohesion imposed by divided jurisdiction; and the difficulties imposed by the closed nature of the system on obtaining timely information on proposed policies. These problems are particularly acute where jurisdiction is shared (agriculture, fisheries, labour, transport) or unclear (consumer protection, environment) (Smiley, 1980, p. 149; Dawson, 1975, pp. 27–58).

A more subtle problem afflicts industrial interest groups. Economic regionalism and the vital necessity for many industries to maintain good relations with provincial regulators inhibit national cohesion and, consequently, influence. Many instances could be cited where national groups remained silent on issues important to their members because of internal disagreement (Jenkin, 1983, p. 26).

Responsiveness to Public Expectations: The General View

In terms of democratic values, the responsiveness of the system to weaker groups and unorganized public opinion is a matter of great importance. The general view is that the complexity of our system insulates decision makers from public pressures, and there is considerable case evidence to support this proposition. As we have seen, however, there is reason to believe that, in broad terms, public expectations tend to be met. In many areas of federal-provincial interaction, however, there is no crystallized public opinion, leaving governmental elites with considerable leeway in developing their positions (Ornstein et al., 1979, p. 106).

It is commonplace for students of federal-provincial relations in Canada to argue, as Smiley does (1980, p. 92), that nationalist and egalitarian sentiments in the postwar period put pressure on the federal government to ensure nation-wide minimum standards in areas deemed vital to the welfare of all citizens. The suggestion is that these pressures led the federal government to initiate shared-cost programs to promote action in areas of provincial jurisdiction. At the same time, writers often take the position that the influence of public opinion in the federal-provincial process is limited (ibid., pp. 152–53). The question, then, is where did these pressures come from, and how were they manifested? Banting (1982, p. 93) notes that in the income security area there has been "intense political pressure on the federal government to treat citizens in all regions equally." He cites direct pressure from regional caucuses of MPs and lobbying by the National Council of Welfare and other client groups. He notes that the latter often seek assistance from the federal government to induce the provinces to live up to national standards.

There is also evidence of a more generalized responsiveness to public expectations, derived, presumably, from electoral considerations and based increasingly on public opinion polling, but this responsiveness has identifiable limits. In the income security field, Banting found that divided jurisdiction limited the impact of the expansionist pressures inherent in democratic politics, except where intergovernmental competition led to expansion (Ottawa-Quebec competition on pensions and family allowance). He found that responsiveness to public pressures was weakened by shared jurisdiction. The federal government was demonstrably responsive to public preferences with respect to exclusively federal programs; mixed jurisdiction, however, insulated decision makers from the full force of public expectations and criticisms (ibid., p. 115; and Leman, 1980, pp. 224–27). Once again the limiting factor is public knowledge. More open discussion of proposals might well increase responsiveness.

In his review of income security policy (1982, p. 106), Banting concluded that:

> The proposition that our federal institutions are particularly sensitive to territorially-based claims, and that they therefore respond more readily to demands for explicit interregional redistribution is simply not sustained by the evidence. . . . Interpersonal redistribution through income security is a much greater spending priority for federal authorities than are special regional programmes.

He notes that some unitary states spend more on regional economic development than Canada does and that there is no reason to believe that the balance would change were Canada to have a more centralized form of government (ibid., p. 106).

It is generally accepted, however, that the provinces have fairly durable and persisting interests, related to linguistic, cultural and economic concerns. The argument is that these interests tend to override partisan and ideological interests in federal-provincial negotiations. The dilemma for the analyst is to discern when provinces are representing the interests of the major economic groups in their territories in response to pressures from those interests and when they are responding to their own self-interest as governments. In many cases, the positions taken are likely to be identical. At the most general level, electoral success in modern democracies tends to be closely related to economic growth and prosperity. Therefore, the provincial governments are usually anxious to promote the interests of their major industries. More specifically, provincial revenues often vary directly with the level of activity in key resource industries. In short, it is quite possible for groups to have influence without necessarily having access. More recently, ideological factors, such as those involved in diagnosing and treating economic difficulties, appear to influence the access of various groups to particular governments.

Unfortunately, reliable propositions regarding responsiveness to interest groups and public preferences remain fragmentary and, in some instances, contradictory. The differences appear to reflect issue and circumstance, however, and suggest the need for more refined propositions. Nevertheless, the general propositions that interest groups have direct influence on federal-provincial negotiations only under special circumstances appears to be sustained. When the crunch comes, governments represent their own interests first. However, electoral considerations do appear to keep governments responsive to widely held public preferences.

OPENING UP THE PROCESS

The case studies turned up a number of promising innovations in federal-provincial collaboration which suggested that structural changes could open the process up to public and interest group representatives in certain circumstances without jeopardizing the negotiations themselves. In particular, the greater use of advisory groups, "tripartite" task forces (federal-provincial-private), pre-conference discussion papers, and investigations by parliamentary and legislative committees all seem worthy of further exploration. The relationship of such innovations to both conflict management and democratic values is explored below.

Accountability:
Stating the Case

It has been fashionable for some time to view with alarm the tendency for federal-provincial agreements to be made with little or no reference to legislative bodies. In many cases, such agreements can be implemented without legislation. Even when legislation is forthcoming, governments are generally unwilling to make changes in hard-won agreements in order to satisfy legislators (Simeon, 1973, pp. 279-80). While there have been examples of effective legislative scrutiny of proposed agreements, mostly at the federal level (such as the constitutional reform package), there is consensus among observers that executive federalism, with its unwritten requirement of unanimity (or near-unanimity under the rules established for patriation) disperses power among eleven governments but helps to concentrate it in the executive of each government (Van Loon and Whittington, 1981, pp. 543-44). Van Loon and Whittington (ibid., p. 542) comment on the "startling lack of attention paid to federal-provincial relations in either Parliament or the provincial legislatures," noting that legislators have little input across jurisdictional lines and that only ministers play any role in federal-provincial bodies. Members of opposition parties are nearly always completely locked out of the process. It is important to recognize that executive federalism is more a consequence than a cause of the general weakness of legislatures in the face of executive dominance in modern parliamentary systems (Stevenson, G., 1979, p. 203). It seems clear, however, that joint programs do help to shield governments from effective legislative scrutiny.

There is little doubt that the practitioners of federal-provincial bargaining prefer secrecy. As Simeon put it more than a decade ago (1973, p. 311):

> The emphasis on *in camera* discussion, so evident among the Canadian decision-makers, seems to imply a belief that the decision-makers themselves share many more common interests than do their constituents, since it is believed that if the conferences were public the participants would be given to public posturings rather than constructive discussion.

Subsequent experience with open (and televised) meetings has done little to change the minds of most practitioners. Indeed, position taking is now a recognized function of open federal-provincial meetings. The prospect of having to explain compromises, i.e., to bargain and make political points at the same time, appears to daunt most ministers.

It must be observed that executive federalism tends to operate in such a way as to shield shared-cost programs not only from parliamentary scrutiny, but also from the scrutiny of central agencies at both levels of government. Program officials achieve a degree of fiscal operational autonomy at both levels because of the joint nature of the activity (Dupré et al., 1973, pp. 94, 109). The weakening of hierarchical authority in these cases also weakens accountability in the larger sense, since departments that have little authority over or information about such joint programs are unable to answer effectively for them, i.e., through the responsible ministers in the legislatures.

It has also been noted by a number of observers that the federal government has been increasingly less able to hold the provinces accountable for the expenditure of transfer funds. The shift to unconditional transfers can be seen as an admission by the federal government of its inability to do more than rely on provincial good will (Smiley, 1980, p. 176). There has been considerable comment on the diversion of funds to purposes other than those contemplated by the transfer. Recent efforts to re-establish controls in the health care field only serve to highlight the extent to which the transfer payments have indeed become unconditional. It should be noted further that, even under conditional grant programs, federal officials often had difficulty acquiring needed information and were thus able to enforce conditions only with difficulty (Dupré et al., 1973, pp. 192ff.). In addition, the limited sanctions available to federal officials (essentially withholding of payment) weakened their control.

A related problem emerges at the federal level with respect to independent regulatory agencies. In a number of cases, federal legislation delegates authority to such agencies, with limited or no review by cabinet. The purpose, of course, was to remove certain decisions from partisan politics. One consequence, however, has been to create areas in which executive federalism cannot operate effectively because the agencies are not accountable to the federal cabinet. Federal negotiators, therefore, cannot negotiate in certain areas because they are unable to guarantee compliance by a regulatory agency, such as the Canadian Transport Commission or the Canadian Radio-television and Telecommunications Commission (Schultz, 1980, pp. 173–78; also Schultz, 1979, pp. 70–92). It should be noted that the federal government has moved in recent legislation to provide the cabinet with directive powers over such agencies, a move which may well strengthen federal departments without improving accountability. However, the directive power may make federal-provincial bargaining easier, by reducing the number of actors involved at the federal level. It is this sort of apparent tradeoff, a tradeoff between effectiveness and accountability or regulatory neutrality, that bedevils reformers.

Federal-provincial negotiators are at best indirectly accountable for their actions at the bargaining table. This, however, appears to be a problem of more concern to theorists than practitioners. The latter tend to resist the introduction of more actors into federal-provincial interactions on the ground that decision making, difficult enough in most circumstances under present conditions, would be more difficult under legislative scrutiny. In examining the cases, we found that parliaments are likely to have a significant role in intergovernmental negotiations only when governments need a mandate to strengthen their bargaining position, or when the issue is of such public concern that governments wish to diffuse responsibility.

With respect to hierarchical accountability, we found considerable agreement that shared-cost programs insulate operational departments from scrutiny by treasury officials at both levels (Dupré et al., 1973, pp. 217–18). Central agents are not able to enforce hierarchical accountability without considerable effort, especially with respect to bilateral programs, and they attempt to do so only when programs become controversial. Dupré and his colleagues found in their case study on policy making with respect to adult occupational training that the compromises between professional perspectives and governmental interests created a barely workable program. The program that emerged was a "fiscal nightmare" in which even the provincial government could not get the information it needed to control its expenditures, one consequence of lack of full agreement (ibid., pp. 192ff.).

Savoie's (1981a) study of the Canada–New Brunswick General Development Agreement makes it clear that bilateralism can have serious implications for accountability. The GDA approach, with decision making dominated by joint committees of federal and provincial officials (based in New Brunswick) locked interest groups out of the process, mainly because they could not get information: "A tacit understanding exists amongst officials which prohibits anyone from discussing or 'leaking' proposals under consideration outside of federal-provincial review committees or DREE-province task forces" (ibid., p. 55). Essentially, officials wanted to retain full control over the process, apparently feeling that special interests and political considerations interfered with rational economic decision making (ibid., pp. 105–106, 145–47). Politicians also lacked information and input.

Despite the emergence of summit federalism, the case studies are virtually unanimous that federal-provincial interaction is a closed bureaucratic loop much of the time. Many of the agreements discussed were implemented without legislation. Where legislation was involved, the implication is that debate was slight and inconsequential. This appears to hold across issues and time periods. Helliwell and May refer to the Syncrude deal as a silent bargain sealed without prior public or parliamentary scrutiny (Helliwell and May, 1976, pp. 178–79). Todres (1977, p. 216) notes that the Ontario Tax Credit scheme was put in place with little input from legislators, who were essentially bypassed by officials and ministers. Glaser (1984, pp. 319–22) sees bureaucratic dominance as typical in the health area. It seems clear that extensive public and legislative debate, as in Simeon's pension case or the constitutional discussions of the 1980s, has been quite rare.

The process of federal-provincial interaction does not itself promote bureaucratic dominance, since ministerial level meetings can set priorities and ratify agreements, but the fact that officials tend to share priorities and have longer-term relationships means that negotiations are more likely to be successful at that level. Especially in bilateral relationships, there is an obvious temptation to try to settle issues before they reach the political level. The problem, as Savoie (1981a, pp. 147–48) points out, is that both parliamentary and hierarchical accountability are eroded by such tactics and that national coordination of programs is also weakened. It appears that to have more accountability, one must have more political oversight and more openness, both of which appear to reduce the chances for harmonious resolution of conflicts. Nevertheless, the case for greater political involvement must be explored carefully. In bilateral relations, joint committees of ministers and officials could operate effectively if there were sufficient incentive for decision.

Responsiveness and Accountability

In many important respects, responsiveness and accountability are linked. In the economic sphere, for example, provincial governments can evade responsibility for many economic decisions by externalizing the consequences to other jurisdictions. The lack of accountability for these consequences provides an incentive for provincial governments to respond more readily to demands from interests with a strong presence in the province — at the expense of others. In principle, the obvious solution is to make each level of government fully accountable for the consequences of its actions, as Trebilcock and his colleagues suggest (1983, p. 560). How this can be done is not obvious, however. Increased jurisdictional clarity might help, but the most promising approaches appear to be those requiring consultation among the governments on all major economic decisions, through reformed central institutions or routinized federal-provincial meetings. Stronger measures, such as a federal-provincial body with the power to veto or delay certain decisions, such as foreign borrowing, would undoubtedly be unacceptable to most (perhaps all) current governments. The gain in influence over other governments would not be adequate compensation for the loss of autonomy.

Brown and Eastman (1981) argue that governments tend to be unaware of the consequences of their disagreements for the private sector and suggest (p. 189) that "a general opening of the federal-provincial process to the scrutiny of Parliament, provincial legislatures and the press may . . . strengthen this awareness." In short, they believe that any measures to open up the federal-provincial process would benefit both responsiveness and accountability. In particular, they suggest that industry consultation processes should be a routine part of federal-provincial interaction on economic policy, with officials meeting regularly with industry representatives through advisory boards, joint planning committees and special task forces.

Woodrow and his colleagues (1980) take the view that the lack of consumer input into federal-provincial decisions on communications policy is related to lack of accountability to Parliament. Better mechanisms for accountability to elected officials would, in their view, increase the incentive to take consumer preferences into account.

While accessibility of decision makers and a relatively open process of making public policy are often held out as central democratic values, openness is not without its difficulties. It is almost axiomatic that the more actors in the process, the more difficult agreement becomes. Therefore, greater access by interest groups would likely produce more immobilism in many circumstances. In addition, public demand rarely concerns itself with the principles of federalism or jurisdictional boundaries as such. Interest-group involvement, therefore, might well promote the erosion of the federal principle. Given the territorial distribution of many interests, decision makers are much more likely to find themselves involved in simultaneous games, trying, for example, to preserve electoral support, to mediate the conflicting demands of interests groups and to optimize their bargaining power in the federal-provincial arena (Simeon, 1973, p. 237ff.). On the other hand, as Van Loon and Whittington (1981, p. 539) suggest, intergovernmental bargaining might be more "honest" i.e., focussed on the issue at hand, when conducted before private-sector representatives, and more legitimate: "By including members of public-interest groups in the early stages of policy development, policy ideas can be 'pre-sold' or legitimized before they enter the political arena through co-opting of non-governmental organizations."

Open Covenants Openly Made?

As we have seen, the routine forms of intergovernmental interaction tend to be carried on with little attention to the legislative process or to interest groups — except where there are well-developed client relationships with particular governments. This is not to say that the officials involved are insensitive to public concerns or to broad government policy but rather to observe simply that the process is often closed. While this situation is probably conducive to effective intergovernmental conflict management, it often appears to mean that policy choices are made within a narrow range and without consideration of alternative perspectives. It is undemocratic not only in the sense that legislators have little influence, but also in the sense that the inequalities of access to decision makers common to liberal democratic systems are exacerbated by the federal-provincial process.

While recognizing the force of the argument that effective collaboration among governments is, to a degree, incompatible with the accountability of federal and provincial governments to their own publics, it is our contention that some reforms could achieve not only greater responsiveness and accountability, but also more effective decision making. Paul Brown (1983) has argued that effective collaboration requires secrecy and executive dominance and precludes legislative oversight. Executive dominance is not likely to be altered without significant parliamentary reform, but measures are possible to encourage greater public and interest-group input, as well as more involvement of legislators in the process. The crucial reforms that should be considered all involve an opening up of the process. It seems clear that, for routine federal-provincial inter-actions, the quality of decisions would benefit from greater public and political input. This could be achieved through a variety of mechanisms. The following three are suggested by the case studies:

- greater use of advisory committees representing affected groups;
- a requirement of public notice of new negotiations on issues of substance (this to be tabled in Parliament and the appropriate provincial legislatures); and
- striking of oversight committees in Parliament and legislatures to receive annual reports from federal-provincial bodies and to ratify new regulations.

The problems of accountability in the federal-provincial process are much like those for delegated legislation generally, and similar solutions seem appropriate.[22] For the sake of controlling costs, it might be possible to consolidate notice of plans for significant policy changes in a periodic publication like "The Regulatory Agenda," published semi-annually on an experimental basis by the Treasury Board. Minor and technical adjust-ments could be dealt with in annual reports and examined after the fact by legislative committees to avoid excessive rigidity.

In fact, technical issues with impact on identifiable interests often per-mit group input, especially when key groups hold necessary information or are needed for effective implementation. However, what might be called government issues, such as equalization, division of revenues and alloca-tion of costs, often have little external involvement. In such matters, responsiveness to groups is clearly less important than accountability to legislative bodies, which could be enhanced by more general oversight of the federal-provincial process.

In bilateral relations, joint committees of ministers could oversee imple-mentation bodies, perhaps with representatives of affected groups. Alter-natively, public hearings or advisory groups might be established. Parliamentary and legislative committees on federal-provincial relations could receive annual reports and exercise post facto oversight.

With respect to more "political" issues, where public controversy could be expected in any case, the most promising approaches seem likely to be those that build on past practice. The striking of ad hoc committees of Parliament (and the legislatures) to investigate policy options, as in the cases of Established Programs Financing and the constitutional accord, holds promise. These mechanisms allow for the canvassing of a wide range of opinions as well as for input from legislators. On more technical issues, committees of officials might canvass the views of interested parties, perhaps even holding public hearings. Special task forces, on the model of the Therrien Committee, might be used to combine federal, provincial and private-sector representation in a process of investigation and recommendation. The case studies suggest that economic decisions, especially those involved in intergovernmental activities to restructure sectors of the economy, would have greater legitimacy if there were mechanisms for group input. None of these reforms would interfere with the final authority of the first ministers, nor would they involve actual opening up of first ministers' conferences, neither of which would likely be conducive to effective decision making.

The major benefits of reforms along these lines would be to increase the range of options canvassed and to make intergovernmental negotiations less remote from the citizenry. Contrary to the views of many practitioners, we believe that a more open process might well produce better decisions. Officials would be under more pressure to anticipate objections and might, therefore, create better articulated proposals. The expectation of political oversight would provide an incentive for officials to put more effort into enforcing a greater degree of hierarchical accountability.

It appears that intergovernmental competition for visibility and legitimacy enhances responsiveness. Greater openness should, then, encourage responsiveness. Improved public understanding of the process might also reduce the tendency to "buck-passing," which reduces accountability and responsiveness in areas of shared jurisdiction. In cases of high public demand, the pressures for settlement might increase the decisiveness of the process, perhaps even promoting compromise in some cases. In others, of course, territorial divisions in the country might well inhibit the emergence of consensus. Certainly, public controversy would be stimulated. However, public debate regarding hard political decisions might well be beneficial, forcing greater awareness, on the part of the public and officials alike, of the tradeoffs required for national policy. In addition, the process might well encourage more careful building of consensus. Failure to reach agreement, when based on real territorial differences of interest, might well lead to effective bilateral bargaining and, perhaps, more sensitivity to such differences on the part of the federal government.[23] In any case, it seems clear to us that the closed and secretive nature of the process is not a functional necessity but rather a convenience for practitioners.

Summary and Conclusions

In this paper, we have tried to glean from the incomplete and often atheoretical literature on federalism and public policy answers to important questions regarding the impact of the federal-provincial process on public policy, its effectiveness as a system of conflict management and its implications for democratic values. In doing so, we have tried to go beyond the literature that suggests that intergovernmental conflict can be resolved simply by the development of appropriate intergovernmental machinery and a greater degree of intergovernmental trust (important as these are) to look at the conditions under which the system works most effectively. From these conditions, we have attempted to derive some lessons that might provide useful directions for reform.

Federalism and Policy Outcomes

It is clear from the case studies that the structure of the federal system has influenced the substance of public policy; the relationship, however, is far from simple. The impact of the federal structure is often indirect or complex, varying by issue, pattern of jurisdiction and interests mobilized. Nevertheless, it is possible to argue that policies would have developed differently had jurisdiction been centralized or decentralized. For example, the strength of provincial jurisdiction in the areas of social welfare and health care has been a conservative force in the expansion of services in those areas, except where intergovernmental competition has spurred innovation and program expansion.[24] Provincial authority over education and some aspects of economic policy has impeded coordination and limited the country's capacity to develop a comprehensive industrial strategy. On the other hand, policies in areas of exclusive federal jurisdiction have often been insensitive to regional differences, and we found instances where provincial jurisdiction was a major factor in protecting regional interests. Many of the administrative problems attributed to federalism (rigidities, delays, duplication, high decision costs) must be seen as the inevitable costs of operating a regionally diverse country. Structural reforms can minimize but not eliminate them, since many are not attributable to the federal system as such.

Also inevitable are a variety of tensions in the system, most of them exacerbated but not caused by the federal structure. The strength of regional interests, for example, creates a variety of tensions which pit particular regional concerns against some broader concept of the national interest. Regional equity often appears to be at odds with international competitiveness. The federal government's commitment to national standards in public services appears to clash with provincial attempts to integrate social programs and respond flexibly to changing needs. These tensions are present in every regionalized country, and the situation in Canada differs only in that they tend to become intergovernmental issues.

In the end, it is necessary to accept the inevitability of these tensions, recognizing, as Savoie (1984a, p. 332) puts it, that "an unrelenting pursuit of 'national efficiency' is not a viable policy option for Canada." However, more flexible intergovernmental arrangements could ameliorate these difficulties and maintain a satisfactory balance. A crucial factor in managing regional tensions successfully is the federal government's capacity to make hard allocative decisions and to fashion appropriate compromises and tradeoffs.

From a broader perspective, the case studies suggest that the intergovernmental policy process has some general effects on the kinds of policies agreed upon. For example, shared jurisdiction and interdependence tend to narrow the range of policies considered, focussing attention on fiscal and jurisdictional issues rather than substantive ones. It also appears that federalism is one factor among many in the system that limits the capacity of governments to make radical changes in the socio-economic order. The requirement of consensus promotes incremental decision making and blocks certain policies where consensus is not possible. Where deep regional divisions are involved, of course, a decision not to act may be the only viable policy. The crucial problem is to ensure that a degree of regional equity is maintained and that regional suspicions, as opposed to real differences, do not paralyze the policy-making process.

Decisions perceived to have differential regional impacts are difficult to resolve through federal-provincial processes, but continual liaison and awareness of possible tradeoffs seem to help. It appears to be particularly important to have visible provincial involvement in major policy decisions of this sort, since regional alienation is, at least partly, a matter of perception. Permanent federal-provincial mechanisms in relevant policy areas might be one way to meet this need.

Systematic biases in the federal-provincial process are difficult to detect, as numerous economic studies demonstrate. It appears, however, that the complexity of the system increases the normal advantage of interest groups with substantial resources over those lacking money and elite membership, but the evidence is scattered. There is also modest support for the allegation that the poorer classes and provinces have been losers in recent years. With the increasing use of bilateral negotiations, poorer provinces may find themselves disadvantaged relative to wealthier ones, since they have fewer resources with which to resist federal government pressures. In addition, decentralization weakens the federal government's capacity to establish national programs and redistribute wealth, which would help poorer provinces.

Economic policy is of particular importance today and poses particular problems for the Canadian federal system. While the issue is complex, it appears that the existence of significant provincial jurisdiction has (as a result of provincial competition for investment) limited provincial tax rates; weakened laws protecting labour; restricted environmental protection laws; hampered federal efforts to reduce regional disparities; and made the development of national fiscal and economic policies more difficult. Here again, however, the effects do not appear to have been drastic, and the jurisdictional factor has only been one among many. Indeed, after reviewing several recent major works on industrial strategy, most of which contend that federalism hampers the development of a national industrial strategy, one scholar concluded that the case was not proven.

In an article published after the bulk of this paper was completed, Michael Atkinson (1984, p. 462) found no conclusive evidence that federalism itself is a serious impediment to the formulation of national industrial policies: "Clearly a federal form of government is no advantage, but often the primary problem lies elsewhere." However, he notes (ibid., p. 465) that the absence of strong national business organizations (arguably a by-product of shared jurisdiction) is an important limitation on the capacity of the federal government to "set industrial policy objectives or harness business to them." Federal-provincial collaboration remains necessary, and in Atkinson's view, quite possible, since he found no incompatibilities among the governmental approaches now in effect at both levels.

Federalism and Conflict Management

In our view, the drift of the federal system, noted by Cairns, toward paralysis as a result of the clash of big governments at both levels is a tendency rather than an inexorable trend. While federalism undoubtedly contributed to the political difficulties of recent years, it was only one among many factors and, probably, not the most important. Nevertheless, the tendency is real, and steps are needed to develop new mechanisms and new approaches to deal with the growing interdependence of governments. Disentanglement is not a realistic option, since it could not be achieved without dismantling much of our economic and social system. Disengagement, however, is possible if governments can be persuaded to focus less on jurisdiction and status and more on the substantive problems at hand in intergovernmental negotiations.

Intergovernmental conflict is inevitable in a diverse federal system, but "no federal system can survive for long in a state that brings federal and provincial governments into continuous confrontation," as Howard Darling put it (1980, p. 240). While some conflicts are too fundamental to be dealt with effectively by institutional reform, it is our contention that much can be done to improve the system's capacity for conflict management. As we have noted, there are no panaceas, but the case studies suggested to us a number of potentially beneficial reforms.

The most useful reforms, in our view, will build on the many successful instances of federal-provincial negotiation, recognizing that the system has continued to function effectively in many sectors even at the height of visible intergovernmental conflict. In addition, it must be noted that interdependence does not mean that governments must solve all problems through collaborative programs. Some issues will be dealt with best by parallel programs, with agreements to consult and minimize duplication or countervailing policies; others will require even less intergovernmental activity, with governments acting independently. In some cases, unilateral action, followed by mutual adjustment of programs, may be necessary.

Effective reforms must also take into account the sources of the high levels of intergovernmental conflict in the 1980s. The general challenge to the regime (posed by independence advocates in Quebec and the prolonged constitutional reform debate) is now quiescent. In any case, the reform of intergovernmental institutions would have limited capacity to ameliorate such fundamental conflicts. Perhaps equally important, however, are the longer-term trends marked by the shift of policy focus from social to economic issues and the increase in interventionist policies by both levels of government. Increased provincial activism transformed regional issues into intergovernmental ones. These trends posed challenges to existing patterns of intergovernmental interaction which were developed to deal with less interventionist social issues, and required some adjustments.

In general terms, reforms to the system must increase incentives for intergovernmental collaboration and develop counterweights to the strong political incentives for provincial leaders to see policies primarily in terms of territorial impact. Given that our customary methods of political representation are primarily territorial, the latter is a major challenge. The problem is complicated by the fact that many of the most difficult intergovernmental issues in the years ahead are likely to revolve around economic development and, therefore, to have fairly clear territorial implications. Two general strategies suggest themselves. The first is the development of an intergovernmental economic council to help frame issues in non-territorial terms or to identify tradeoffs. The second is continuous consultation on economic policy, without regard for jurisdiction. In this context, the federal government must reduce the widespread feeling at the provincial level that it is insensitive to provincial interests in its own areas of jurisdiction. More effective mechanisms for consulting provincial governments are clearly needed.

In the course of our discussions, we have identified a number of strategies for more effective intergovernmental collaboration. Some are general, and some are specific to particular jurisdictional patterns and policy issues. In areas like communications and transportation policy, the case studies suggest to us the desirability of regulatory sharing, with the federal government giving up some authority to ensure effective provincial input. Similarly, we identified a need for more federal involvement in education policy. Both levels must consult more with other governments if economic and fiscal policy are to be effectively coordinated. In areas such as energy policy and regional economic development, bilateral negotiations appear to be the only hope, given the sharp regional differences involved.

Seen in a broader context, however, there is a need for permanent intergovernmental bodies to identify externalities and possible tradeoffs, as well as to put bilateral agreements in national perspective. Where regulation is concerned, there is a variety of mechanisms available to ensure better intergovernmental coordination, from joint boards to parallel agencies with regularized consultation. For new subject areas, federal-provincial working groups show promise.

With respect to industrial policy, we have suggested the need to break down the issues into more manageable segments, either by limiting the issues through sectoral planning or by limiting the players through bilateralism. These approaches seem best suited to a political system with deep regional divisions of economic interest in which important segments of society are wary of large-scale economic intervention. The danger is that sector-specific or bilateral agreements will be made by "small, closed policy communities . . . far away from the parliamentary stage" (Atkinson, 1984, p. 466), threatening accountability and responsiveness to broader interests. It seems clear that mechanisms for political oversight and public input are necessary, and these, in our view, are not incompatible with effective conflict management. For example, bilateral agreements are more likely to serve national needs and to be politically legitimate if they are made within a widely accepted national program. The latter might involve a multilateral umbrella agreement or simply a federal policy worked out in bilateral talks with all the provincial governments.

In more general terms, our survey of case studies confirmed the conventional wisdom that conflict management is most effective when certain conditions are met. The most important of these are mutual trust, a shared perception of the issue (common vocabulary and perspectives), and a shared commitment to reaching an agreement. In institutional terms, these conditions are most likely to be fostered by mechanisms for continual consultation. In areas where joint programs are well established, especially where regional differences are not great, councils of ministers backed by intergovernmental secretariats hold promise. The proliferation of intergovernmental bureaucracies is not itself a panacea, however. In many cases, small bodies to which minor regulatory decisions could be referred would be helpful in permitting rapid adjustment of joint programs. In other cases, monitoring groups would be helpful. In difficult areas, joint task forces would be helpful in clarifying issues and proposing solutions. With respect to the hard political questions, better preparation for meetings, with the assistance of joint bodies, might improve the chances for agreement.

The existence of intergovernmental bodies would not, in many cases, lead to agreement on highly political matters, but it might well help insulate less controversial areas from the mistrust often generated by the hard issues. Such agencies, with staff support, can keep issues on the agenda and frame issues in such a way as to minimize politicization. Well-developed ministerial councils might help to focus first ministers' conferences on broad issues and encourage them to establish frameworks for more detailed negotiations by ministers and officials. In short, we believe that efforts to improve intergovernmental mechanisms for both routine adjustments and the debate of fundamental questions would pay off.

In summary, it is our view, based on the case studies, that the Canadian system of intergovernmental relations could achieve better conflict management by developing new mechanisms; trying new approaches; and disengaging in some areas, through the implementation of parallel rather than contractual programs. For the latter approach to be most effective, there would have to be a new willingness to consult with other governments, but each level would get full credit (or blame) for its own programs. Recent government spending restraint programs fall into this category. Of course, effective conflict management requires a degree of consensus on values and the acceptance of Canada as a legitimate political community (at least for some purposes).

Federalism and Democratic Values

An important question remains, however: How compatible are such new mechanisms and approaches with democratic values? In examining this question, we began with the patterns we could identify in the operation of existing mechanisms and approaches. We found that both direct public input and accountability to legislative bodies have generally been limited. In particular, the intergovernmental process is most likely to exclude outside influences when the interests of governments become primary (with negotiations revolving around jurisdiction or sharing of revenues and allocation of costs) and when the pressures for agreement are strong. We noted the special burdens imposed by shared jurisdiction on groups attempting to monitor government actions and to gain access to decision makers. In particular, mixed jurisdiction and joint programs result in a reduction in responsiveness and accountability by making it difficult to determine responsibility for decisions. Looking at the issue more broadly, however, we found that strong public preferences tended to be reflected in the substantive policies agreed to. It seems that electoral considerations have made governments attentive to public opinion and to the views of powerful groups, expressed directly and through politicians and officials. Nevertheless, we found that the general lack of access has narrowed the range of policy options considered and probably exacerbated inequalities of influence among groups and reduced the legitimacy of agreements. The system does appear to be more professionally open than democratically open, as Doern has suggested; nonetheless, professionals seem often to have represented the views of unorganized groups in society.

While executive dominance is a constant in our parliamentary system, we believe that greater openness and accountability can be achieved without reducing the effectiveness of conflict management. In our view, the secrecy surrounding the process, like that surrounding budget making, is outmoded and is now more a convenience for participants than a functional necessity. Indeed, we believe that secrecy has at times contributed to shortsighted policies and that policy outcomes have at times been improved by parliamentary and public involvement, as in the Constitution case. In the past, parliamentary or legislative involvement has tended to be greatest when governments wanted a mandate to support their bargaining positions or wished to diffuse responsibility for difficult decisions. The difficult decisions ahead may well call for more such involvement.

What we advocate is greater openness in the process leading up to intergovernmental negotiations and greater willingness to submit decisions subsequently to parliamentary and legislative scrutiny. The conventional view that bargaining sessions themselves must remain closed seems to us correct. The conflicting pressures on participants would make compromise difficult to achieve. However, the use of such mechanisms as advisory groups, public hearings, pre-conference discussion papers, and investigations by parliamentary and legislative committees might well have actual benefits for the policy-making process as well as serving democratic values. The key is to involve groups in the process at the early stages, so that all legitimate viewpoints are canvassed. The expectation of post facto oversight might well improve both hierarchical accountability and the quality of preparation for conferences. Better mechanisms for continual private-sector consultation would help to ensure that the federal-provincial agenda encompassed all major concerns.

It would be unrealistic to expect that new mechanisms for and approaches to intergovernmental relations will prevent intergovernmental conflict. Our thesis is that better mechanisms and approaches, geared to greater public input and accountability, will produce better and more legitimate decisions. In addition, we believe that more openness would help to counter both unrealistic expectations and cynicism regarding federal-provincial relations without impeding effective conflict management. In the end, appropriate reforms must evolve through the operation of the federal-provincial process itself. We hope that some of the ideas explored here will assist in that process.

Notes

This study was completed in November 1984.

The authors gratefully acknowledge the research assistance of Robert Everett, Joan Boase, Deborah Stienstra and Robert Speller. We have also benefited immeasurably from the advice and encouragement of Richard Simeon, without whose boundless creative energy this paper would have been much less penetrating (and much easier to complete). The comments of the Commission's anonymous reviewer and the Research Advisory Group for this section were also most helpful. Errors and omissions remain our responsibility, and we hope that the authors of the many case studies we have reviewed will forgive us our debts (and our trespasses).

1. These criteria for assessing public policy making — decisiveness, responsiveness, and conflict management — are suggested by Murray (1983, p. 138).

2. For recent evidence on this point, see Elkins and Simeon (1980) and Fletcher and Drummond (1979).

3. This is set out in Banting (1982, chap. 5).

4. Various attempts to do so are reported in Trebilcock et al. (1983). See also Tupper (1982); Scott (1976); Bryan (1980).

5. *Globe and Mail*, 11 July 1984.

6. Objective economic analysis suggests that western anger regarding freight rates is largely unjustified, indicating that the issue is a surrogate for more general regional alienation. See Darling (1980, pp. 235–41). On the more general issue, see Norrie (1976).

7. Banting (1982, pp. 69–76) also notes the expansionist dynamic created by competition between governments — especially Ottawa and Quebec — to occupy jurisdictional gaps and to gain public support.

8. Banting (ibid., pp. 84ff.) summarizes the arguments of leading federalism specialists, including Alan Cairns, Richard Simeon, Donald Smiley and Milton Moore.

9. This summary is distilled from the following sources: Jenkin (1983); Tupper (1982); Thorburn (1984); Brown and Eastman (1981); Savoie (1981a); Scott (1976b); Trebilcock et al. (1983); Bryan (1980); Doern and Phidd (1983, chaps. 15, 16).

10. Some of these ideas are derived from Van Loon and Whittington (1981, pp. 534, 547–48).

11. The differing assessments of Berry and Laxer regarding the energy issues are a case in point. The disagreement between Dyck and Hum may be explained by their focus on process (Dyck) or substance (Hum).

12. For an excellent summary of Smiley's views, see Smiley (1979).

13. In this section, we have received considerable inspiration from an unpublished manuscript kindly made available to us by Peter Leslie, entitled, "Federal State, National Economy".

14. See Fletcher and Fletcher (1979); Schultz (1982, pp. 104–106); Stanbury (1982, pp. 12–13); Buchan and Johnston (1982, pp. 117–66); Lesser (1982, pp. 169–224); Woodrow et al. (1980).

15. See also Westmacott (1973); Westmacott and Phillips (1979); Schultz (1980, pp. 206–207).

16. In the current period of restraint, public opinion may be more divided than in the past, but general support for these programs appears to remain strong.

17. This distillation is drawn from a long list of sources, the most important of which are: Scott (1976b); Swainson (1979); Laxer (1983); Doern and Phidd (1983, pp. 453–87); Ontario Economic Council (1980, vol. 2); Thur (1981); Caplan (1970); Simeon (1980).

18. See, for example, Brown and Eastman (1981, pp. 186ff.); Thorburn (1984, pp. 212–17); Simeon (1979); Trebilcock et al. (1983, pp. 5, 48–50); Tupper (1982, pp. 83ff.).

19. The Committee on the Extension of Services to Northern and Remote Communities (chaired by Réal Therrien) was created by the federal minister of communications and the Canadian Radio-television and Telecommunications Commission (CRTC) in the fall of 1979 to examine television service extension via satellite and pay-TV.

20. We have in mind here the influence of women and native groups in the constitutional negotiations in the 1980s.

21. The Royal Commission on Taxation (or Carter Commission) was appointed by the federal government in September 1962 to make recommendations on the reform of the federal tax system.

22. The fact that only a few parliamentarians might approach the task of oversight with any diligence does not negate the value of establishing the principle and the improvement in the flow of information that would accompany it. See Jackson and Atkinson (1980, pp. 102–105).

23. Similar arguments with respect to regional development are made by Savoie (1984b) and by Aucoin and Bakvis (1984).

24. We found little evidence to support the view of the public choice theorists that intergovernmental competition produces a better bundle of services for the citizenry to choose among. While competition produced more consumer-oriented policies in some cases, it favoured business interests in others.

Bibliography

Armitage, Andrew. 1975. *Social Welfare in Canada: Ideas and Realities.* Toronto: McClelland and Stewart.

Atkinson, Michael M. 1984. "On the Prospects for Industrial Policy in Canada." *Canadian Public Administration* 27: 454–67.

Atkinson, Michael M., and Marsha A. Chandler, eds. 1983. *The Politics of Canadian Public Policy.* Toronto: University of Toronto Press.

Aucoin, Peter, and Herman Bakvis. 1984. "Organizational Differentiation and Integration: The Case of Regional Economic Development Policy in Canada." *Canadian Public Administration* 27 (3) (Fall): 348–71.

Babe, Robert E. 1974. "Public and Private Regulation of Cable Television: A Case Study of Technological Change and Relative Power." *Canadian Public Administration* 17: 187–225.

Banting, Keith G. 1982. *The Welfare State and Canadian Federalism.* Montreal: McGill-Queen's University Press.

Bella, Leslie. 1979. "The Provincial Role in the Canadian Welfare State: The Influence of Provincial Social Policy Initiatives on the Design of the Canada Assistance Plan." *Canadian Public Administration* 22: 439–52.

Berry, Glyn R. 1974. "The Oil Lobby and the Energy Crisis." *Canadian Public Administration* 17: 600–35.

Birch, Anthony. 1955. *Federalism, Finance and Social Legislation in Canada, Australia and the United States.* London: Oxford University Press.

Brown, Paul M. 1983. "Responsiveness Versus Accountability in Collaborative Federalism: The Canadian Experience." *Canadian Public Administration* 26: 629–39.

Brown, D.M., and J. Eastman. 1981. *The Limits of Consultation: Ottawa, the Provinces and the Private Sector Debate Industrial Policy.* Kingston and Ottawa: Queen's University, Institute of Intergovernmental Relations, and Science Council of Canada.

Brunelle, Dorval. 1982. *L'État solide: Sociologie du fédéralisme au Canada et au Québec.* Montreal: Éditions Sélect.

Bryan, Ingrid. 1980. *Economic Policies in Canada.* Toronto: Butterworth.

Bryden, Kenneth. 1974. *Old Age Pensions and Policy-making in Canada.* Montreal: McGill-Queen's University Press.

Buchan, J., and C. Christopher Johnston. 1982. "Telecommunications Regulation and the Constitution: A Lawyer's Perspective." In *Telecommunications Regulation and the Constitution,* pp. 117–66. Montreal: Institute for Research on Public Policy.

Buchan, Robert J., C. Christopher Johnson, T. Gregory Kane, Barry Lesser, Richard J. Schultz, and W.T. Stanbury. 1982. *Telecommunications Regulation and the Constitution.* Montreal: Institute for Research on Public Policy.

Bucovetsky, M.W. 1975. "The Mining Industry and the Great Tax Reform Debate." In *Pressure Group Behaviour in Canadian Politics,* edited by A. Paul Pross, pp. 87–114. Toronto: McGraw-Hill Ryerson.

Byers, R.B., and Robert Reford, eds. 1979. *Canada Challenged: The Viability of Confederation.* Toronto: Canadian Institute of International Affairs.

Cairns, Alan C. 1977. "The Governments and Societies of Canadian Federalism." *Canadian Journal of Political Science* 10: 695–725.

——. 1979. "The Other Crisis of Canadian Federalism." *Canadian Public Administration* 22: 175–95.

Cameron, David M. 1981. "Regional Economic Disparities: The Challenge to Federalism and Public Policy." *Canadian Public Policy* 7: 500–505.

Campbell, Harry F., W.D. Gainer, and Anthony Scott. 1976. "Resource Rent: How Much and for Whom." In *Natural Resource Revenues: A Test of Canadian Federalism,* edited by Anthony Scott, pp. 118–36. Vancouver: University of British Columbia Press.

Caplan, Neil. 1970. "Offshore Mineral Rights: Anatomy of a Federal-Provincial Conflict." *Journal of Canadian Studies* 5: 50–61.

Careless, Anthony. 1977. *Initiative and Response: The Adaptation of Canadian Federalism to Regional Economic Expansion.* Montreal: McGill-Queen's University Press.

Chandler, Marsha A., and William M. Chandler. 1979. *Public Policy and Provincial Politics.* Toronto: McGraw-Hill Ryerson.

Clarke, Harold D., Jane Jenson, Lawrence LeDuc, and Jon H. Pammett. 1984. *Absent Mandate: The Politics of Discontent in Canada.* Toronto: Gage.

Corry, J.A. 1958. "Constitutional Trends and Federalism." In *Evolving Canadian Federalism,* edited by A.R.M. Lower. Durham, N.C.: Duke University Press.

Courchene, T.J. 1976. "Equalization Payments and Energy Royalties." In *Natural Resource Revenues: A Test of Canadian Federalism,* edited by Anthony Scott, pp. 74–107. Vancouver: University of British Columbia Press.

Courchene, T.J., and James R. Melvin. 1980. "Energy Revenues: Consequences for the Rest of Canada." *Canadian Public Policy* 6 supplement (February): 192–202.

Darling, Howard. 1980. *The Politics of Freight Rates.* Toronto: McClelland and Stewart.

Dawson, H.J. 1975. "National Pressure Groups and the Federal Government." In *Pressure Group Behaviour in Canadian Politics,* edited by A. Paul Pross, pp. 27–58. Toronto: McGraw-Hill Ryerson.

Doern, G.B. 1977. *Regulatory Processes and Jurisdictional Issues in the Regulation of Hazardous Products in Canada.* Ottawa: Science Council of Canada.

Doern, G.B., and V.S. Wilson, eds. 1974. *Issues in Canadian Public Policy.* Toronto: Macmillan.

Doern, G.B., and P. Aucoin, eds. 1979. *Public Policy in Canada: Organization, Process and Management.* Toronto: Macmillan.

Doern, G.B., and R.W. Phidd. 1983. *Canadian Public Policy: Ideas, Structure, Process.* Toronto: Methuen.

Dupré, J. Stefan, David M. Cameron, Graeme H. McKechnie, and Theodore B. Rotenberg. 1973. *Federalism and Policy Development: The Case of Adult Occupational Training in Ontario.* Toronto: University of Toronto Press.

Dyck, Rand. 1976. "The Canada Assistance Plan: The Ultimate in Co-operative Federalism." *Canadian Public Administration* 19: 587–602.

Elkins, David J., and Richard Simeon, eds. 1980. *Small Worlds: Provinces and Parties in Canadian Political Life.* Toronto: Methuen.

Fletcher, Frederick J., and Robert J. Drummond. 1979. *Canadian Attitude Trends, 1960–78.* Montreal: Institute for Research on Public Policy.

Fletcher, Martha, and Frederick J. Fletcher. 1979. "Communications and Confederation: Jurisdiction and Beyond." In *Canada Challenged: The Viability of Confederation,* edited by R.B. Byers and Robert Reford, pp. 158–87. Toronto: Canadian Institute of International Affairs.

Gillies, J. 1981. *Where Business Fails.* Montreal: Institute for Research on Public Policy.

Glaser, William A. 1977. *Federalism in Canadian Health Services: Lessons for the United States.* New York: Columbia University.

——. 1984. "Health Politics: Some Lessons from Abroad." In *Health Politics and Policy,* edited by J. Litman, pp. 305–39. New York: John Wiley and Sons.

Guest, Dennis. 1980. *The Emergence of Social Security in Canada.* Vancouver: University of British Columbia Press.

Helliwell, John, and Gerry May. 1976. "Taxes, Royalties and Equity Participation as Alternative Methods of Dividing Resource Revenues: The Syncrude Example." In *National Resource Revenues,* edited by Anthony Scott, pp. 153–80. Vancouver: University of British Columbia Press.

Hum, Derek. 1983. *Federalism and the Poor: A Review of the Canada Assistance Program.* Toronto: Ontario Economic Council.

Ivany, J.W.G. 1981. "Alternative Structures for the Governance of Education: Some First Steps." In *Federal-Provincial Relations: Education Canada,* edited by J.W.G. Ivany and M.E. Manley-Casimir, pp. 110–116. Toronto: OISE Press.

Ivany, J.W.G., and M.E. Manley-Casimir, eds. 1981. *Federal-Provincial Relations: Education Canada*. Toronto: OISE Press.

Jackson, Robert J., and Michael M. Atkinson. 1980. *The Canadian Legislative System*. 2d ed. Toronto: Gage.

Jenkin, Michael. 1983. *The Challenge of Diversity: Industrial Policy in the Canadian Federation*. Ottawa: Science Council of Canada.

Kwavnick, David. 1972. *Organized Labour and Pressure Politics: The Canadian Labour Congress 1956-68*. Montreal: McGill-Queen's University Press.

——. 1975. "Interest Group Demands and the Federal Political System." In *Pressure Group Behaviour and Canadian Politics*, edited by A. Paul Pross, pp. 69–86. Toronto: McGraw-Hill Ryerson.

Laxer, James. 1983. *Oil and Gas: Ottawa, the Provinces and the Petroleum Industry*. Toronto: James Lorimer.

Leman, Christopher. 1980. *The Collapse of Welfare Reform: Political Institutions, Policy and the Poor in Canada and the United States*. Cambridge, Mass.: MIT Press.

Lesser, Barry. 1982. "The Implications of the Federal and Provincial Proposals for Regulating Telecommunications." In *Telecommunications Regulation and the Constitution*, pp. 169–224. Montreal: Institute for Research on Public Policy.

Lévesque, René. 1977. "For an Independent Quebec." In *Canadian Federalism: Myth or Reality?*, 3d ed., edited by Peter Meekison, pp. 483–93. Toronto: Methuen.

Mallory, J.R. 1954. *Social Credit and the Federal Power in Canada*. Toronto: University of Toronto Press.

McCorquodale, Susan. 1983. "The Management of a Common Property Resource: Fisheries in Atlantic Canada." In *The Politics of Canadian Public Policy*, edited by Michael M. Atkinson and Marsha A. Chandler, pp. 151–71. Toronto: University of Toronto Press.

McInnes, Simon. 1978. "Federal-Provincial Negotiation: Family Allowances 1970-76." Ph.D. dissertation, Carleton University.

Meekison, Peter, ed. 1977. *Canadian Federalism: Myth or Reality?* 3d ed. Toronto: Methuen.

Morin, Claude. 1976. *Quebec Versus Ottawa: The Struggle for Self-Government 1960-72*. Toronto: University of Toronto Press.

Murray, Catherine. 1983. *Managing Diversity: Federal-Provincial Collaboration and the Committee on Extension of Services to Northern and Remote Communities*. Kingston: Queen's University, Institute of Intergovernmental Relations.

Norrie, K.H. 1976. "Some Comments on Prairie Alienation." *Canadian Public Policy* 2: 211–24.

OECD. 1977. "Education: Governments, Goals and Policy-Making." In *Canadian Federalism: Myth or Reality?*, 3d ed., edited by Peter Meekison, pp. 416–29. Toronto: Methuen.

Ontario Economic Council. 1980. *Energy Policy for the Eighties: An Economic Analysis*. 2 vols. Toronto: OEC.

Ornstein, Michael, Michael Stevenson, and Paul Williams. 1979. "The State of Mind: Public Perceptions of the Future of Canada." In *Canada Challenged: The Viability of Confederation*, edited by R.B. Byers and Robert Reford, pp. 57–107. Toronto: Canadian Institute of International Affairs.

Phidd, Richard W., and G.B. Doern. 1978. *The Politics and Management of Canadian Economic Policy*. Toronto: Macmillan.

Poel, Dale. 1983. "Determinants of Legal Aid in Canada: Actors, Policies, Programmes and Futures." In *The Politics of Canadian Public Policy*, edited by Michael A. Atkinson and Marsha A. Chandler, pp. 69–91. Toronto: University of Toronto Press.

Pratt, Larry. 1976. *The Tar Sands: Syncrude and the Politics of Oil*. Edmonton: Hurtig.

Presthus, Robert. 1973. *Elite Accommodation in Canadian Politics*. Toronto: Macmillan.

Pross, Paul A., ed. 1975. *Pressure Group Behaviour in Canadian Politics*. Toronto: McGraw-Hill Ryerson.

Safarian, A.E. 1980. *Ten Markets or One? Regional Barriers to Economic Activity in Canada*. Toronto: Ontario Economic Council.

Savoie, Donald J. 1981a. *Federal-Provincial Co-operation: The Canada-New Brunswick General Development Agreement*. Montreal: McGill-Queen's University Press.

——. 1981b. "The General Development Agreement Approach and the Bureaucratization of Provincial Governments in the Atlantic Provinces." *Canadian Public Administration* 24: 116–31.

——. 1984a. "The Toppling of DREE and Prospects for Regional Economic Development." *Canadian Public Policy* 10: 328–37.

——. 1984b. "L'harmonie fédérale-provinciale est-elle toujours essentielle?" *Policy Options* (November): 13–14.

Schultz, Richard. 1979. *Federalism and the Regulatory Process*. Montreal: Institute for Research on Public Policy.

——. 1980. *Federalism, Bureaucracy, and Public Policy: The Politics of Highway Transport Regulation*. Montreal: McGill-Queen's University Press.

——. 1982. "Partners in a Game Without Masters: Reconstructing the Telecommunications Regulatory System." In *Telecommunications Regulation and the Constitution*, pp. 41–114. Montreal: Institute for Research on Public Policy.

Scott, Anthony. 1976. "Who Should Get Natural Resource Revenues." In *Natural Resource Revenues: A Test of Canadian Federalism*, edited by Anthony Scott, pp. 1–51. Vancouver: University of British Columbia Press.

Simeon, Richard. 1973. *Federal-Provincial Diplomacy: The Making of Recent Policy in Canada*. Toronto: University of Toronto Press.

——. 1979. "Federalism and the Politics of a National Strategy." In *The Politics of an Industrial Strategy: A Seminar*, pp. 5–43. Ottawa: Science Council of Canada.

——. 1980. "Natural Resource Revenues and Canadian Federalism: A Survey of the Issues." *Canadian Public Policy* 6: 182–91.

——. 1982–83. "Criteria for Choice in Federal Systems." *Queen's Law Journal* 18: 131–57.

Smiley, D.V. 1976. "The Political Context of Resource Development in Canada." In *Natural Resource Revenues: A Test of Canadian Federalism*, edited by Anthony Scott, pp. 61–73. Vancouver: University of British Columbia Press.

——. 1979. "An Outsider's Observations of Federal-Provincial Relations among Consenting Adults." In *Confrontation and Collaboration — Intergovernmental Relations in Canada Today*, edited by Richard Simeon, pp. 105–113. Toronto: Institute of Public Administration of Canada.

——. 1980. *Canada in Question: Federalism in the Seventies*. 3d ed. Toronto: McGraw-Hill Ryerson.

Soderstrom, Lee. 1978. *The Canadian Health System*. London: Croom Helm.

Spector, Norman. 1984. "Federal-Provincial Professionalism." *Policy Options* (November): 44–46.

Sproule-Jones, Mark. 1975. *Public Choice and Federalism in Canada and Australia*. Canberra: Australian National University Press.

Stanbury, W.T. 1982. "Telecommunications Regulation and the Constitution: The Main Themes." In *Telecommunications Regulation and the Constitution*, pp. 1–19. Montreal: Institute for Research on Public Policy.

Stevenson, Garth. 1979. *Unfulfilled Union: Canadian Federalism and National Unity*. Toronto: Macmillan.

——. 1981. "The Political Economy Tradition and Canadian Federalism." *Studies in Political Economy* 6: 113–33.

Stevenson, Hugh A. 1981. "The Federal Presence in Canadian Education." In *Federal-Provincial Relations: Education Canada*, edited by J.W.G. Ivany and M.E. Manley-Casimir, pp. 3–18. Toronto: OISE Press.

Swainson, Neil A. 1979. *Conflict over the Columbia: The Canadian Background to an Historic Treaty*. Montreal: McGill-Queen's University Press.

Taylor, Malcolm G. 1978. *Health Insurance and Canadian Public Policy: The Seven Decisions that Created the Canadian Health Insurance System*. Montreal: McGill-Queen's University Press.

Thorburn, H.G. 1984. *Planning and the Economy: Building Federal-Provincial Consensus.* Toronto: James Lorimer.

Thur, Livia, ed. 1981. *Energy Policy and Federalism.* Toronto: Institute of Public Administration of Canada.

Todres, E.M. 1977. "Adaptive Federalism: Taxation Policy in Canada." Ph.D. dissertation, University of Pittsburgh.

Trebilcock, M.J., J.R.S. Prichard, T.J. Courchene, and J. Whalley, eds. 1983. *Federalism and the Economic Union.* Toronto: Ontario Economic Council.

Trudeau, P.E. 1968. *Federalism and the French Canadians.* Toronto: Macmillan.

Tupper, Allan. 1982. *Public Money and the Private Sector: Industrial Assistance and Canadian Federalism.* Kingston: Queen's University, Institute of Intergovernmental Relations.

Tupper, Allan, and G. Bruce Doern. 1981. "Public Corporations and Public Policy." In *Public Corporations and Public Policy in Canada*, edited by A. Tupper and G.B. Doern, pp. 1-50. Montreal: Institute for Research on Public Policy.

Van Loon, Richard. 1979. "Reforming Welfare in Canada." *Public Policy* 27: 469-504.

Van Loon, Richard, and Michael S. Whittington. 1981. *The Canadian Political System: Environment, Structure, and Process.* 3d ed. Toronto: McGraw-Hill Ryerson.

Weller, Geoffrey R., and Pranlal Manga. 1983. "The Development of Health Policy in Canada." In *The Politics of Canadian Public Policy*, edited by Michael M. Atkinson and Marsha A. Chandler, pp. 223-46. Toronto: University of Toronto Press.

Westmacott, Martin. 1973. "The National Transportation Act and Western Canada: A Case Study in Co-operative Federalism." *Canadian Public Administration* 16 (Fall): 447-67.

Westmacott, Martin, and D.J. Phillips. 1979. "Transportation Policy and National Unity." In *Canada Challenged: The Viability of Confederation*, edited by R.B. Byers and Robert Reford, pp. 293-315. Toronto: Canadian Institute of International Affairs.

Wharf, Brian. 1981. "Social Welfare and the Political System." In *Canadian Social Welfare*, edited by J.C. Turner and F.J. Turner, pp. 70-86. Toronto: Macmillan.

Whitaker, Reginald. 1983. *Federalism and Democratic Theory.* Kingston: Queen's University, Institute of Intergovernmental Affairs.

Woodrow, R. Brian, Kenneth Woodside, Henry Wiseman, and John B. Black. 1980. *Conflict Over Communications Policy: A Study of Federal-Provincial Relations and Public Policy.* Montreal: C.D. Howe Research Institute.

Gérard Bélanger is Professor in the Department of Economics, Université Laval, Quebec.

Frederick J. Fletcher is Associate Professor in the Department of Political Science, York University, Toronto.

Garth Stevenson is Professor in the Department of Political Science, University of Alberta, Edmonton.

Donald C. Wallace is Lecturer in the Department of Political Science, York University, Toronto.

John D. Whyte is Professor in the Faculty of Law, Queen's University, Kingston.

THE COLLECTED RESEARCH STUDIES

Royal Commission on the Economic Union and Development Prospects for Canada

ECONOMICS

Income Distribution and Economic Security in Canada (Vol.1), *François Vaillancourt, Research Coordinator*

Vol. 1   Income Distribution and Economic Security in Canada, *F. Vaillancourt* (C)*

Industrial Structure (Vols. 2-8), *Donald G. McFetridge, Research Coordinator*

Vol. 2   Canadian Industry in Transition, *D.G. McFetridge* (C)
Vol. 3   Technological Change in Canadian Industry, *D.G. McFetridge* (C)
Vol. 4   Canadian Industrial Policy in Action, *D.G. McFetridge* (C)
Vol. 5   Economics of Industrial Policy and Strategy, *D.G. McFetridge* (C)
Vol. 6   The Role of Scale in Canada–US Productivity Differences, *J.R. Baldwin and P.K. Gorecki* (M)
Vol. 7   Competition Policy and Vertical Exchange, *F. Mathewson and R. Winter* (M)
Vol. 8   The Political Economy of Economic Adjustment, *M. Trebilcock* (M)

International Trade (Vols. 9-14), *John Whalley, Research Coordinator*

Vol. 9   Canadian Trade Policies and the World Economy, *J. Whalley with C. Hamilton and R. Hill* (M)
Vol. 10 Canada and the Multilateral Trading System, *J. Whalley* (M)
Vol. 11 Canada–United States Free Trade, *J. Whalley* (C)
Vol. 12 Domestic Policies and the International Economic Environment, *J. Whalley* (C)
Vol. 13 Trade, Industrial Policy and International Competition, *R. Harris* (M)
Vol. 14 Canada's Resource Industries and Water Export Policy, *J. Whalley* (C)

Labour Markets and Labour Relations (Vols. 15-18), *Craig Riddell, Research Coordinator*

Vol. 15 Labour-Management Cooperation in Canada, *C. Riddell* (C)
Vol. 16 Canadian Labour Relations, *C. Riddell* (C)
Vol. 17 Work and Pay: The Canadian Labour Market, *C. Riddell* (C)
Vol. 18 Adapting to Change: Labour Market Adjustment in Canada, *C. Riddell* (C)

Macroeconomics (Vols. 19-25), *John Sargent, Research Coordinator*

Vol. 19 Macroeconomic Performance and Policy Issues: Overviews, *J. Sargent* (M)
Vol. 20 Post-War Macroeconomic Developments, *J. Sargent* (C)
Vol. 21 Fiscal and Monetary Policy, *J. Sargent* (C)
Vol. 22 Economic Growth: Prospects and Determinants, *J. Sargent* (C)
Vol. 23 Long-Term Economic Prospects for Canada: A Symposium, *J. Sargent* (C)
Vol. 24 Foreign Macroeconomic Experience: A Symposium, *J. Sargent* (C)
Vol. 25 Dealing with Inflation and Unemployment in Canada, *C. Riddell* (M)

Economic Ideas and Social Issues (Vols. 26 and 27), *David Laidler, Research Coordinator*

Vol. 26 Approaches to Economic Well-Being, *D. Laidler* (C)
Vol. 27 Responses to Economic Change, *D. Laidler* (C)

* (C) denotes a Collection of studies by various authors coordinated by the person named.
  (M) denotes a Monograph.

POLITICS AND INSTITUTIONS OF GOVERNMENT

Canada and the International Political Economy (Vols. 28-30), *Denis Stairs and Gilbert R. Winham, Research Coordinators*

Vol. 28 Canada and the International Political/Economic Environment, *D. Stairs and G.R. Winham* (C)

Vol. 29 The Politics of Canada's Economic Relationship with the United States, *D. Stairs and G.R. Winham* (C)

Vol. 30 Selected Problems in Formulating Foreign Economic Policy, *D. Stairs and G.R. Winham* (C)

State and Society in the Modern Era (Vols. 31 and 32), *Keith Banting, Research Coordinator*

Vol. 31 State and Society: Canada in Comparative Perspective, *K. Banting* (C)

Vol. 32 The State and Economic Interests, *K. Banting* (C)

Constitutionalism, Citizenship and Society (Vols. 33-35), *Alan Cairns and Cynthia Williams, Research Coordinators*

Vol. 33 Constitutionalism, Citizenship and Society in Canada, *A. Cairns and C. Williams* (C)

Vol. 34 The Politics of Gender, Ethnicity and Language in Canada, *A. Cairns and C. Williams* (C)

Vol. 35 Public Opinion and Public Policy in Canada, *R. Johnston* (M)

Representative Institutions (Vols. 36-39), *Peter Aucoin, Research Coordinator*

Vol. 36 Party Government and Regional Representation in Canada, *P. Aucoin* (C)

Vol. 37 Regional Responsiveness and the National Administrative State, *P. Aucoin* (C)

Vol. 38 Institutional Reforms for Representative Government, *P. Aucoin* (C)

Vol. 39 Intrastate Federalism in Canada, *D.V. Smiley and R.L. Watts* (M)

The Politics of Economic Policy (Vols. 40-43), *G. Bruce Doern, Research Coordinator*

Vol. 40 The Politics of Economic Policy, *G.B. Doern* (C)

Vol. 41 Federal and Provincial Budgeting, *A.M. Maslove, M.J. Prince and G.B. Doern* (M)

Vol. 42 Economic Regulation and the Federal System, *R. Schultz and A. Alexandroff* (M)

Vol. 43 Bureaucracy in Canada: Control and Reform, *S.L. Sutherland and G.B. Doern* (M)

Industrial Policy (Vols. 44 and 45), *André Blais, Research Coordinator*

Vol. 44 Canadian Industrial Policy, *A. Blais* (C)

Vol. 45 The Political Sociology of Industrial Policy, *A. Blais* (M)

LAW AND CONSTITUTIONAL ISSUES

Law, Society and the Economy (Vols. 46-51), *Ivan Bernier and Andrée Lajoie, Research Coordinators*

Vol. 46 Law, Society and the Economy, *I. Bernier and A. Lajoie* (C)

Vol. 47 The Supreme Court of Canada as an Instrument of Political Change, *I. Bernier and A. Lajoie* (C)

Vol. 48 Regulations, Crown Corporations and Administrative Tribunals, *I. Bernier and A. Lajoie* (C)

Vol. 49 Family Law and Social Welfare Legislation in Canada, *I. Bernier and A. Lajoie* (C)

Vol. 50 Consumer Protection, Environmental Law and Corporate Power, *I. Bernier and A. Lajoie* (C)

Vol. 51 Labour Law and Urban Law in Canada, *I. Bernier and A. Lajoie* (C)

COMMISSION ORGANIZATION